PEAKY BLINDERS

Professor Carl Chinn, MBE, PhD, is a social historian, writer, public speaker, and teacher. An off-course bookmaker himself until 1984, he is the son and grandson of illegal bookmakers in Sparkbrook, whilst his mother's family were factory workers in Aston. His writings are deeply affected by his family's working-class background and life in the back-to-backs of Birmingham, and have earned him a national following. He believes passionately that history must be democratised because each and every person has made their mark upon history and has a story to tell. *Peaky Blinders: The Real Story* is his thirty-third book.

PEAKY BLINDERS

THE LEGACY

**The real story of Britain's most
notorious 1920s gangs**

CARL CHINN

JB

First published in the UK by John Blake Publishing
An imprint of Bonnier Books UK
80-81 Wimpole Street, London, W1G 9RE
Owned by Bonnier Books
Sveavägen 56, Stockholm, Sweden

www.facebook.com/johnblakebooks
twitter.com/jblakebooks

First published in paperback in 2020

Paperback: 978-1-78946-293-7
Ebook: 978-1-78946-294-4
Audio: 978-1-78946-311-8

A catalogue record for this book is available from the British Library.

Design by www.envydesign.co.uk

Printed and bound in Great Britain by Clays Ltd, Elcograf S.p.A

3 5 7 9 10 8 6 4 2

John Blake Publishing is an imprint of Bonnier Books UK
www.bonnierbooks.co.uk

CONTENTS

INTRODUCTION

THE PEAKY BLINDERS' LEGACY

The Roaring Twenties of the popular imagination is an exuberant, joyous, fashionable and, above all, youthful decade encapsulated by the self-indulgent Bright Young Things. A mixture of rich aristocrats and bohemians disdainful of social norms, they delighted in their wild behaviour, spectacular parties, expensive cocktails, drug-taking and outrageous excesses. This impression of the 1920s is infused with the riches and privilege of a tiny minority, yet the decade was an exciting one for many more who relished new-found freedoms. Released from their stays and hoops, young women known as 'flappers' went out more confidently in skirts shortened to the knee and with bobbed hair covered trendily by bell-shaped cloche hats worn low on the forehead. Smoking and drinking like young men, they too embraced the jazz craze, the dance craze, the cinema craze, the Charleston craze and all the other crazes of the decade.

As for the middle-aged middle class, the 1920s may not have

been roistering but they were pleasurable. Growing in numbers and secure in their employment, they could afford to buy modern semi-detached houses in the suburbs and to spend their disposable income on the cars that took them to and from work and on day trips. Yet millions faced a harsher reality. Britain was riven by gender and class inequalities. Working-class women may have gained the vote in 1928 but they were far from equal in education, health, the workplace and opportunities; huge numbers of working-class people still lived in badly built and overcrowded housing in polluted neighbourhoods; and working-class men were much more likely than others to suffer the indignities and hopelessness of unemployment. The older industries that had propelled Britain into industrial supremacy were in rapid decline, and the closure of cotton mills, iron works, coal mines and shipyards devastated whole communities across Britain. In a land of plenty, unhappily the only abundant thing in the lives of the poor was poverty. The Roaring Twenties may have been a party-time for a few, but for countless numbers it was a hard and hungry time.

These grim realities are ignored in dramatised versions of the decade, which are also deeply affected by Hollywood's portrayals of 'Jazz Age' America with its mobsters and their molls, singers, dancers, bootleggers, decadent socialites, speakeasies, shootouts, and escapades. Gangsters, in particular, have become ingrained in the popular consciousness as a peculiarly 1920s American phenomenon, but more recently a stylish, peak-capped and charismatic British version has arisen through the acclaimed television series, *Peaky Blinders*. These gangsters take their name from real peaky blinders, who also wore flat caps, but, unlike their fictional counterparts, they were neither well-dressed nor alluring. Vicious thugs, they had made Birmingham notorious as one of the most violent cities in Britain, not in the 1920s but in the late nineteenth and early twentieth centuries. Belonging to numerous street gangs, they revelled in fighting each other, attacking the police and preying upon the decent majority of the poor amongst whom they lived.

As explored in *Peaky Blinders: The Real Story*, they disappeared before the First World War, thanks to stronger policing, sterner sentences for violent crime and the provision of youth and sports clubs for lads. Yet though their reign of ruffianism was ended in Birmingham, they passed on a violent legacy because men who had been peaky blinders sparked the first major gangland war in Britain. Belonging to a loose combination of villains known as the Birmingham Gang, by 1920, they controlled the pickpocketing of racegoers and the blackmailing of bookmakers on most of England's racecourses. Such criminality was lucrative and the Birmingham Gang's dominance was quickly challenged in the South by London's Sabini Gang. The resulting Racecourse War of the spring and summer of 1921 was a new and shocking phenomenon. Previously, street gangs within one city had brawled with each other simply to assert which was the hardest; now, two gangs of criminals from different cities clashed over making money illegally. The fighting between them was brutal, provoking headlines in newspapers across the country. Men were scarred by slashes from cut-throat razors; others were shot; and many were battered with hammers and other weapons. And at the forefront of the fighting were former peaky blinders.

During their heyday in the 1890s, it was noticed that 'senior peaky blinders' had become racecourses rogues, travelling the country during the more thrilling Flat racing season of the spring and summer.[1] Racecourses were 'happy hunting grounds'

3

for them because of the large amounts of money carried by bookmakers and punters. Cash betting was illegal anywhere else, a factor that encouraged rising attendances at Flat meetings in a period when there was an expanding middle class and an extending railway network that facilitated travel. The result was an extraordinary growth in ready-money betting.[2] This was a magnet to thieves, who were able to rob and intimidate virtually with impunity because of the lack of control on racecourses. Too few police were employed to keep order and some of them were susceptible to bribes 'to look the other way'.[3] This state of affairs made it easy for gangs of six, seven and eight men to surround and trip up their victims to rob them or else to snatch purses, watches and chains. Travelling to and from the racecourse by train, teams from each gang also worked as card sharps upon gullible fellow passengers.[4] Such pickpockets and card sharpers increasingly intimidated bookmakers to pay into 'collections', and they were joined by welching gangs. Two or three men, protected by several others, would set up as bookmakers, disappearing before they had to pay out winning bets.[5]

Racecourse pests, as the police termed them, were known colloquially as 'the Boys', and the Birmingham Boys, also called the Brummagem Boys, ranged wide, but they were not alone. In Scotland, crews of roughs from the East End of Glasgow and 'other notorious regions were foremost in a reprehensible system that had been in vogue at Scottish race meetings for a considerable time – forcing money from bookmakers'.[6] South of the border, the Newcastle Boys plagued the racecourses of the North-East, extorting 'protection' money from bookies; whilst another gang, the Mexborough Boys from South Yorkshire, focused on 'megging' – an expression for the three-card trick, also called 'find the lady'.[7] Yet it was the 'Brums' who were the most feared, and for a short time they were brought together into a fearsome force under the overall leadership of Billy Kimber.[8]

Portrayed in the series *Peaky Blinders* as a small, dapper Londoner, in reality he was a burly Brummie with a formidable reputation as a street fighter. Born in 1882, he had been a peaky blinder but, by his early twenties, he had followed others in moving away from backstreet rowdiness and into pickpocketing. Under Kimber, the medley of small gangs that made up the Birmingham Boys came together as a slightly more coherent entity known as the Birmingham Gang or Brummagem Gang. By the early twentieth century, it ruled with a rod of iron the racecourses of the Midlands and the North of England, up to the border with the Newcastle Boys. But Kimber had bigger ambitions. He wanted to organise and control the highly profitable rackets on the more numerous racecourses of southern England, leading him to abandon his family and move to London in 1910. He achieved his ambition, and although racing was curtailed during the First World War, he reasserted his dominance in 1920. But his success was short-lived because the Birmingham Gang's takeover fuelled the resentment and envy of London gangs, and violence soon broke out.

A world city and centre of the British Empire, London expanded massively in the 1920s. Propelled by the expansion of the railway and underground systems, it burst out of its bounds, rapidly overlaying the surrounding countryside with large-scale suburban development. In sharp contrast to the comfortable homes, pleasant settings and prosperous lives of the suburbanites, the poor of London's older central districts endured unfit housing and insanitary conditions and struggled to get by on low-paid and intermittent work. Just as Britain was a nation rent apart by class so too was London, perhaps more starkly so, as the wealth of the City and the West End was so close to some of the most deprived neighbourhoods in the country. It was from these poorer areas which emerged the gangs that became embroiled in the Racecourse War of 1921. Like Birmingham, parts of the capital had also been infested by backstreet gangs in the later nineteenth century. Commonly known as hooligans, they had much in common with the peaky blinders in that they were territorial, motivated by asserting their fighting prowess, and fought with belts and knives as well as fists and feet.[9] But there were also crucial differences. There was a wider use of revolvers and pistols in London, where neighbourhood gangs also emerged – and some of these developed into more organised criminal groupings. They included the Titanics, a pickpocketing gang from Hoxton, and the Elephant Boys of South London, which became an important ally of Kimber through his friendship with two of their top men – brothers Wag and Wal McDonald. In a city decisively split by the River Thames, Kimber cleverly secured back-up from the other side of the divide thanks to George 'Brummy' Sage, who would go on to lead the Camden Town Gang.

During a period when 'un-Englishness' was despised, when foreigners were demeaned as inferior, and when Eastern European Jewish immigration was restricted by laws targeting 'undesirable' aliens, racism coursed through the Birmingham Gang and their London allies. They especially hated Jewish bookmakers, who were subjected even more than others to blackmailing for 'protection'. It was the brutish beating of one of them that was the catalyst for conflict. The victim was Alfie Solomon. Dramatised in *Peaky Blinders* as Alfie Solomons, and as if he were from an Orthodox Jewish background, he actually belonged to a secular Anglo-Jewish family. After his mauling in March 1921,

Solomon and other Jewish bookies turned turned to another gang leader for help, this leader would later be portrayed in the drama – Darby Sabini. Depicted on screen as a smartly dressed Italian gangster, he was really an Anglo-Italian who identified as an Englishman. He led a gang of men like himself from London's Little Italy in Clerkenwell, but the gang also included those from solely English backgrounds and Anglo-Jewish men from the East End. At its core, though, the Sabini Gang was tightly organised under one clear leader bolstered by an intimate inner circle that included two of Sabini's brothers, as well as close friends with whom he had grown up.

The bloody conflict between the Sabini Gang and the Birmingham Gang and its London allies was marked by serious outbreaks of violence at Alexandra Park racecourse, which led to the death of a Jewish bookie; at the Epsom Road Battle, in which several mostly Jewish bookmakers were savagely assaulted, and at Bath races, where there were wild scenes when the Birmingham Gang went on the rampage. The nation watched on in horror as the gangs clashed not only on southern racecourses but also on the streets of North London. But in the autumn of 1921, and in a startling turn of events, the Birmingham Gang and the Sabinis declared a truce and agreed to divide the racecourse rackets between them on a regional basis. However, Kimber's London allies were left out of the agreement. Determined to wrest power back from the Sabinis, in 1922, Sage formed the Camden Town Gang, which was supported by Hoxton's Titanics and the Elephant Boys. Another violent confrontation broke out in North London and on racecourses around the capital. Yet again the Sabinis were the winners, and for a short period there was peace. Then, in 1925, the Sabini Gang was again challenged fiercely within

London whilst in Sheffield a man was murdered in a war between the Mooney Gang and the Garvin Gang. Both leaders were racing men who had belonged to street gangs and both were embedded in poor districts close to the centre of a city famed for its production of steel. But their bitter quarrel was not over racecourse rackets – it was over control of a gambling site close to Sheffield city centre.

That gang war was put down by forceful policing and, in another unexpected twist, and for a variety of reasons that will be made clear, the racecourse gangs of London and Birmingham soon faded away. They had caused mayhem, terrorised bookmakers and racegoers, inflicted terrible wounds, triggered fearful headlines, and had seemed all but invincible. Yet now some of the gangsters sought legitimacy for themselves and respectability for their families; others carried on as petty criminals; and a handful became leading figures in London's gangland. Most have been all but forgotten, and none have been glamorised in gangland mythology – none except for Darby Sabini. He has been depicted as if he were a 1920s-type American mobster, a Mafia-style don and 'Britain's Godfather' from whom later London gang leaders took inspiration. He was no such thing. Nor were the other 1920s gangsters audacious and exciting anti-heroes. They were dangerous, nasty, mob-handed racketeers who blackmailed, intimidated and maimed. Yet they were as noticeable and important a feature of the Roaring Twenties as the dissolute Bright Young Things, the carefree young flappers and jazzers, the few glamorous wealthy, the favoured suburbanites, and the unfortunate many who were unemployed and poor. This is the story of those real gangsters. It is the story of Britain's most notorious 1920s gangs and of the legacy of the peaky blinders.

Chapter 1

PEAKY BLINDERS TO THE BIRMINGHAM BOYS

THE EPSOM ROAD AMBUSH

On Friday 3 June 1921, *London's Evening News* carried the attention-grabbing headline: 'The Epsom Road Ambush'. In an alarming report, readers were told of how, after that day's racing at Epsom, a battle had caused panic and, in a dramatic raid, a charabanc (motor-coach) party of men had been surprised in a beer garden by a force of a hundred police. They had made twenty-eight arrests, including two men with loaded revolvers. A vivid, attention-grabbing spread told of an attack the previous afternoon next to the Brick Kiln pub at Ewell Corner when a gang had assaulted a group of men in a vehicle, some of whom were hospitalised. The attackers had then easily escaped because racegoers leaving the Epsom meeting had fled from them. People shouted in fright at their drivers to turn around and many scuttled back to Epsom or took other routes home. One startled resident saw what had happened. Opposite the pub, a private car had been running and beside it a man with a pair of field glasses was watching the road. When he said,

'Here they come, boys,' the car was driven at full speed across the road. Its front tyres burst with loud bangs as it crashed into an oncoming vehicle, whose occupants were attacked by a gang of ten to fifteen men wielding hammers, hatchets, bottles, bricks and hedge sticks. There was a charabanc nearby and then many of the gang jumped in and made off.[10]

With the newspapers carrying daily reports of the guerrilla conflict between British forces and Irish republican fighters in the Irish War of Independence, fears were heightened, and so a few witnesses actually believed that some sort of terrorism was afoot – one telephone caller warning the local police that a Sinn Fein riot was taking place.[11] Gathering a number of officers, a detective inspector immediately made his way to the scene. By the roadside, he found three men suffering from wounds, as well as two badly damaged cars. He transmitted details of the attackers' charabanc to all stations in the Metropolitan Police area.[12] A young PC noticed a motor tallying the description at the George and Dragon hotel on Kingston Hill. After he passed on this information, over twenty uniformed and plain-clothes policemen hurried to the hotel on bicycles and in commandeered vehicles. Reinforcements swiftly followed in police motor tenders, and altogether the force numbered about a hundred.[13] They surrounded the pub and garden where the men from the charabanc were drinking. One officer pulled out the vehicle's spark plugs so it couldn't be driven and then others approached the lawn. Sergeant Dawson was the first to confront the men. Holding up his revolver, he announced, 'I will shoot the first man that tries to escape.' After the arrests were made, the police saw that the charabanc floor was smeared with blood and covered with broken glass; they found a loaded Mauser pistol, hammers, large stones, a chopper and a hammer with the handle missing as if it had been broken off in the fight.[14]

The next day, twenty-eight men were charged with committing grievous bodily harm to ten others. But they were not members of Sinn Fein and they had nothing to do with the Irish War of Independence. As the *Evening News* revealed, they were well known on racecourses, although they were not bookmakers.[15] These observations were well founded. Most of them belonged to the Birmingham Gang, which was battling London's Sabini Gang over control of the rackets on southern England's racecourses. However, the victims were not Londoners; they were bookmakers from Leeds. Previously regarded as allies of the Birmingham Gang, they'd recently switched allegiance to the Sabinis and therefore, in the eyes of the Birmingham Gang, had to be punished. The Epsom Road Ambush was a major event in that struggle for supremacy. Involving a large number of attackers, it was well planned and was a bloody warning to bookmakers of what would happen if they deserted the Birmingham Gang. And as the victims were mostly Jewish, it was also an opportunity for venomous anti-Semitism.

Yet the Epsom Road Ambush did not work out as the Birmingham Gang had intended. It ensured that London's bookmakers, Jewish and non-Jewish, would look even more towards the Sabini Gang for protection. It attracted widespread condemnation in the press; it energised the police against the gang; and it resulted in the imprisonment of seventeen of the most menacing of the Birmingham Gang. The disturbing details of their attack and the sentences passed on them will be recounted later, but it is important here to emphasise that most of them had been peaky blinders, and that a discussion of their early lives informs an understanding of how the legacy of the peaky blinders was both the Birmingham Gang and Britain's first major gangland war.

BANKS'S MOB

Amongst the men arrested and convicted was Edward Banks, formerly Edward Pankhurst, and the man who had arranged the trip to Epsom.[16] Born in 1878 and the eldest of a big family of siblings, Banks was short at 5 foot 3 inches. Despite this, he was ever ready to brawl, and by 1904 he had received seven convictions for fighting and assault. One of them in particular highlighted his volatile nature. In December 1903, after a policeman had remonstrated with him for using bad language, Banks ran into his house and, from the attic window, threw a soda-water bottle that hit the officer in the chest.[17] By then, he had also been found guilty of petty theft and warehouse breaking, whilst he had been fortunate to have been given the benefit of the doubt on a charge of loitering. Under the 1824 Vagrancy Act, the police were allowed to arrest those they suspected of frequenting public spaces with the intent of committing an arrestable offence. This section also applied to those loitering with intent and was regularly applied to suspected pickpockets. By now, Banks was one of the Birmingham Boys and, like them, he moved across the Midlands to rob. In 1904, he and an accomplice were found guilty of breaking and entering a shop in Nottingham and stealing gold and silver watches, gold rings and other items worth £100. He was sent to prison for twelve months.[18] The court was told that Banks was the leader of a gang of Birmingham thieves and that he was a very bad character.[19]

He was indeed and, once released, he became embroiled in the infamous Garrison Lane Vendetta.

As detailed in *Peaky Blinders. The Real Story*, this was an especially violent backstreet gang war that was regarded as 'The End of the Peaky Blinders'.[20] Fought between 1908 and 1912 by men who were near neighbours in Bordesley and Deritend, close to the city centre, it pitched the disreputable Sheldon brothers, the inspiration for the Shelby family in the series *Peaky Blinders,* against a hard man called Billy Beach and his pals.[21] Banks was with the Sheldons, and in January 1909, men brandishing revolvers forced their way into his house looking for him. They did not find him.[22] The next year, in August 1910, Banks was arrested for possessing a loaded firearm whilst drunk. In his defence, he said that three evenings previously, his enemies had again broken into his house, kicking in the door and smashing the windows. Afterwards, he had bought the revolver to prevent a recurrence. Banks denied that he had threatened to shoot Beach, but after he was sentenced to one month with hard labour, he vowed, 'I will get twelve months for him when I come out, or swing for him.'[23]

As it was, Banks did not swing for Beach, and over the next decade he seemed to transform his life. He was not arrested for any serious offence and his economic standing improved markedly. Formerly a hawker who made a precarious living traipsing the streets selling vegetables from a handcart, he had lived in badly built back-to-backs; however, by 1921, Banks had a greengrocery shop at 67 Digbeth, just below the Bull Ring markets, and he and his wife lived on the premises. Nearby, he had another shop selling fish and rabbits.[24] In total, he employed fourteen people, and after his arrest he was able to bail himself for the huge sum of £1,000 and secure seven sureties totalling £3,000.[25] His success was most unusual and, given his previous and later criminality, it is likely that it was achieved from illegal activities.

It was apparent that Banks also headed a group within the Birmingham Gang. Although the notorious Billy Kimber may have been its main leader, this gang was nothing like that of a modern organised crime syndicate, and nor did it have the compactness of the Sabini Gang. It was a rowdy assortment of small bands of rogues. Because of this splintering, due to the Birmingham Gang being based neither in one neighbourhood nor around one family, and because it operated outside the city and did not spawn a successor gang, it has not passed into folklore, and memories of the gang all but disappeared after the Second World War. However, back in the late 1980s, an anonymous letter was sent to me stating that one of those arrested after the Epsom Road Ambush was Billy Hayden, who came out of Sherlock Street, one of 'Banks's mob . . . he used a chopper in the big battle when it went down.'[26]

Hayden was arrested at the scene in Epsom. Though just over 5 foot 5 inches, Hayden could mix it in a fight. In 1909, he was involved in a street melee with a father and son he had rowed with in a pub. After seeing Hayden knock the older man to the ground twice, a witness ran for a constable. When they returned, Hayden had been stabbed by the son at the top of the left cheekbone, a wound a doctor later described as very dangerous.[27] A year later, Hayden was one of a number of men arrested for playing pitch and toss, a favourite pastime of the peaky blinders, on a Sunday afternoon.[28] He also had two convictions for larceny, yet he was not a habitual criminal and was a very different character to most of the other arrested men. By 1911, he was a butcher aged twenty-four; his wife,

Annie, was a factory worker, and they had a young daughter and son.

A working man, Hayden also served his country loyally. After seven years with the Special Reserve, he left in 1912 but then volunteered to join the 10th Battalion Royal Warwickshire Regiment in September 1914, soon after the outbreak of the First World War. He was accepted before the height standard was raised and was posted to France in July 1915. Towards the end of the war, his wife was notified that he had been killed in action, but this was a mistake and soon afterwards she was informed that he was a prisoner of war. A lance corporal, Hayden had already seen plenty of action at the battles of Albert, the Menin Road Ridge and Passchendaele, among others. Then, from 21–23 March 1918, his battalion was involved in the Battle of St Quentin, where he was captured, after which he was made to work down German mines.[29] Following his discharge, Hayden must have struggled to get by as a hawker, and so during the coal strike of 1921, he went to the Black Country to draw out crop coal – inferior coal close to the surface. It was a long trek from his home for hard, dirty and low-paid work. Perhaps the opportunity of making easy money on the racecourses was too tempting for him and led him to join Banks's Mob.

Hayden was from a street near to where Banks lived, as were several other men convicted of the Epsom Road Ambush, and it was likely that they too were part of his Mob. They included William Bayliss from Barford Street – one of the first streets in Birmingham to have a gang of sloggers, the forerunners of the peaky blinders.[30] He had convictions for living on the earnings from prostitution and was also anti-Semitic, a prejudice infecting the Birmingham Gang.[31] In 1892, Bayliss was nineteen when he and two other roughs were involved in what was condemned as a small-scale *Judenhetze*, a persecution of Jews.[32] Without any reason, they had formed an intense hatred for a German Jew and had 'threatened that they would half murder him' when they came across him. When they did so, they kicked him in the stomach and Bayliss struck him with his buckled belt. Afterwards, the victim was menaced with serious injury if he gave evidence. He was so scared that he refused to identify his tormentors until the magistrates assured him, 'that the law in Birmingham was strong enough to protect foreigners, and if any attempt was made to continue the assault the Police should be communicated with'.[33]

Five years later, Bayliss was one of a gang of drunken roughs standing at a street corner quarrelling and using bad language. When a policeman ordered them to move on, he was violently assaulted. A crowd gathered to watch but the only person to help was a lady who blew the officer's whistle to signal help. Bayliss kicked her on the arm and was sentenced to six weeks' hard labour for each assault.[34] Undeterred from violence, in July 1914 he hit a policeman with the back of a chair. He was given four months' imprisonment with hard labour. Now following only intermittent employment, Bayliss was viewed by the police as 'addicted to drink and when under its influence is regarded as being very violent. He is constantly in the company of low-class thieves and prostitutes.'[35]

Three other men arrested at Epsom appear to have been in Banks's Mob, as they also came from streets near to his home and business. They were Thomas Conway, Thomas Eivers and Alfred Jackson. In 1919, Conway was fined twenty shillings for running a crown and anchor board at Gosforth Park races in the North East. This was an illegal gambling game favoured by other members of the Birmingham Gang because the odds were stacked in their favour.[36] As for Eivers, he had convictions for wilful damage and assault and was a thief and frequenter of race meetings.[37] Neither man did regular work.[38] Nor did Alfred Jackson, another associate of low thieves. In March 1914, aged twenty-three, and soon after he had been arrested for frequenting in Burnley, Jackson was found guilty of housebreaking and stealing jewellery in Liverpool. Because he did not have a serious record and appeared to have got among a body of men worse than himself, he was imprisoned for only six months.[39] He had indeed fallen amongst bad men and he would become as bad as them. Allegedly a carter, in June 1919, he was one of several Birmingham pickpockets arrested in Newcastle. Now calling himself Alfred John Thomas, he stole £3 from a man boarding a bus to Gosforth races. Pickpocketing gangs operated with an 'obstructor', who took up a position at the entrance to a racecourse bus, and a 'tickler', who actually picked the pockets of the 'lamb', who was squeezed between them. Others in the gang acted as a 'cover up' for their companions.[40] On this occasion, Jackson was the tickler. He was sentenced to three months in prison, having other convictions for larceny and wounding.[41]

SLOGGERS AND PEAKY BLINDERS

The coach trip to Epsom organised by Banks included men from other bands within the Birmingham Gang, one of which was that of the three Tuckey brothers. Unlike the pickpockets and sharpsters connected with Banks, they were not from the markets area but came from Aston, to the north of the city centre. Nor were they career criminals. Two of them were bricklayers and another was a wire drawer and it seems they didn't go racing regularly. When they did so, it was not as thieves but as blackmailers, intimidating bookies into giving them money. Hard men, they emphasise that the Birmingham Gang was the legacy of the peaky blinders, as two of them had been in a notorious street gang. The eldest brother was fifty-three-year-old Thomas Tuckey, who had been a slogger like Bayliss. Raised in badly built and insanitary back-to-back housing, as a nineteen-year-old in 1887, Tuckey had thrown a glass at the back of the head of a detective called to a pub disturbance. He was sentenced to three months' hard labour. Hard fare, hard board and hard labour, such as stepping on the treadmill for relentless hours a day, failed to reform him. Two years later, Tuckey and a friend were called sloggers when arrested for assaulting a policeman taking a man into custody. In the company of well-known members of the slogging gang, they'd beaten the officer 'savagely about the head and body, destroying his hat, and inflicting a wound which bled profusely'. This time, Tuckey was imprisoned for nine months' hard labour.[42]

He came from the Aston Cross locality, which was notorious for its slogging gang, and it is apparent that Tuckey was a leading figure within it. So too was his younger brother, Henry 'Harry' Tuckey. Aged eighteen in September 1894, Harry Tuckey and a friend were charged with violently assaulting a third man. All three had been at a fight between rival slogging gangs by the canal. Afterwards, they were walking along the towing-path when Tuckey struck the victim, who was then kicked. He was fined merely ten shillings with costs.[43] A violent man, Tuckey was also a petty thief, as were many peaky blinders. In particular, he and his younger brother, Edward, had a liking for stealing bicycles. In 1908, they took two in Bristol and each was given three years' hard labour. Six years later, in October 1914, they were found guilty of breaking and entering a house, after which they rode away on bikes. In passing lengthy sentences of hard labour for both of them, the judge remarked that 'the prisoners were not only brothers in name, but, judging by their past records, they were also brothers in crime'.[44] They were indeed, and Harry Tuckey's misdemeanours continued after his release. In February 1918, when he was in a relationship with a serviceman's wife, he attacked her husband, kicking him in the mouth, loosening four teeth and causing a wound needing three stitches.[45]

At 5 foot 9 and 5 foot 8 inches respectively, Thomas and Harry Tuckey were tall for sloggers and peaky blinders. Most of them were smaller like Edward Tuckey, who was 5 foot 5 inches, and who joined his brothers at Epsom. According to his great-grandchildren, Lesley and Robert Staight:

> Despite the evidence he was a very bad lad, he was considered a good man to the family. There is no history or stories of any domestic violence. Of course, he did drink bucket loads and we know he'd be off out with his brothers and 'clan' lots. He'd get his brick hammer out sometimes and disappear out on 'business'. His tools seemed to be stored in the coal shed for long periods (possibly when he was doing time) but he is remembered as a hard worker in his job as a bricklayer.

Tuckey's wife, Florence, was 'a lovely lady, always with a chuckle and humming. A strong matriarchal figure, known to regularly send Teddy off to bed if he was drunk, to sleep it off.' Their only child, Violet, was 'positively spoiled. Piano lessons, ballet, and both she and Florence had very nice clothes. Florence had fur stoles.'[46] The part-time blackmailing of bookmakers obviously paid well for Edward Tuckey, but it's likely that he and his brothers were drawn to join Banks's Mob in the Epsom Road Ambush less by the chance of making money on this occasion and more by the prospect of having a row with Londoners. That would also seem to have been the motivation of other former sloggers-cum-peaky blinders such as Jack Allard.

Born in 1870, Allard was from Sparkbrook, two miles to the southeast of the Bull Ring. At 5 foot 9 inches he was also tall for his background, and with scars from fighting between his eyes and on his forehead, he was a frightening man. Like all peaky blinders, he hated the police, and when he was twenty-three he had struck a constable on the nose and kicked him.[47] Two years later, he was named as the ringleader of a trio of burglars when sentenced to twenty-one months in prison.[48] But it was as a fighting man that Allard became notorious. One Thursday in February 1907, he was drinking in a pub with some out-of-work bricklayers. Generously, he paid for several rounds of drinks. Then the bricklayers demanded that he give them half-a-crown. He refused, and in the ensuing row he ran amok with a heavy stick in his hand. Leaving the pub, he hit two other men before he was arrested. The magistrates were lenient – for drunkenness and assault, they fined him ten shillings with costs or one month's hard labour.[49]

Ostensibly a plumber, from about 1900, Allard had become an associate of low-class racing men and one of the Birmingham Boys. Over the next eleven years, he was convicted for frequenting at Lincoln races and, under an alias, at Brighton and Bath.[50] It seems likely that a dispute relating to racing led to his next crime – the manslaughter of Charles Cutler, a racecourse bookmaker's assistant. Both men lived close to each other: Allard on the Ladypool Road, Sparkbrook and Cutler just off this shopping thoroughfare. There had already been some bother between them, in which Cutler's head had been cut and his ear bitten, and on the afternoon of the fatal attack on 29 February 1912, Cutler told his mother that he'd met Allard, who had vowed to 'bodge his eye out with his umbrella if he were by him'. Later that evening, Cutler walked his girlfriend to her house nearby, and soon after Mrs Cutler heard the sound of police whistles. Going out into the street, she found her son lying in the gutter. He was bleeding and dying. There was a crowd, and she saw Allard held by a policeman. She heard him say words to the effect of: 'I have been waiting for him all day; I've done him, and I meant to', and 'I will blow the policeman's brains out'. Her account was corroborated by the arresting officer, who added that Allard had sworn: 'If I had my revolver I would have blown his brains out and done for him.'

A witness explained that he had passed Cutler and Allard in the street and then heard a thud and a groan followed by the words, 'Take that, you dirty dog.' Turning round, he saw Cutler lying in the gutter. Allard was standing over him with an umbrella in his hand as though he were about to jab or had jabbed. When the constable arrived, Allard swore that, 'It's a matter of getting your own back, and I have – well got mine back.' (The use of the dash in newspaper reports indicated a profanity.) Cutler was rushed unconscious to the General Hospital. He was bleeding freely from the nose and had a deep wound on the inner angle of the right eye. Internally, the wound extended to a fracture of the bone forming the inner wall of the eye socket. There was another fracture of the base of the skull, with a half-inch piece of bone detached. Grievously injured,

Cutler died of laceration of the brain following the penetration of some instrument through the wall of the eye socket into the skull. It was a terrible injury, and a doctor reported that it could have been caused by an umbrella point, although that would have required the exertion of considerable force.

On the afternoon of the killing, another witness had been in a pub in Birmingham city centre drinking with Cutler, who had pulled out a knuckleduster. When questioned if 'that is the gentleman you are going to do Allard in with', Cutler had replied, 'What do you think I've got it for?'[51] A bloodied knuckleduster was found beside the unconscious Cutler, and this provided Allard with part of his defence when charged with manslaughter. He claimed that Cutler had threatened him on several occasions. They had met earlier on the day they clashed, and Cutler had supposedly vowed that he would 'put him through it' at the first opportunity. That night, after having plenty to drink, Allard stated that he was returning home when the two men came face to face. Cutler drew his hand back and was wearing a knuckleduster. Saying, 'You dirty dog. Take that,' he went to hit Allard. Trying to ward off the blow, Allard reckoned that he had held up his umbrella and that Cutler had rushed onto it so that the point penetrated his eye.

The jury accepted this unlikely explanation, finding Allard guilty not of murder, for which he would have hung, but of manslaughter and, despite all the evidence, somehow recommended the judge to show mercy. He did so by imposing a sentence of only seven years' imprisonment.[52] After his release, Allard worked at the Austin Motor Company from October 1917, where he was a good timekeeper, and his general character was given as good. Subsequently, he was unemployed, so he bought a horse and cart to hawk vegetables around the streets. Yet, as the Birmingham police stressed, he remained 'an associate of racecourse thieves and with them attends the majority of meetings'.[53]

Purportedly a painter, John Lee was another murderous member of the Birmingham Gang and was also tall for the period, at just over 5 foot 10 inches. He was from Bordesley, which adjoined Sparkbrook where Allard lived; he had also been in a gang of peaky blinders, and in 1899, aged nineteen, he was sentenced to twelve months in prison for manslaughter. One of his accomplices was Arthur Griffiths, and two years later they assaulted a carter.[54] After he was convicted for another attack in January 1902, Lee must have fallen out with Griffiths, for he was later found guilty of maliciously wounding his former friend. Despite a sentence of eighteen months' hard labour, Lee was now infused with violent behaviour, and in September 1903 he was charged with having attempted to murder Charles Connor, who was soon to be involved in the Garrison Lane Vendetta mentioned earlier.[55]

There was bad blood between their friends, and in the Sailor's Return in Bordesley on the August Bank Holiday, Lee had attacked a man with a chopper. Later that evening and armed with a revolver, he met Connor in Garrison Lane and shot him in the arm and leg. In court, when a witness called Julia Kane was called, Lee's rage 'knew no bounds. He used the most filthy and violent language, and to the surprise of everyone . . . took from his pocket a large road stone and with an oath slung it viciously at the woman.' Fortunately it missed, as did a second stone. Clambering over the dock from all directions, eight policemen strove to stop Lee. Mad with rage, he fought savagely until he was overpowered and cried for mercy. Hands cuffed behind his back, he was forced to sit but carried on swearing at the witnesses and violently threatening them and the police. He shouted that even if he got twenty years he would not forget them, and if he had a shooter he would die for them at once. Lee reserved special hatred for Kane, whom he vowed to kill straight away if he could reach her.[56]

Found guilty of wounding and attempted murder, he was sentenced to five years' penal servitude. After his release, he lived with a young woman called Ada Bailey, whom he abused. Still only twenty-seven, in February 1908, Lee was charged with unlawfully wounding her. Witnesses said that she had been in a butcher's shop when he had rushed in and stabbed her between the ribs and in the thigh. Despite this, when Bailey came out of hospital, she went back to live with Lee, who continued to ill-treat her. Yet even after his arrest she brought him food in his cell. Obviously fearful of him, at first Bailey denied that he had knifed her, telling the improbable story that she had fallen on a spike. She later withdrew this account. Lee refused to accept his guilt, saying that Bailey had charged him out of jealousy because he would not live with her any more as she was a drunk. His appeals were ignored and he was imprisoned for another five years.[57]

Lee was irredeemable, returning to crime after his release. Like others in the Birmingham Boys, he travelled far and wide, and in July 1917 he was found guilty of housebreaking and the theft of £350 worth of jewellery in Surrey. Because he had a long record of crime, he was sent to prison for five years.[58] He was released shortly before the Epsom Road Ambush. So too was Joseph Witton, another man inured to violence who lived in the same street as Lee. Born in 1886, Witton had scars on his right temple, forehead and beneath his left eye. Distinguished by tattoos of Buffalo Bill and a pugilist on his right arm and by a wreath and flowers on his left forearm, Witton was convicted fourteen times between his first offence in 1900, when he was fourteen, and 1908. His crimes ranged from stealing three tins of brawn and a tin of sardines to the theft of a purse; from using indecent language to drunkenness, and from loitering to assault.

A vicious and dangerous man, in March 1909, Witton was convicted on two charges of robbery with violence.[59] The previous October, he had been one of three men who had attacked a manufacturer on a street close to Snow Hill Station. The victim 'was rendered insensible by kicks on the head, and practically all the contents of his pockets were stolen'. In the judge's opinion, it was one of the worst cases of its kind that he had met with. Five months later, in February 1909, Witton was one of seven or eight men 'who made a murderous attack upon a dealer in precious stones in a house in a low quarter of the city'.[60] It seems that racism also played a part in the assault, for the victim was Ismail Razagoff, who was named as a Muslim. Visiting Birmingham on business, he had gone with a woman to a house in Thorp Street, a locality that had long been notorious for its street gangs. When Razagoff tried to leave, the woman and a gang of men set about him and robbed him. For this and the previous attack, Witton was sentenced to four years' imprisonment and fifteen lashes of the cat.[61]

The cat o' nine tails was brutal. A rope whip consisting of nine knotted thongs, it was used to flog prisoners and could only be inflicted for robbery with violence. As a punishment, it had gained widespread publicity in 1887 when Justice Day had sentenced members of the High Rip Gang of Liverpool to flogging; but it had not been passed in Birmingham for many years. The decision was praised in a local newspaper's editorial. It pronounced that unfortunately there were 'some members of the criminal class who are so little removed from barbarians to be impervious to any other form of punishment' and for them flogging was a deterrent. It was not. In Liverpool robberies with violence had increased after Day's sentences, whilst in Birmingham Witton went on to commit more violent crimes.[62]

Following his four-year stretch, he was given eighteen months' hard labour for stealing a purse in March 1914.[63] Previously a part-time soldier, after his release he joined the Worcestershire Regiment in June 1915. He served in France and Gallipoli and was wounded, but his military character was classed as 'indifferent'. In August 1916, when on leave, he was named as a soldier in a fracas after a policeman was attacked.[64] Two years later, he had deserted and was arrested for shopbreaking. In mitigation, it was disclosed that he had saved a comrade's life in Gallipoli, but still he was sentenced to twelve months' hard labour.[65] Released from prison in July 1919, Witton was unable to steer himself away from criminality. Within days he was arrested for loitering at a tram terminus in Birmingham. He and his accomplice were described as the associates of thieves and pickpockets and part of a well-known gang. When arrested, Witton told the detective, 'I am a fool. I have only been out of prison six days, and I know what this will mean for me.' He was a fool but a dangerous one. After serving twelve months' hard labour, Witton was sent back to prison in September 1920 for larceny in Worcester.[66] He now stated that he was a commission agent. Because of their knowledge of horse racing, some men did make a living as agents, placing bets for others and taking a commission for doing so. However, the term commission agent was also a favourite catch-all used by racecourse pickpockets, thugs and fraudsters like Witton to disguise their criminality and to give them a semblance of legitimacy.

A CITY-WIDE GANG

Although coming from different parts of Birmingham, racing men like Witton, Allard and the Tuckeys would have met travelling across the country to different racecourses and drinking in the same pubs. As recalled by Mr Gilliver, who knew members of the Birmingham Gang, 'the Birmingham mobs used to hang around just there in town by the Fish Market and the Rag Market and that's where they used to hang around when there was no racing on'.[67] Such 'hanging around' would explain the involvement in the Epsom Road Ambush of Ernest Hughes, who had no fixed abode and who had also been fined for running a crown and anchor board, in his case at Warwick races in 1919.[68] It also explained the inclusion of William Henry 'Harry' Stringer, the only arrested man from the Ladywood district to the west of the city centre, and another deserter and rogue. Having previously been a part-time soldier in the Militia, he joined the Worcestershire Regiment in 1907 when he was eighteen. It is noteworthy that on his attestation papers he was unable to record where his father or mother lived, and later he would also be noted as being of no fixed abode. His Army record was grim, and within weeks he was charged with being absent without leave. A few months later, he was in detention for using insubordinate language, after which he deserted. Sentenced by a civilian court to six months' imprisonment for theft, Stringer was discharged from the Army in January 1909.[69]

Like others of those arrested, he was a constant associate of thieves and racing men, and by 1912 he had accumulated nine convictions for obstruction and other minor offences, and three for stealing, one of which was in Dover and another in Cheltenham. That year he was imprisoned for twelve months for uttering base coins (trying to pay for something with counterfeit coins). Reoffending after his release, he was branded a dangerous thief.[70] In January 1916, Stringer once again joined the Worcestershire Regiment but, as before, went on to desert. Soon after, he was convicted in Liverpool as well as Birmingham.[71] Then in January 1920, and stating that he was a bookmaker's clerk, he was sentenced to twelve months' hard labour for loitering at tram queues in Birmingham.[72] Damned in court as an 'incorrigible rogue', he was discharged from the Army with the military character of 'bad'.[73]

William O'Brien was of the same ilk. Born in 1892, he was from Small Heath, not far from where Lee and Witton lived. At a little over 5 foot 4 inches, O'Brien joined the Army Reserve in 1910, and four years later he was called up to serve with the Lincolnshire Regiment. In October 1914, days after reaching the Western Front, he was wounded on his right hand whilst being shelled. He was discharged in November 1915 to work in munitions and his character was given as 'very good'.[74] It did not stay that way. In July 1918, he was arrested for loitering in Manchester city centre. Saying that he was an Army pensioner, he was bound over to be of good behaviour for twelve months.[75] A few days later, though, O'Brien was apprehended in Blackpool as one of a gang of notorious Birmingham pickpockets who had been giving the police a lot of trouble. After he was arrested, he appealed to the two detectives with him to, 'Give us a chance; let me go this time, and I will give you all the money I have got and leave the town.' His plea fell on deaf ears and he was sentenced to three months' hard labour.[76] On his release, he returned to Birmingham and pickpocketing, and at the end of December 1918 was imprisoned for loitering in the city centre. A detective told the court that O'Brien had not been following any employment for the previous three months and instead had been working tram queues with other men.[77]

Two of the arrested men who were convicted did not fit into the categories either of travelling pickpockets like O'Brien or former sloggers-cum-peaky blinders such as Bayliss. They were William Goulding and Arthur Vincent. Aged forty-five, Goulding was a widower from Aston and had no previous convictions. After his arrest, his daughter stated that he had worked as a labourer on the construction of a large factory but had to leave at Easter 1921 because of ill health. Since then he had been out of work. The Birmingham police knew nothing detrimental about him and he appeared to be well respected in the district where he lived. Goulding was clearly the odd man out and struggling for money; he may have been pulled into the Epsom Road Ambush by a connection with the Tuckeys, who were also from Aston.

As for Arthur Vincent, like Hayden he was an ex-serviceman who had done his duty and who had grown up in poverty. The only convicted man from Hockley, in 1901 and aged twelve, Vincent was living with his mother, Elizabeth, his older sister and younger brother. Elizabeth was forty-four and, although married, she was recorded as the head of the household – indicating that her husband had deserted her and their children. A hardworking woman, she kept them out of the hated workhouse through working as a charwoman, cleaning the houses of the better off. Her wages for long hours and laborious work would have been pitifully low and the household income was supplemented by her daughter, who worked in a factory, and by rent from a boarder.

Six years later, Vincent was working for a metal merchant when he joined the Militia. He was called up from the Reserve in August 1914 to join the Coldstream Guards. Immediately drafted to France as one of the British Expeditionary Force, Vincent was in the Retreat from Mons and was severely wounded at the Battle of the Aisne in September 1914.[78] Discharged, he was awarded an Army pension and the British War Medal and Victory Medal.[79] Additionally, he was entitled to wear the Silver War Badge, issued to service personnel who had been honourably discharged from military service due to wounds or sickness. His Army character was praised as very good. Vincent went on to keep a fruiterer's shop and do some hauling with a van. Birmingham's police indicated that he was in 'a sound financial position, but he commenced to associate with well-known thieves and others and attended race meetings playing "Crown & Anchor". Eventually he lost his business.' Married with a wife and four children under nine, Vincent had convictions only for street betting and was regarded as 'more or less a tool of the party' in the Epsom Road Ambush.[80]

As can be noted from the different characters explored above, Banks's charabanc trip for that attack drew in tough nuts from across poorer working-class Birmingham and from different mobs within the Birmingham Gang, including several of the twenty-eight arrested men who were not convicted of the Epsom Road Ambush. Such a large gathering was unusual and was driven by the need to make a show of strength against the Sabini Gang. Behind this rallying of rogues, as the Birmingham Police emphasised, was a syndicate that had provided the money for this affray and others. Waxing wealthy through their illegal earnings, it's most likely that Kimber and his closest associates were that syndicate. In the immediate aftermath of the First World War, through his fighting prowess and leadership qualities, he had brought the shifting conglomeration of the Birmingham Boys into a slightly more ordered grouping able to enforce the paying of tribute by bookmakers on a much wider scale.[81] He was not the kind of man to give up that powerful position and the riches it brought. Once a peaky blinder and a pickpocket, Kimber was now England's first gangland leader on a national scale, and his determination to resist the challenge of Sabinis was the catalyst for the Racecourse War of 1921.

Chapter 2

THE BIRMINGHAM GANG LEAVE THEIR MANOR

THE BIRMINGHAM GANG TAKES LIBERTIES

'Racing Roughs Held Off by Armed Man' shouted the *Evening News* headline on 23 March 1921. Exciting scenes had unfolded at Greenford Trotting Track the previous afternoon when a man was attacked by 'Twenty Birmingham Racing Pests'. A police inspector had been in the betting ring when he heard shouting and saw Charles Sabini facing a crowd of men. There were cries of 'Shoot the –!' Some of the crowd had pieces of wood and others empty beer bottles. There was a shot and smoke arose from above Sabini's head. In his hand was a revolver. The inspector ran towards him and commanded him to drop the weapon, but the crowd was trying to rush him and Sabini was pointing it from right to left, from left to right, saying, 'I'll shoot.' He then ran backwards and a police sergeant threw his arms around him, securing him. But the crowd rushed on top of them. Men struck at Sabini with bottles and one had a piece of wood about three feet long. He was holding it above his head with both hands, shouting, 'I'll murder him!' There was a struggle to get the weapon from Sabini, but eventually a constable managed it. During the melee, he heard the hammer of the revolver click. Because of the menacing attitude of the crowd, the police took Sabini to the local station, where he told them, 'I had the revolver given to me to-day when I looked like getting murdered. I don't know by whom. About twenty of those Birmingham racecourse pests got hold of me. I did not shoot anyone; I did it to frighten them.' When the revolver was examined, one empty cartridge was found and four live ones. Three had been struck by the hammer, which had misfired.[82]

Charles Sabini was actually Octavious Sabini, although he was rarely known by these names and was best known as Darby Sabini or Fred Handley and sometimes Ottavio Sabini. The attack on him signalled the start of the Racecourse War of the spring and summer of 1921. It also heralded the surge to power of the Sabini Gang and the end of the Birmingham Gang's short-lived domination of the racecourse rackets in the south of England. That control had arisen from the ambitions of former peaky blinder, William 'Billy' Kimber. Hailing from Birmingham's Summer Lane neighbourhood, well known for its gangs, he was engaged in 'peaky blinderism' throughout his teenage years as a violent petty criminal who assaulted the police and gambled illegally. At just over 5 foot 8 inches, he was sturdy and physically strong. Quickly, he gained a reputation as a fearsome street fighter. But unlike most peaky blinders, he did not stay a backstreet thug. Instead, he and his brothers, Joe and Harry, formed the core of a travelling pickpocketing gang, one amongst many in the Birmingham Boys. Possessed of clear leadership skills, through his thieving Kimber palled up with equally tough men from the capital: the McDonald brothers of the Elephant Boys in South London, and George

'Brummy' Sage from North London, who will be discussed in more detail later.

Fully aware of the richer pickings from crime on the racecourses around the capital, Kimber moved there in about 1910, abandoning his Birmingham wife, Maude, to live and die in poverty.[83] Swiftly, Kimber and Sage became well known as racing men and habitués of boxing events.[84] Before the First World War, as highlighted by the noted referee Moss Deyong, 'the seamier side of boxing and racing were one and the same thing. The same tough crowd of racketeers and hoodlums that frequented and at one time terrorized race tracks were, for a period, an inseparable part of the boxing scene. When they were not operating at racecourses, they were at the boxing shows.'[85]

Kimber was a key figure amongst these men, as recognised by the celebrated bookmaker, Thomas Henry Dey. On one occasion at Newbury Races, Dey refused to take a £10 bet from 'Joe', one of the 'Boys'. No payment was offered, and instead Dey was ordered to, 'Put it down for "Issy" for whom I am working, I will go and get the money and bring it up to you in a minute'. Dey insisted that there was no bet, even after 'Joe' returned with the cash. With a flood of expletives, the gangster flung the £10 at the bookie, who let it flutter to the floor. Throughout the race, the gangster stood beside the joint, making himself a nuisance and exclaiming at the top of his voice that he had a bet. As it was, the horse lost and then 'Joe' demanded 'his' £10 back as it had been no bet. Ignored by Dey, 'he stormed and ramped and raved, and threatened me with all sorts of penalties, threatening to tear the money out of [his] hand'. After racing, Dey boarded his train, followed by 'Joe', who explained in detail what he would do when they reached London. Nothing happened, but worried that he would face vengeance, at the next meeting Dey sought out Billy Kimber, telling him what had occurred. This 'gentlemen interviewed Joe, and gave him to understand that I was not to be molested'.[86]

It is likely that Dey had employed Kimber as a minder to protect him from gangs of the 'Boys' until racing was mostly ended during the First World War. Kimber joined up but soon deserted and went to Ireland, where racing continued, and he was arrested for pickpocketing in a Dublin railway station on the day of the Leopardstown races. Dey sent his chief clerk to the court, explaining that Kimber was employed to collect large sums of money that was owed. He always acted honourably and 'racing being quiet in England, some of the people owing debts to Mr Dey had come over to Ireland, and Kimber crossed over from Liverpool to meet those people'. Dey's clerk added that the bookmaker had 'full knowledge of the past career of Kimber who had been an honest man for the seven last years' – which, of course, he had not been. Dey was prepared to keep Kimber employed and give the substantial sum of £50 for bail.[87]

Kimber's authority with ruffians like 'Joe' and the respect from bookies such as Dey rested on his reputation as a very hard man. Tommy Garnham's father, John, led a small gang from the Chapel Market locality in Islington and was a close friend of Kimber. Growing up, Tommy heard many stories about Kimber.

> He was the boss. And when he come down [to Warren Street] everyone used to lock their doors. Of course he aint going to do nothing but they just kept away. Me Dad always used to say he was coming up once to some race, I don't know if it was Cheltenham or what

race track, or York I can't remember, and him and the Wizard was on the train going up and it was gambling weren't it and on the train was a couple of these hard bastards, big fellas. They had a game of cards and they took all their money. They was in the compartment with them. They went up overnight and the blokes said, 'We want our money back'. The Wizard said you won't get your money back so they said, 'We'll see you at the track'. That's where they were all going and when they get in there they went straight over to Bill, 'See them two over there. Took their money off them last night and they want their money back'. 'Alright'. Bosh, bosh. And they were both carried out, both, yeh. Bill Kimber on his own.

His favourite punch was up the solar plexus. My Dad said he didn't like a tool and my Dad never used a tool. He [Kimber] weren't a tool merchant. Punch up the solar plexus. And my Dad's said three or four, he's been there, shit themselves. Completely shit themselves. He's hit them so hard you lose it. Shit yourself. He's carried a few out the race tracks, my Dad.

Garnham used to say of Kimber, 'He was a dangerous bastard. Some dangerous man. I've seen him being horrible to people. Look he was a dangerous man. When he hurt a person they hurt bad. But he was a respected man. Well respected.'[88] Kimber was indeed a most dangerous man and, contradicting the belief that he did not use weapons, he and Sage were tooled up in a callous assault on another racing man in a Whitechapel pub in 1913. Both were arrested for cutting and wounding their victim, who was in a serious condition in hospital suffering from stabs to the neck and face. When arrested, Kimber became violent and on the way to the police station, he dropped a brass harness buckle.[89] He and Sage were soon discharged, as the publican's daughter stated that she could prove the stabbing had been done by the Kidderminster Kid.[90] It was an improbable story, and it's more likely that she had been intimidated into coming up with this account to exonerate Kimber and Sage.

Brian McDonald's uncles were the leading family in the Elephant Boys and they admired Kimber. In his important and insightful book on the gangs of London, he praised the Brummie as having 'a reputation for brains and brawn, that desirable combination that produced many a gang boss'. McDonald believed that soon after Kimber's move to London in 1910, a compromise was reached between race organisers and rogues. In effect, if the 'Boys' regulated themselves they would be allowed to operate their enterprises unchecked. Kimber was acknowledged as their leader because of his cunning and strength, and because he had the backup of the strongest gang from Birmingham. Crucially, he also had the support of many London gangsters.[91]

It is impossible to verify this arrangement as if it had been made there would have been no records. But McDonald's work is well informed and it's interesting to note that between 1910 and 1914, there were few reports on racecourse rogues and no outcry about ruffianism on the turf as there had been in 1898. The belief in Kimber's authority before the First World War is bolstered by Arthur Harding's unique memories of the East End underworld. He recalled that most of the racing people were from South London, with some from Islington. Billy Kimber was their gaffer, and by 1910 he had control of 'all the racecourse meetings down south – Newbury, Epsom and all the

Park meetings belonging to London – Alexandra Park, Earls Park, Kempton Park'.[92]

Whatever rackets Kimber and Sage were involved in, they ended soon after the First World War started. With railways crucial to the movement of troops, transportation to racecourses was disrupted, and increasingly it was regarded as unpatriotic to enjoy sport. Attendances tumbled, and in May 1915 all racing was abandoned except at Newmarket, the home of racing. Although a few meetings were sanctioned thereafter, the 'Boys' had lost their livings.[93] Like Kimber, some joined up, and like him many deserted.[94] With the end of the war in 1918, all restrictions were lifted. The public was looking for entertainment and many found it in horse racing. The Flat season began at Lincoln in the following March and there was a massive attendance. Captain Eric Rickman was there and, after making his first bet, he was unable to move away because of the press of the crowd. 'And there I had to stay for the rest of the afternoon, pushed by the surging multitude a few yards this way and that, and just managing to be carried towards my bookmaker when I wanted to make a bet or draw over the two winners I backed.'[95] Attendances boomed everywhere, so much so that this 'abnormal interest in racing' was one of the most remarkable features of the immediate post-war period.[96]

As Rickman observed, racegoers 'were spending their war-made wealth freely and thousands of demobilized servicemen having received their gratuities in lump sums and not having any immediate employment, began at once to dissipate this money'. Unsurprisingly, the bookmakers had the time of their lives. Many of them were taking so much cash that instead of putting it in their satchels they employed 'cashiers'. Standing each side of their joints, they held 'a huge bundle of bank and treasury-notes as much, perhaps, for advertisement as for convenience'. But where so much money was spent so liberally, so too was it a magnet to racecourse pests and, rapidly, 'welching, pocket-picking, blackmail and even robbery with violence developed to an extent unprecedented in modern England'.[97]

In the Midlands and the North, the Birmingham Gang reasserted its control over the major rackets on the racecourses – up to the limits of their allies, the Newcastle Boys. Smaller gangs of rogues from other places were allowed to operate as card sharps and the like, probably subject to paying tribute. But there was no doubting the Birmingham Gang's dominance, as emphasised by Tom Divall, a former chief inspector at Scotland Yard employed to keep order at various racecourses. During the first meeting at Doncaster after the war, he took charge of the ten-shilling ring. An enormous crowd attended and the queues on the main day's racing almost reached from the course into the town. In the middle of the afternoon, there was what Divall euphemistically called a 'misunderstanding about a bet'. It was more likely a case of welching.

A lot of men lost their tempers, and high words and ugly threats passed between some miners and bookmakers' runners. Both the course officials and the police quite lost all control of the mob. I was fearful of an awful scrimmage taking place, when up came Billy Kimber, a host in himself among his fellows, and he soon settled the disturbance between the bookmakers and their discontented backers. What would have occurred if Kimber had not offered his most timely help, I can't imagine; nor do I like to conjecture, for there were thousands of men about and most of them of the roughest class. Billy afterwards came up to me and calmly told me that what he had done was to save me from any trouble and worry.[98]

The evidence strongly suggests that Divall had an 'arrangement' with Kimber.

In the South things were different. There was no dominant gang and violent thugs from across London and elsewhere swept across the racecourses. In September 1919, newspapers reported on 'a desperate hand-to-hand encounter' between three detectives and about fifteen crooks returning from Alexandra Park races. Having smashed several sticks for weapons, the villains kicked and rained heavy blows at the policemen, and one shouted 'Who has a shooter? Let them have one!' Eventually, six men were arrested. They were identified as members of a Sheffield gang considered as one of the most dangerous combinations of racecourse sharps in the country.[99] But only one actually came from Sheffield; the rest were from London. Three of them were imprisoned for grievous bodily harm.[100]

In July the next year, the *Daily Mail* covered 'disgraceful scenes' at the Salisbury races. 'Pests' had arrived from across the kingdom 'to plunder, where and whom and how they can'. Some of the largest and worst gangs came from the Midlands and Lancashire, and pickpockets and rowdies infested the open part of the course, which wasn't enclosed and so was free for spectators to stand. Later in the day, knots of roughs forced chauffeurs of hired cars to take them to the railway station. Those who refused were badly manhandled.[101]

These shocking events prompted *The Times* to call for immediate action against 'rogues of the racecourse'. It thundered that since the war, rowdyism and robbery had been going on to an ever-increasing extent at practically all the race meetings up and down the country. There had never been so many rascals making a living by preying on racegoers, and undoubtedly they were capitalised because they used a new form of transportation – luxurious motor cars. That way, they avoided the London police watching for them on trains; whilst the local police were unable to cope as they didn't know the ruffians and nor could they spare the resources to supervise racecourses properly. Differing from three-card tricksters and other conmen, these organised gangs maltreated punters and bookmakers alike and openly robbed with violence in the rings, covering each other to allow the workers of the more desperate assaults to escape.[102]

The police agreed with this assessment. In August 1920, five men were arrested at Hurst Park for obtaining money by threats and picking pockets. Detective Inspector Grosse of Scotland Yard explained that they were members of an organised gang that frequented the outside of racecourses and railways. Each was found guilty and sentenced to various terms of hard labour.[103] Brian McDonald has shown that they were members of Alf White's King's Cross Boys and Jack 'Dodger' Mullins's Bethnal Green Gang.[104] The same month, another gang of racecourse roughs from London was convicted for terrorising bookmakers at Brighton. Emphasising the fluidity of the gangs, two of them would become connected to the Birmingham Gang, but the third, James 'Jim' Ford, would become a major figure in the Sabini Gang.[105] Brian McDonald believed that the racecourse managements in the London area were concerned that neither they nor the police could counter the widespread gangsterism that had erupted, which was making race-going an alarming prospect. Consequently, once more they turned to Billy Kimber to restore order.[106] He did so and this takeover by the Birmingham Gang was noteworthy. Ali Harris, a bookmaker from the East End of London, remembered they 'come down here because obviously there was money down the South'. Other gangs 'wouldn't really leave their own manor. The only time I've heard of them leaving their own manor was when the Birmingham Boys come to London . . . because they were probably the strongest.'[107] Importantly, Kimber was again supported by the McDonald brothers and the Elephant Boys, and by Brummy Sage. This partnership expelled the other gangs, including a small one led by Joe Sabini.[108] Its success was facilitated by a falling out between Alf White's King's Cross Gang and the Bethnal Green Mob, who also lost their leader, Dodger Mullins, for unlawful wounding. His imprisonment in June 1920 was a crucial factor contributing to Kimber's takeover.[109]

Although later describing himself as a bookmaker from Bordesley, in reality Kimber was nothing of the kind.[110] As bookie Sam Dell explained, at each meeting Kimber controlled the most prominent five or six pitches, the ones taking the most money and thus the most profitable. On them he put either his own men or bona fide bookmakers for a return of 'ten bob in the pound' – 50 per cent of the winnings.[111] A police report divulged another money-making racket: buying up portions of the open areas at racecourses. These were sub-let as pitches to bookmakers 'at exorbitant prices almost amounting to blackmail'. In addition, a daily toll was levied on practically all the bookmakers on the course, who paid up 'for the sake of saving their skins'.[112] The going rate was between £5 and £20 per day.[113]

Dell well remembered that to get their pitches, bookmakers had to arrive at a meeting early in the morning to stake a claim and 'you had to be prepared to bung or be prepared to fight'. But that was not the end of the scams, because 'to be a successful gangster they had to have money coming in to pay their hirelings see. You had to have plenty of money coming in to keep a team together. Once they couldn't keep the team together well that was the end of the gang.'[114] Kimber did make plenty of money and kept his team together supported by one of the key figures in the Birmingham Gang, Andrew Towey. Also known as Cochrane, Towey was a mysterious figure but was another convicted Midlands thief who moved south to be closer to the busiest racecourses. Dell declared that he was 'a man of great respect . . . a tremendous gambler. In those days he'd have a monkey (£500) on a horse and he used to sit there on a stool, I can see him now, and they'd come and give him information about the prices and he'd send them away to have a bet. But he was the one they all looked up to in Birmingham, and of course Billy Kimber.'[115] Charles Maskey, a well-known racing man from Hoxton in London, once benefitted from Towey's advice when he and his friend, Dick, were at a night race meeting at Kempton Park:

> We'd got about eight bob between us and we'd put it on the one (horse) and that come up and we got about six quid, so Towey says 'How y'doin' Dickie boy?' So he says, 'Well we've had a bit of a double up'. So Towey says, 'Now back this one'. The big race was the third race so we had odds of 50 to 3½ that one (£3.50 to win £50). Oh fuckin hell (it won). Oh Andrew, lovely boy. Andrew 'back this one' Andrew Towey.[116]

It was Towey who either came up with or developed the idea of selling dots and dashes cards for each race. This was a simple operation whereby each horse on the card was pricked with symbols to alert bookies to its form and its chances in the race. In fact, this 'service' told the bookmaker nothing more than he knew already and it was merely a means to obtain money. Jim Cooper was a bookie from 1926 onwards and, as he clarified, there would be 'a dot here, that would be the favourite, and a cross there, that was a tip'.[117] Then there was the selling of tissues with the names of the jockeys on them and the payment for the calling out of the numbers of the horses in a particular race. The runners were declared three days in advance and printed on a race card, but between then and the race itself some horses were pulled out. About half an hour before the 'off', one of the course officials would put up on a board the numbers of the horses that would actually run. These would be marked on a race card by touts or 'runners' paid by the gangs, and they would run around the bookies, trying to take in about ten at a time, shouting out the numbers of the horses.[118]

Bookmakers were also 'encouraged' to 'cough up' for 'tools of the trade': pieces of chalk to mark up the prices of the horses on their blackboards; water from buckets and sponges with which to rub them out; and stools on which to stand. Dell emphasised that 'it was the Birmingham mob that used to run the stools at Cheltenham and places like that. And they used to have to cart the stools from track to track and they used to have a big van to do it in. And then when they got there, they were collapsible stools, used to have to bang the legs in, and they used to have to set all the stools up.' Excessive prices could be charged, as if a bookie did not have a stool to stand on to shout to the crowd, he was at a disadvantage. Bookies usually paid 2s 6d for each 'facility', and with between 200 and 300 of them at many meetings, this added up to a lot of money.[119]

There was one other money-making racket and it was entrusted to John Garnham and his small team from Chapel Market. His son, Tommy, was told that his father was 'a watch-out' for pickpockets who had not sought Kimber's permission to work the meeting and who had not paid tribute. One of Garnham's men was Henry Thorne, who was well in with Kimber and better known as 'the Wizard'. He would report back on which pickpocketing gangs were around: 'He was like the Wizard of Oz, he'd go and spy on some gangsters somewhere.' Then there was Pio, 'who always had my Dad's back', and Scouser, who was 'a bit of a back-up for my Dad. Any problems he was always there'. If 'unauthorised' pickpockets were spotted, John Garnham would go over and look for their boss, 'the fuckin main man'. He would give him a good hiding in front of the others, in effect saying to them, 'This is your fuckin boss, look what I've done to him.' With him beaten the rest would go, but if Garnham thought that he couldn't handle the hard man of the pickpocketing gang, then he would call for Kimber as no one messed with him.[120]

Given the chaos that had pervaded southern racecourses in 1919 and early 1920, it's likely that Kimber did bring some order. But the demands of the Birmingham Gang and its allies were resented. Born in 1901, Lou Prince was a racecourse bookie with a Jewish father, and although he regarded Towey as a gentleman and respected Kimber, he was contemptuous of the roughnecks who took liberties.

These Birmingham tearaways come down South and terrorised the bookmakers down here. It was common practice for them to kick the bookmaker's tools out of their rightful position and institute their own favoured one in that pitch. It had gone on for years, blackmail and what have you, demanding money and monopolising anything that was profitable. [121]

Former chief inspector Divall revealed that some of these liberties were taken by 'three low blackguards, always more or less full of liquor'. These 'loonies' visited the cheap ring and 'terrified and blackmailed a small number of East End bookmakers. If the latter did not shell out, they were cruelly assaulted and badly damaged'.[122] The bookies were Jewish, and those who terrorised them were Elephant Boys. They were arrested in April 1921 at Kempton Park, where, with hammers on view in their coats, they had demanded money from bookmakers. One of them was George Moss, the maddest man in South London when he was in drink – hence why he was called Mad Mossy. He was imprisoned for twelve months' hard labour.[123]

But it was not the 'Loonies' who provoked the racecourse war of 1921. It was an enforcer from the Birmingham Gang with a vicious attack on Alfie Solomon, a Jewish bookie from Covent Garden. Unlike Kimber and most gangsters, Solomon had served loyally throughout the First World War and then followed two of his brothers into racing.[124] On 12 March, ten days before the attack on Sabini at Greenford, Solomon was bookmaking at Sandown Park. Boxing referee Deyong saw what happened. Solomon called out odds of 11 to 4 on a horse called Morganatic Marriage. As he was doing so, a mobster passed and shouted, 'I'll lay 33 to 12 on!' – meaning that he wanted a bet of £12 to win £33 if the horse won. Solomon knew the gangster as one who betted 'on the nod', collecting if he won and refusing to pay up if he lost, and so he snapped back, 'No bet!' But the horse won and, after the race, the mobster came looking for his money. Solomon steadfastly refused to pay, saying that he had not laid the bet. Suddenly the gangster swung his race-glasses, heavy and solid, into Solomon's face. Falling to the ground, his 'assailant promptly stepped on his unprotected face', immediately afterwards slipping away into the crowd. Solomon was picked up, his face a bloody mass and with several teeth missing. In Deyong's words, 'from that moment the gang wars between the North and South began in earnest'.[125]

Another Jewish bookmaker was attacked soon after. Aged fifty-three and from Whitechapel, Philip Jacobs died a few months later. At the inquest, his widow said that he had returned from the Sandown Park meeting with his head bandaged, telling her that he had been struck on the head with a hammer. His injury was explained by Samuel Hirschowitz, who had been with Jacobs and a man called Abraham Joel. Someone named Armstrong had struck Joel and the two began to scuffle. As Hirschowitz tried to separate them, he was also hit by Armstrong, who forced him to the ground and 'kicked him for all he was worth'. There were plenty of people about, but they were all too afraid to intervene – all that is, bar Jacobs. As he did so, he was hit on the head and then struck with a chopper. Badly injured, he received medical aid from the ambulance men. After all the evidence had been heard, the widow of Jacobs stated clearly, 'Everybody knows Armstrong. He is a big and desperate man. My husband told me that after he had been assaulted Armstrong said to him, "I am very sorry, Phil. I did not know it was you."' [126]

The day after the inquest, Thomas Samuel John Armstrong was charged with the wilful murder of Jacobs. He was arrested in Birmingham, telling a detective:

> I know I had a fight with two men in the small ring at Sandown Park on that day, and I know I hit one of them and knocked him down. I didn't hit him with a hammer, because if I had I should have killed him then … I had been on the booze all that day, and don't know what I did. I was at a club all the night before. I got laid out myself at Brighton after the last meeting there, and they nearly did me in. I was knocked unconscious, and in Brighton Hospital for two or three days.[127]

At the remand hearing, Armstrong was now charged with manslaughter through striking Jacobs and occasioning or hastening his death. Another witness in the various court proceedings was Morris Forman, a bookmaker from Brixton. At first, he said that he not seen anything in Armstrong's hands in the fight, but he contradicted this later, stating that Armstrong had hit Jacobs on the head with a pair of field glasses. When challenged about changing his evidence, he replied that he had been threatened with his life if he spoke the truth, after which he had asked for police protection. Despite this new evidence, Armstrong denied that he had struck Jacobs and was found not guilty.[128] Given Forman's information about the field glasses, it is most likely that Armstrong was the mobster who had beaten Solomon.

Although stating he was a bookmaker, Armstrong was a habitual criminal. However, unlike others of his age in the Birmingham Gang, there is no indication that he had been a slogger or peaky blinder. Born in 1875 and from Aston, at aged fifteen he was sentenced to four months in prison for breaking into the house of his uncle. He was no longer living with his parents and he had been in trouble before for petty theft and sleeping out. [129] Two years later, he joined the Militia. He was just under 5 foot 6 inches, sallow complexioned, brown haired and blue eyed.[130] Armstrong married Alice Fisher in 1895, but by 1911 it appears that he had abandoned her and their three children, as they were living without him in overcrowded conditions with Alice's mother, her two sisters and brother. In October 1915, Armstrong joined the Royal Garrison Artillery but deserted two years later. A few months afterwards, he was arrested for loitering in Bolton. Thereafter, Armstrong became one of the most alarming men in the Birmingham Gang with a nominal address in Highgate, Birmingham.[131]

THE SABINIS TAKE UP THE CUDGELS

Alfie Solomon's youngest brother, Simeon Solomon, had started up as a bookie in 1919 but because of anti-Semitism he betted in the name of Simmy Lewis, as 'if I'd put up Simmy Solomon I wouldn't have took a penny'. After his older brother was beaten up by the Birmingham Gang, it became 'us against them, the North against the South. They came down here. We were not up North. They came down here'.[132] The targeting of the Jewish bookies was stressed by Alan Harris, who was bookmaking at Brighton races when 'some Birmingham people had had a row with some Jewish people and they came along, the Birmingham mob, and cut everybody up, everybody was just running about and they just cut them'.[133] But it was the attack on Solomon that provoked a fierce backlash. Dell insisted that the 'Jews were very game. In the old days, in the poverty-stricken days, every fighter was a Jew. Nearly every champion was a Jew. Why? Because they were poverty-stricken. I could run through them all. Johnny Brown, Kid Lewis, Kiddy Berg, all of them.'[134] Fellow bookmaker Prince agreed, indicating that a Jewish team emerged and that 'they found their power in strength and gameness. They wouldn't be dictated to.' This team involved Alfie Solomon, who was transformed into a gangster by his mauling, and the tearaways attached to Edward Emanuel because he was 'a financial power' and 'the guvnor before Darby Sabini'.[135]

Emanuel was indeed a power, with Arthur Harding saying that he governed the whole Jewish underworld: 'He was the Jewish Al Capone – everything was grist to his mill – he got in the spieling business and through that with the racing. He used to fix the boxing fights and all.' Emanuel's group of terrors included Jackie Burman, a man called 'Do-Do', Bobby Nark and Bobby Levy.[136] They were from the Jewish East End, as was Ralph L. Finn. He noticed that as they grew up, the local youths who gambled with cards and dice joined the race gangs. They gathered in the forecourt of Aldgate East Station at the corner of Golden Street. The most feared of these was the Aldgate Mob, 'a razor slashing gang of hoodlums who protected bookmakers – for a fee – and fleeced those who would not be protected. The lucky punter coming away from the races discovered to his cost that winnings were not meant to be won permanently. They were only on loan. The race gang would take his money. Or cut him up. Or both.'[137] The Aldgate Mob were also pickpockets, as Dell remembered.

They were led by a face among them called Dychell. Right villain and he was the leader. And they used to operate mostly on bank holidays and high days and holidays and they'd be 20 handed . . . and what they would do, they would lift a guy in the air, someone would take his money. And I've seen 'em come up to your joint and as you see their hands, Bank Holiday Monday, you'd see their hands coming out to give them, you know, their stake (protection money).[138]

For all that the Aldgate and other Jewish tearaways were 'terrors', they were not strong enough to take on the Birmingham Gang. As one of the city's newspaper admitted, 'its members were utterly unscrupulous. They visited racecourses in the Midlands and the South, blackmailed bookmakers and any members of the public who were unfortunate enough to fall into their clutches, and generally made themselves so terrifying that the bookmakers in self-defence engaged for their protection a number of men of a similar character from the King's Cross and Saffron Hill districts.'[139] Those men from Saffron Hill were the Sabinis, 'the Italian push' as Prince put it, and they were called in by Emanuel as he was 'pally' with them. As Divall recognised, the persecution of the East End Jewish bookmakers had become unbearable and 'the Sabinis took up the cudgels in their defence'.[140] A mixed gang quickly emerged, with all the Jewish terrors joining the gang led by Darby Sabini.[141] He justified his involvement because the Birmingham Gang of very tough and rough people was 'blackmailing these Yiddisher people for years'.

The Jews had all these best pitches. To stop in those pitches they had to pay money to these people. If they did not pay money to these people, they could not bet, or they were set upon. They used to charge £10. If you did not give them the £10, you would very likely be knocked down and you would not bet anymore.[142]

But Sabini's motives were not as benevolent as he made out, for he saw an opportunity to wrest control of the rackets on the southern racecourses from the Birmingham Gang.

Born in 1888 to an English mother and a father from the villages around Parma in northern Italy, Sabini had been a minder at spielers, illegal gambling clubs for mostly Jewish businessmen. The main operator of these was Emanuel, and it's likely that it was through this connection that the two men came together.[143] Harding mentioned that he first heard of the Sabini Gang about 1910–11, and certainly within a few years it was an established force in Clerkenwell.[144] In her major study of London's criminal underworlds, Heather Shore suggested that like the other London gangs of the 1920s, the Sabini Gang may have had roots not only in the territorial street-fighting gangs that had long been a feature in areas like Clerkenwell, but also in forms of defence against incursions from other local youths. Bound together by a shared background and neighbourhood loyalty, the Sabini Gang was strengthened by personal relationships and blood, for as Shore has discerned, 'the most enduring "structure" connecting the Sabini Gang was family and kinship'.[145] To a large extent, the core of the gang was so connected. It included Darby's two youngest brothers, Joe and Harry, nicknamed 'Harryboy'; his childhood friend, Angelo Gianicoli, better known as Georgie Langham; and two of the Cortesi brothers. Yet it also included Jewish toughs led by Alfie Solomon, and those with a solely English heritage like Alf White and Jim Ford.

In his book *Gangs of London: 100 Years of Mob Warfare*, Brian McDonald includes a rare and important photograph from his family's collection. Taken in 1919, it shows leading gangsters, 'when the Brummagems, McDonalds, Cortesis and Sabinis were still friends'. It includes Darby, Harry and Joe Sabini; Harry and George Cortesi; Wal, Jim, Tom, Bert and Wag McDonald; and Billy Kimber. Well dressed in suits and ties, they are sporting a mixture of straw boaters, flat caps and bowlers, and all of them have a flower in their jacket buttonhole. It is apparent they are going off on 'a jolly', most probably to a race meeting, and that they are on sociable terms.[146] That friendly relationship broke down when Kimber and his pals found out Sabini had been called in by the Jewish bookmakers, and that knowledge led to the attack on him at Greenford on 22 March.

Charged with shooting at persons unknown with a revolver, Sabini disclosed that he'd been employed by George Harris, one of the biggest bookmakers in London. Bail was granted for the large sum of £200 from Sabini himself and a surety of £200. His ability to pay, and the support of Harris, suggests that Sabini also had the backing of big London bookies who had tired of the Birmingham Gang's extortion.[147] In the final hearing of his case, a police officer reported that when Sabini was arrested, he was very agitated and in fear of his life; whilst a police inspector stated that his character had previously been good. The charge of shooting at persons unknown with a revolver was dismissed and he was fined £10 for possessing a gun without a certificate. The magistrates appeared more concerned to prove that the men who had attacked Sabini were not from Greenford and were pleased to learn that they were from Birmingham and belonged to a violent and dangerous gang who would do anything, even shoot to kill.[148]

The leniency shown towards Sabini and the favourable police report led Brian McDonald to believe that 'money changed hands' – an allegation given support by Arthur Harding's recollections that Emanuel 'had the police buttoned up' and could get criminals out of trouble.[149]

It is unlikely that Sabini would have turned up at Greenford without support and nor did he. Two men from his gang were arrested for disturbing the peace and loitering with intent to commit a felony. They were Sandy Rice, real name Alex Tomaso, and Fred Gilbert. It was alleged that they had led an attack on the police and incited others to join them. During the disturbance, after Sabini had fired, a policeman saw Rice and Gilbert fighting their way through the crowd. Rice said that he was trying to reach Sabini to help him, but some of the attackers spotted him and shouted, 'Here is one. I then had help myself and I ran in self-defence.' Seeing Gilbert, the Birmingham gangsters called out, 'Here is a pal of one of them.' They knocked him to the ground and kicked him. He denied attacking the police, maintaining they were his friends that day. Gilbert's account was corroborated by Harry Joel, a bookmaker: 'How he escaped being killed I don't know. Both of us were attacked by the mob.' Gilbert and Rice were discharged.[150]

Three days after the fracas at Greenford, Robert Charles Harvey and 'a number of other racecourse frequenters' were beaten with a baton at London Bridge Station. The Railway Police intervened and the attackers boarded the train to Plumpton races. Harvey was taken to hospital with scalp wounds and body bruises. He told the police that he had no idea as to who had assaulted him, and if he had known he would not prosecute. This was to become a common refrain. However, the police believed that Harvey had welched at the Greenford Trotting meeting and was associated with the Birmingham Gang. [151] With the violence escalating, the gangs approached each other to try to settle their differences. Accompanied by the McDonalds and Sage, on 27 March Kimber went to Sabini's house. [152] The meeting was dramatised in *Britain's Godfather*, Edward T. Hart's biography of Sabini, which, ignoring his Englishness, imaginatively depicted him as a Mafia-style godfather.

> Darby welcomed Billy Kimber politely to his home, but without any display of warmth. He seated him at a table laid in the Italian tradition ... a freshly baked loaf, great chunks of cheese and a carafe of anisette, a liquorice-flavoured wine. As a concession to Kimber's essential Englishness, there were also six bottles of beer. [153]

Heather Shore has described Hart's book as 'the pulp fiction account of Darby Sabini's life', and his representation of the meeting with Kimber does read as sensationalised and swayed by images of American gangsters. [154] According to Hart, the meeting turned sour over the terms of a truce and Kimber went for the gun hidden in his powder-blue suit. But Sabini was swifter and pulled out his own big, flat gun and shot Kimber, whose 'own hand hadn't even reached his gun butt'. The force of the bullet drove Kimber backwards, toppling the chair and sending him sliding to the floor. He groaned and lay still, but as if Sabini were a gunslinger, Hart claimed that 'even during the reflex action of firing Darby had been careful to aim for a non-lethal part of the human body, the thigh'. Hart was not at the meeting and had never met either Sabini or Kimber, and he wrote that this incident occurred at Sabini's home in Little Italy in Clerkenwell and after the Epsom Road

Ambush.[155] Neither statement is correct. The two gangsters met before that event and after Sabini had been saved by the police at Greenford, and by then he was no longer living in Little Italy but in Collier Street, King's Cross. And whilst Kimber was shot it was not by Sabini.

In his reminiscences, ex-Detective Chief Superintendent Greeno was also prone to colourful language.

> Sid F–, second-in-command of the Birmingham boys, went to Darby's £2 6s 6d-a week three-roomed flat at King's Cross to 'shake hands and make up'. That's what he said. Darby wasn't home but his wife, having been round to the Prince of Wales for two dozen Guinness, was throwing a party. Sid arrived at midnight and at 2 a.m. he was found lying in the street with a bullet in his right side and a cut over the eye. 'Who did it? I never come copper on anyone and I ain't starting now.[156]

Sid F– was Kimber, not the second-in-command but the overall chief of the Birmingham Gang.[157] In court, he recounted that late on the evening of 27 March, he had gone with Darby Sabini to his house in Collier Street, where others arrived. There was plenty of drink and Alfie Solomon was among the company. They had a few songs and the party broke up about 2am. When Kimber was leaving, someone hit him on the eye, others assaulted him, and 'I was shot by a third party, but all I saw was a shadow'.[158] The only witness to give evidence remembered the events differently. This witness stated that Solomon arrived later and was spotted by Kimber and his pals when they moved into the passageway. One of them then turned round, demanding, 'What do you want, you Jew!'[159] Shots were fired and Kimber was later found unconscious on the pavement. He had suffered a wound in the side and was rushed to hospital.[160]

Handing himself in to the police, Solomon was charged with unlawful wounding. He accepted that he had shot Kimber, but insisted that it was an accident after the head of the 'Birmingham gang of terrors' had shouted, 'What are you doing here, you Jew? Get out or I'll shoot you.' He knocked a revolver out of Kimber's hand, and in the struggle, the weapon went off. Frightened, Solomon ran away. Throughout the court hearings, Kimber continued to maintain that he did not know who had shot him, declaring that if Solomon 'said that he shot me then he is a coward. Only cowards carry revolvers. I would rather blow out my brains than use one on anyone.'[161] With Kimber refusing to say anything and acting as a hostile witness, the judge at the trial at the Old Bailey directed the jury to return a verdict of not guilty.[162]

Although he had appeared at Solomon's trial, Kimber was out of action over the next couple of months whilst he recovered from his wound. Given his hatred of Jews, especially of Solomon, and of the necessity of striking back to show that he was still a force to be reckoned with, it is likely that Kimber brooded over taking revenge. Tommy Garnham heard a larger-than-life story of how he supposedly did so.

> When Bill (Kimber) got shot they surrounded the hospital, the gangsters, you know. Dad was down there. They surrounded the hospital. The police was outside, you know. In case they wanted to come and get him again, do him in the hospital. So he got out, they asked him questions and he didn't want to know about who done it.

Then he got a bit better, down here in Grant Street (Islington) he got dressed up in a right load of old clothes, like a tramp, this is the story how my Dad told me. He went down Clerkenwell looking in bins and he see him (Solomon) come out – it weren't the 'Griffin' – it was a place somewhere round the back. He knew where they was. And he'd been waiting a week just to get him on his own. And he got him and he said 'all I want to do is put him in a wheelchair. I don't want to kill him but I want to do him because the c**t shot me in the back'. And he done it Kimber. Battered him badly. Really badly. And I said 'why didn't he kill him, Dad?' and he said he didn't want to kill him he wanted him like a cabbage. He'd remember what shooting him in the back was like.[163]

There is no evidence that Kimber did avenge himself on Solomon in this way, but the creation of the story itself reinforces Kimber's position as 'the head of a gang of desperadoes', a position which clearly inspired a fervent loyalty as much as dread. And he would go on to brutally assault Solomon in the future.[164]

Days after the shooting of Kimber, the police received a tip-off, as Greeno put it, that 'the Sabini Gang and the Brummies planned a showdown at Alexandra Park on 4 April. Police swarmed all over the track and at every railway station en route, but at one o'clock a gang surrounded a couple of bookmakers' touts from Birmingham and felled them with bottles. Then they "put the boot in".[165] The Sabini Gang was cleared from the silver ring but the Birmingham Gang and their allies were also there in big numbers. Deyong evoked the taut atmosphere:

'shots were fired that day, iron-bars and lead-sticks crashed on defenceless and often innocent heads, and the knuckledusters and razors ripped and slashed to deadly purpose'.[166] Lou Prince was bookmaking when the violence erupted.

> Things moved on rapidly and Alexandra Park could have been a right to-do. The Birmingham Mob marched through Tattersall's in Indian file about 20 strong and a couple of them carrying shooters. They marched right through Tattersall's looking for any member of the opposition but found none and then went onto the small ring. I will never forget those scenes for when the search started the ring was packed and as it moved on everyone dived out of the way and believe me, three quarters of the attendance did just that and likewise it was the same in the cheaper ring.[167]

One of the Birmingham Mob carrying a shooter was Anthony 'Curly' Martin. Aged forty-two, he was charged with attempting to murder a Londoner called James Best, one of two taxi-drivers who had driven the Sabini Gang to the meeting and were attacked as a result.[168] A police witness described the scene: 'I saw a number of men chasing another man and I saw the man hit on the head from behind and knocked down. While he lay on the ground I saw the prisoner (Martin) take out a revolver and point it at the man the ground. He then fired and ran away.'[169] This account, however, cannot be wholly trusted, as whilst a revolver was found after Martin's arrest, it was rusty and had not been used recently, therefore if Best had been fired at, the shot had missed for he had been taken to hospital with two wounds caused instead by a blunt instrument. In court, he said that he did not know who had hit him and nor did he know Martin, whose good character was affirmed by two bookmakers and the police in Birmingham.[170] They disclosed that he was a professional backer of horses and did not know the Birmingham Gang.[171]

Yet Martin lived in Bridge Street West, close to where Kimber had grown up and where his parents still lived. Given that, and that he was also a racing man, it is most unlikely that Martin did not know members of the Birmingham Gang. Described as thick-set and clean-shaven, his son, Joe, remembered him 'as always a smart feller'. He recalls that 'he always had a bowler hat, y'know, he always got the brush and put it over the steam of the kettle and steamed it and pull his hat on. And the old lady always looked after him, polished his boots.'[172] Like the Sabinis, Anthony Martin was the son of a mixed marriage, with his mother an Englishwoman and his father an Italian from Genoa.[173] He recorded himself as a fish hawker in 1911, but as his son recalled, 'My Dad wasn't a bookie, he was what you called a minder, really.' He did have a revolver, although, 'You could bet your life it wasn't loaded, I'm positive of that y'know, really. If he had, it would have been a flash, really, a frightener.'

Martin was a freelance minder, although often he protected one particular bookmaker, and he used to mix with other racing men at Howard's pub by Birmingham's Snow Hill Station. Like them, he was rarely at home and his wife had to bring up their family with his uncertain and irregular income: 'She had a struggle, I can tell you that. Her had a struggle 'cus her had nothing coming in but somehow my mother went on and her had a big family . . . It wasn't a regular wage but somehow or other he must have earnt something.' Martin died in 1938 aged fifty-eight. His son Joe, born in 1914, went on to become a bookie as did his older brother, Alfie.[174]

Following the affray at Alexandra Park, on 20 April, an undercurrent of violence between the gangs threatened to burst out into full-scale warfare in London. There was a fight between two groups outside Mornington Crescent tube station, close to where Brummy Sage lived. They were thought to have belonged to racing gangs, one from Birmingham and the other from the neighbourhood of King's Cross – which is where Darby Sabini lived. A shot was fired and several men tried to get away in a taxicab when the police intervened. One of the officers jumped onto the footboard of the cab and directed the driver to a police station. Three men were arrested, with one of them having a bludgeon made out of the case of a German grenade tied to short stick. Two of them were discharged, including Jim Ford, who was now a main tough in the Sabini Gang. The third was merely fined 20 shillings.[175] Later that month the Birmingham Police were informed that someone had been offered a job to bomb a nightclub owned by one of the Sabini Gang.[176] According to the city's chief constable, 'a number of race course frequenters were going to London for the purpose of carrying out some raid, and that they were going to obtain Mills Bombs from Uxbridge'.[177] The bombing did not happen, but Edward Banks was named as the leading participant in the plot. A few weeks afterwards, he took a similar role in the Epsom Road Ambush – an event that would soon become known as the Epsom Road Battle.

Chapter 3

THE BIRMINGHAM GANG AND SABINI GANG AT WAR

THE EPSOM ROAD BATTLE

Throughout the spring and summer of 1921, the racecourses of southern England were wracked by a bloody gang war. This feud was nothing like the brawls of the street gangs of the past – the peaky blinders of Birmingham, the hooligans of London and the scuttlers of Manchester and Salford. The Racecourse War between the Birmingham Gang and the Sabini Gang was on a much bigger and wider scale, pitting as it did two gangs of criminals from different cities against one another in a fight for control of highly profitable money-making rackets. A new phenomenon, it triggered alarming press headlines: 'Racecourses Infested with Ruffianly Gangs'; 'Blackmail Gangs on Racecourses'; 'Bookmaker's Fatal Injury'; 'Racecourse Riot'; 'Shooting and Fighting with Fists'; 'Bookmaker Acquitted of Murder'; 'Racecourse Fracas' – and more.[178] The disturbing stories of violence sparked speculation about the identities of the gangs, and it was quickly revealed that a London group composed exclusively of foreigners was waging a vendetta against a Midlands combination.[179]

But there was confusion as to the actual make-up of the two gangs. *The Times* believed that the London gang consisted of Italians, whilst the Birmingham Gang was 'mostly foreign Jews'. It found some satisfaction that these roughs were 'wretched foreigners' who could not fight cleanly, using as they did 'knives, life preservers – falsely so called – and apparently pistols'.[180] A better-informed correspondent in the *Sporting Times* condemned both gangs and hoped they would decimate each other in their vendetta. But inferring that the Midland gang was English, he claimed that by comparison with the London gang it was 'more human than a collection of foreigners'.[181] Anti-Semitic language and disdain for foreigners would sully the reporting of the Racecourse War of 1921 and of the race gangs thereafter. Yet the Birmingham Gang was not made up of 'foreign Jews'. It was an overwhelmingly English grouping that did not fight fairly in an 'English' way. Mob-handed, they wielded hammers, hatchets, revolvers and sandbags, and it was Jewish bookmakers whom they beat up most eagerly.

It is likely that the Birmingham Gang was supported at least tacitly by some local bookmakers, as suggested by a statement issued to a Birmingham newspaper in June 1921 by a well-known racegoer. Infused with anti-Jewish prejudice, it played upon notions of 'Englishness'.

> We strongly resent the allegation that Birmingham men are blackmailers and tricksters. We do not claim to be 'little white angels', but we do claim to be good sportsmen and to be no better or worse than other

men attending race meetings. What was alleged is that a comparatively new group of Jews have been attempting to set themselves up as masters of the situation, especially in the south of England and they have been employing hooligans to make the atmosphere unhealthy and dangerous for Birmingham racing men. That is the root cause of the trouble, and the Birmingham boys would welcome any action on the part of the authorities which would remove it. Anyone is at liberty to come to Birmingham or the Midlands. Why should Birmingham racing men who go elsewhere be subject to violence, instigated, as we allege, by jealous rivals.[182]

After the Alexandra Park incidents, and with Kimber injured, the Sabini Gang had quickly become the dominant force on its 'home patch'. Fearful of what might happen to them, most Birmingham bookies stayed away from southern racecourses. Hilda Burnett grew up in the 1920s by Birmingham's markets, in the same neighbourhood as Banks's Mob. Her mother's brother was one of them and she was told that 'the London gang did not want the Birmingham bookies down there working their territory. The Birmingham bookies thought different so decided to do something about it. So they all got together and off to the south they did go. They all met up at the Epsom Racecourse and it was given its name the Epsom Vendetta.'[183] In response to the successful takeover by the Sabinis, the Birmingham Gang did resolve to go down south and make a massive show of strength at the Epsom Derby meeting in the first week of June. It was the biggest racing event of the year, attracting tens of thousands of people, and a victory there in

Surrey, so close to London, would finish off the Sabini Gang. That decision led to the Epsom Road Battle on 2 June 1921. Only it wasn't a battle, it was a one-sided battering of ten men unconnected to the Sabini Gang.

A tabloid-style retelling of this 'fight' was very different. Published a generation after the affray, it began with a call to Reuben Bigland, a wealthy Birmingham businessman nicknamed 'Telephone Jack' because he had set up a telephone service providing racing results to credit bookmakers.[184] The caller was Horatio Bottomley, the financier, editor of the highly popular *John Bull* magazine, and populist politician. He began a rant about a scandalous wrong done to brave British boys who had been serving their country in the trenches. London's bookmakers had returned to find that their rightful pitches had been stolen 'from under their noses by alien scrimshankers'. Supposedly the aggrieved bookies looked to Bottomley, as a patriot and patron of sport, to protect their interests against the capital's two biggest gangs, the Sabinis and Solomons. Seeing an opportunity to establish absolute 'Brummagem supremacy' on England's racecourses, Bigland called a meeting of Birmingham's gangs, including the two biggest, the so-called Mancinis and Vendetta boys. The account stated that a temporary truce was agreed and arrangements were made for an outing to Epsom for 'doing in' the London gangsters.

Very early on Derby Day, 1921, a party of 39 thugs and mobsters armed with razors, coshes, knuckledusters, hammers, axes, spanners and even a few revolvers assembled outside the 'Malt Shovel' public house in Milk Street, Birmingham. They were waiting bunched together in little knots, for the charabanc that was to take them to the Epsom Downs. Some were taking a swig at bottles of Scotch (recently raised to the iniquitous price of 12s 6d) from their mackintosh pockets. One or two were practising 'putting in the leather', i.e. kicking a man on the ground round the base of a lamp-post. Presently the dark blue coach, driven by one of their own boys, turned the corner of the street and came wheezing along through the pearly dawn haze. They climbed in and drove off singing *K-K-K-Katie* and *O Sole Mio*. All in all, it was, as one of them, the philosophical Brummy Sage, remarked to another, his gypsy friend known as the King of Digbeth, 'as promising a start to a nice day's racing as you could wish for under the circs' (circumstances).

This fictionalised account went on to explain how the Birmingham mob watched the Derby with 'a modest decorum that amazed the police and anyone else who knew them', but left Epsom early. Arriving at a suitable corner on the Ewell Road, they blocked it with their charabanc and took up battle stations in the hedge. The first cab to appear carried a lone Leeds bookie. Trying to defend his day's take, he lost three fingers 'from a Brum boy's meat axe'. Then came the real target: five taxi-loads of London bookmakers protected by their own minders and members of the Sabini and Solomon gangs. They were surprised and their vehicles were overturned. The bookies ran for their lives, and although the minders and gangsters fought it out with the Birmingham Boys, they were routed with heavy casualties and a total of over 400 stitches between them.[185]

Despite some connections with real places and events, most

of this account is incorrect. Brummy Sage was a Londoner and did not go racing from Birmingham. The gypsy King of Digbeth did not exist. There was neither a Mancini gang nor one called the Vendetta Boys in Birmingham. The Sabinis were not the ones attacked. Those London bookmakers who first turned to the Sabini Gang for protection may have been Jewish, but non-Jewish bookies were also backing them against the Birmingham Gang. Finally, while the MP Horatio Bottomley was widely known for his patriotic speeches in the First World War and was a betting man friendly with Reuben Bigland, there is no evidence to link Bigland with the Birmingham Gang, nor with its leaders like Billy Kimber, Andrew Towey and Edward Banks. Yet one aspect of this account does resonate with reality – the prejudice against 'aliens' who had supposedly shirked their duty in the Great War. Actually, it was Kimber and others in the Birmingham Gang who were the scrimshankers, while Alfie Solomon and Sabini's brother, Joe, had served their country patriotically.

What then was the reality? The Birmingham Gang did go to Epsom mob-handed, ostensibly to affirm the rights of Midlands' bookies to work southern racecourses, but in reality to violently reassert their control of the rackets. The coach trip arranged by Banks was one of several groups that were involved, and his Mob did meet at the Malt Shovel pub in Milk Street. It was a favourite rendezvous for some of the Birmingham Gang and, as recalled by Steve Nicholls, the son of one of them, 'a chara (charabanc) would tek them. But they could all scrap. But I mean they'd got to be all tooled up 'cus look what they was up against. I mean the London mob was always tooled up. I mean you way [sic] it up, London's a bigger place than this so you might know how they'd got to go on.'[186]

On this occasion, Banks's party teamed up not on Derby Day but beforehand, on Tuesday 30 May. They stayed in London and went racing for the next three days but left early on Thursday 2 June, the day after the Derby, so as to make their attack.

When their charabanc reached Ewell Corner by the Brick Kiln pub at about 4.30pm, they ordered their driver to pull over and then guarded him with a revolver.[187] Others from the Birmingham Gang were already there, five of them having arrived in a taxi driven down from Birmingham the day before.[188] Then a Crossley tender came in sight. A former Royal Flying Corps personnel carrier, it had seven men in the back and three in the front. They were bookmakers from Leeds. As the vehicle approached, it was hit with a shower of bricks and someone inside shouted, 'It's the Brummagem gang,' before it collided with the taxi. Those in the tender were attacked by what they thought was sixty to seventy men, although it is likely there was not as many and that the numbers were understandably exaggerated in the minds of the victims through a petrifying experience in which the assailants wielded choppers, hammers, bars of iron and bricks. One even held a revolver and shouts of 'Kill them!' were heard.[189] Amongst those injured was Samuel Barnet, who was knocked senseless and received wounds all over his head, arms and leg. Another was Solomon Levinson, who was hit twice on the head but did not know whether it was with a hammer or a hatchet.[190] Isaac Lewis was also rendered unconscious by his beating, whilst his brother Michael was struck on the eye and body as he heard men shouting 'Kill the Italians'.

A fifth man, Lazarus Green, received blows from a hammer just above the eye and right ear, and his arm was fractured. Struggling down the road and covered in blood, he was followed by a man with a hammer and pleaded with him, 'You have made a bloomer. We are Leeds men.' The attacker retorted, 'God blimey, I hope we have not. Anyway, get into the field and lie behind the trees, or else they will kill you.'[191] These statements suggest it was a mistake to attack the Leeds bookies as they were allies of the Birmingham Gang. Such an interpretation has been followed by the majority of gangland authors, particularly Hart, who insisted that Sabini deliberately arranged for the Leeds men to take his gang's taxis as a ruse to fool the Brummies.[192] But it wasn't a mistake. The victims were mostly Jewish bookmakers and they were bludgeoned because they had abandoned Kimber for the protection of the Sabini Gang.[193]

None of the beaten men were gangsters, but amongst them was one Londoner called Charles 'Deafy' Schwartz, also known as Woolf Schwartz. Although working for one of the Leeds bookmakers, he lived in Whitechapel.[194] Another deserter from the Army, he admitted that he had been imprisoned six times and it was feared that might taint his evidence in court. It did not. Alone of the victims, he was able to identify some of the attackers – twelve in total.[195] He stated that after men had clambered into the Crossley tender, he was struck on the back. Turning around quickly, he put his hands out and caught hold of a chopper wielded by a man known as 'Big Jock', shouting, 'Go on, kill the Bastards.' Schwartz managed to jump out of the car and flee to hide in the pub. Watching from safety what was going on, he recognised a number of men, all of whom were from Birmingham. After the attack, a large number of them got into the charabanc, but two taxis arrived to take away others. Schwartz had been at Alexandra Park when the shooting affray had taken place and knew that 'for sometime past, from conversations I have had with members of the Jewish fraternity, that the Birmingham gang would in all probability assault anyone of us at a favourable opportunity. I think this particular assault was arranged so that the first party of Italian or Jewish racing men coming along should be assaulted.'[196]

A few hours after the attack, twenty-eight men were arrested at the George and Dragon hotel. Most had been involved and had left the scene in a charabanc. A day later, the handcuffed prisoners were taken from Kingston Police Station to the court in Epsom. They wore a careless air, with many of them smoking cigarettes as they were driven away escorted by forty policemen, many of whom were armed.[197] Brought to trial at Guildford on 19 July, they were charged with conspiring to cause grievous bodily harm to ten men from Leeds and with conspiring with persons unknown to commit unlawful and malicious wounding. All bar one were also charged with being in possession of arms and ammunition. James Berrett, a divisional inspector at Brixton, was responsible for policing the whole of the Epsom course, and therefore was actively involved with the legal proceedings after the 'battle'. Berrett reported that behind the scenes 'various threats were constantly made to me, but they had no effect'. His account further demonstrates that the prisoners were a vicious crowd who made remarks at every opportunity. At the end of each day's proceedings, they were taken by bus back to prison and 'as we passed through Epsom the prisoners swore at everybody they saw'.[198]

By the end of the trial, several men had been discharged or found not guilty. Berrett emphasised that some of them were 'very fortunate indeed as they have very bad criminal records, and if they had been found "Guilty" would no doubt have received severe sentences'.[199] There was a strong police presence in the court as the verdicts were read to prevent a demonstration by the crowd of racing men in the gallery. The seventeen men found guilty were those whose early lives were previously discussed. Each was given a term of hard labour. Arthur Vincent was sentenced to nine months, because he had no previous convictions and a good Army record. Thomas Conway also had a good character and he received a similar term along with William Goulding, who had no previous convictions, Ernest Hughes and Thomas Tuckey.[200] The Assistant Commissioner of the Police at New Scotland Yard was disappointed. He recognised that 'the sentences varied according to the past records of the Prisoners, some of them having very bad records, though we must admit a sentence of nine months even for men with an unblemished record, who were found guilty of this murderous attack, appears to us to be lamentably inadequate'.[201]

William Hayden was given ten months and William Bayliss and William O'Brien were each sentenced to twelve months. Thomas Eivers was committed to fourteen months, as was Alfred Jackson, under the name of Alfred John Thomas. He shouted at the judge, 'That is a miscarriage of justice!' Edward Banks and Edward Tuckey were each imprisoned for fifteen months. Given Banks's leading role in the attack, and the failed bombing plot on a Sabini nightclub, he must have counted himself lucky not to have been given a stiffer sentence. Henry Tuckey, Harry Stringer and John Allard were each sent down for eighteen months. Finally, sentences of three years each were passed on Joseph Witton and John Lee, who remarked 'thank you' and left the dock with a loud laugh.[202] Berrett himself realised there was no direct evidence against any particular prisoner, whilst the Assistant Commissioner of the Metropolitan Police acknowledged that the seventeen convictions had been secured with 'evidence none of the strongest'. However, although wishing that each prisoner had been imprisoned for a minimum of three years, overall he was satisfied with the result and 'we sincerely trust that it may be a heavy deterrent to the Birmingham gang who undoubtedly for the past few months have been carrying on outrages on London bookmakers and racecourses generally'.[203]

Three other Birmingham gangsters were arrested separately at the Epsom Meeting for demanding money from bookmakers with threats. They were Ernest Mack, a dealer aged fifty-six; William Darby, a haulier, thirty-nine; and Charles Franklin, a metal worker, forty-one. A police witness had watched them going through lines of bookmakers, stopping in front of each one and pushing through the crowd to reach them. Invariably as Darby put out his hand, Franklin ordered, 'Give us a pound, come on.' Because they were obviously terrified, most bookmakers gave them some silver, but if any refused the men's attitude became aggressive, with Darby warning, 'Come on, we are four-handed.' (One of them was not arrested.) An aggrieved bookmaker actually shouted at the men, 'Why don't you stand up for your living like we do? If you have not got the guts for that – well welsh, but don't come blackmailing.' A threat was also made to knock over a bookmaker's joint. The men had made a lot of money from their bullying as they had intimidated fifteen bookmakers and afterwards they went into a booth and joined the 'Birmingham Mob', who numbered about a hundred.[204] As mentioned earlier, such estimates of the size of the gangs need to be treated with caution, even when arising from police sources, but what is certain is that they reflected a large number of men.

Darby had no previous offences and was fined £25, but Mack and Franklin were habitual criminals and each was sent down for three months. Mack was yet another one of the Birmingham Gang who had been a slogger-cum-peaky blinder. In 1883, aged twelve, he was one of a number of youths who so violently assaulted a local man that his arm was broken in two places. Belonging to a gang of young roughs who were the terror of Aston, he was sentenced to two months' imprisonment with hard labour.[205] He went on to serve time for two assaults on police constables and also for theft, housebreaking and gaming. Then, in 1907, he was found not guilty of uttering base coins. He was most fortunate for his accomplice, Samuel Sheldon, was imprisoned for five years.[206] Sheldon was one of three brothers who were the driving forces in the infamous Garrison Lane Vendetta. Interestingly, Mack's accomplice at Epsom, Charles Franklin, had been in the opposing gang and had been sentenced to ten years for attempting to murder Sheldon in 1912.[207]

However, the Birmingham Gang didn't have it all its own way at Epsom as Andrew Towey, a key personality in the gang, was struck on the head with a mallet and a bottle, probably by the Sabinis.[208] Receiving first aid, he was asked by the police to identify his attackers. He replied 'that he knew them and would murder them when he recovered but absolutely declined to give the Inspector the names of his assailants and added that if the men were arrested he would decline to identify or prosecute them'.[209]

Towey lived in Kingston, where the five unknown men who had arrived in a taxi had stayed the night before the Epsom

Road Battle.[210] Given that they and others of the Birmingham Gang were never captured, it is not surprising that there were concerns that most of the ringleaders had escaped.[211] Such suspicions were well founded. Donald Mark, the leader of the Newcastle Boys had also been there.[212] So too was Charles 'Wag' McDonald of the Elephant Boys. Soon afterward, he fled to Canada and thence the USA to escape arrest. He went on to become a bodyguard to Jack Dragna, the Mafia boss of Los Angeles, and set up a service for protecting film stars. His exploits are stirringly told in Brian McDonald's book, *Elephant Boys*.[213] But the main ringleaders who got away were from the Birmingham Gang.

In the lead-up to the trial, Birmingham's CID received information from a very reliable source that an Arthur Denny from Smethwick, a town adjoining Birmingham, had been sitting next to the taxi driver before it was driven at the vehicle of the Leeds men. He managed to return to Birmingham on the evening of the attack. William Cunnington from Ladywood was also named as one of the organisers of the affray. However it was thought that although Cunnington may have taken a very active part in the organisation, he was possibly acting as one of their intermediaries for the syndicate, which the police believed was behind the Birmingham Gang's affrays.[214] However, there was too little evidence to take action against either him or Denny. Still, the Staffordshire Constabulary disclosed that both men were almost inseparable and had been attending race meetings together for a considerable time, making a book in the name of Arthur Williams Junior.

Denny himself was distinguished by his smart appearance, having '3 or 4 suits in his possession including a blue pin stripe, a light check and a brown, and he nearly always wears a light velour trilby hat, collar and bow tie, appears very respectable.'[215] Little else is known about him, although in January 1921, he was summoned for deserting his wife. Married six years before, she explained that her 'husband was a bookmaker's clerk, but she had never been able to find out how much he made by that calling. However, he boasted that he was in the habit of paying 5s. 6d. for his meals when he dined out.' Elsie Denny produced a bill to prove this. Taken as evidence of his means, he was ordered to pay her £2 a week. A few months later, he was imprisoned for two months for failing to comply with this order.[216]

As for Cunnington, he lived in a back-to-back house in Nelson Street, Ladywood, a poor quarter of the town, and was recalled as 'a real character'.[217] He was usually known as Cunny, not only through the shortening of his surname but also because he was regarded as a cunning man. Born in 1890, he was the youngest of five sons.[218] His parents separated when he was a child, and by 1901 his father was lodging with another family, whilst his mother and her four younger sons was boarding with a single man. Her eldest boy was twenty-two, married and living nearby. He was a habitual criminal, and by 1908 had been imprisoned ten times for theft – having received his first conviction when he was fifteen.[219] Another brother was also a thief, as was his mother's brother, and in 1913 both were found guilty of uttering counterfeit coins.[220] There is no evidence that William Cunnington followed his older brothers into thieving and he was charged for only one offence. In May 1918, he obstructed the police when they had been searching for deserters in a hotel bar in Birmingham city centre. Coming outside, Cunnington went up to the officers, saying, 'This a nice thing; don't you stand it.' Appearing to be greatly excited, he pointed to his discharge papers from the Army and a crowd gathered, allowing the deserters to abscond. Cunnington had served with the military for seven years, and admitting that he had given the policemen 'a bit of lip', he was fined twenty shillings.[221]

A bookmaker from Brixton identified another Birmingham man as having been at the Epsom Road Battle. After the races, the bookie was in a car with five people, including a child. They passed a vehicle going in the opposite direction and in which they noticed was an injured man. Soon afterwards, they heard someone call out, 'Go back or you will be killed.' The bookmaker's party turned their car around but, within a few hundred yards, seven or eight men ran towards them. Although they came close, they did not catch them but a shot from a revolver was heard. Mo (Moses) Kimberley was recognised as one of the men.[222] He had a long criminal history. In the ten years from 1907, he was convicted of theft, loitering and assault – not only in Birmingham but also in London and Waterford in Ireland, where some pickpockets had moved because horse racing had continued there during the First World War.[223] Then, in 1917, he was sent down for fourteen months' hard labour for a robbery committed in Athlone with other Birmingham men who had very bad records.[224] In the bookmaker's statement, Kimberley was described as broad built, clean-shaven, and dressed smartly in a dark-brown suit and cap. Generally, though, he wore a bowler hat – and the billycock, a type of bowler hat, was the headgear of the first peaky blinders in the early 1890s. Given the meagre evidence against him, Kimberley wasn't charged. However, like Banks he had his own mob within the Birmingham Gang, and so did Cunnington. Allies at the Epsom Road Battle, they later fell out after the Birmingham Gang fractured and were involved in one of the outrages to be discussed later, which precipitated the Home Secretary into declaring war on the race gangs in 1925.

WILD SCENES AT BATH

Berrett asserted that the sentencing for the Epsom Road Battle put an end to warfare between the racing gangs, which had been greatly exaggerated but undoubtedly had kept many people off the racecourses.[225] The bookmakers who suffered blackmailing and those who were razor-slashed and beaten up by the gangs would have disagreed that the violence was exaggerated. Furthermore, it's clear that Berrett was mistaken that the racecourse war had ended. On 5 July 1921 there were disturbances at Salisbury Races, despite the extra precautions that had been taken as a result of the widespread disorder the previous year.[226] After the racing, as related by Brian McDonald, his uncles, Wal and Bert, led the Elephant Boys in an attack on a gang of Sabinis led by Jim Ford, who was arrested by the police after they intervened to stop the fighting. This provoked more violence and eventually eight more men were arrested. None of the arrested were Elephant Boys.[227] In court, the prisoners were presented as 'young men from London, of no great stature but sturdily built and flashily dressed'. Five of them were imprisoned for short terms. Most were from the East End, some were Jewish and a few gave themselves as bookmakers. However, Thomas Mack, a commission agent, was from Clerkenwell, the heartland of the Sabinis.[228] In the strange relationships of gangland, it's possible he was a relative of Ernest Mack of the Birmingham Gang.

The Racecourse Feud, as it was now mostly termed, was attracting widespread publicity. Rickman named one journalist who especially drew the ire of the gangs, recounting what happened to him at the mid-July Newmarket meeting:

> J. M. Dick, who was then the travelling racing correspondent of the *London Evening News* and no longer a young man, was set upon in the streets of Newmarket by a mob who pelted him at close range with paper-bags full of flour and yellow ochre and otherwise assaulted him. His clothes were ruined and he was severely bruised and shaken. Dick had been writing courageously for some time about the lack of protection to the race-going public, and he went further than most of his confrère calling for the suppression of those who endeavour to sell 'tips' on or in the vicinity of the racecourse. I have always understood that it was this particular feature of his campaign that prompted the attack on him.[229]

The police believed that Dick was assaulted by the Sabini Gang. His ordeal highlighted the arrogance of the racecourse gangs, who felt that they could attack a journalist without fear of recourse from the law.

Obviously, the Birmingham Gang had been weakened by the imprisonment of so many of its fighters after the Epsom Road Battle, but once Kimber recovered from his gun wound he fought back hard, causing 'Wild Scenes' at the Bath meeting on 17 August.[230] The next day, the local newspaper reported on the sensational sights when London bookmakers were attacked by Birmingham men with sandbags and hammers. It was the most pronounced display of open violence that had ever occurred in the city and arose from a well-organised plan of campaign.[231]

During the morning, it was said that nearly five hundred of the Birmingham Gang had stationed themselves near the Great Western Railway Station, 'where they scrutinised the large crowds of men coming from the trains from London. In this way they hoped to pick out the rival gang, which is composed largely of foreigners from the East End.'[232]

The first attack occurred just after 10am when a small crowd hustled a man with hammers and sticks. Soon after, George Hall, a bookmaker, and his clerk, Frank Heath were set upon. Both were from Brighton and Hall was treated for scalp wounds, a broken finger, and cuts on the left hand. Heath, a tall stalwart man, described how he and Hall had been walking up the hill towards the racecourse when, suddenly, he had received a violent blow on the head from behind. Knocked to the ground, he was struck again and kicked. Though dazed and frightened, he managed to pick himself up from the unexpected onslaught. Shouting for help, he ran as fast as could downhill, passing a constable on point duty who took no notice of him. But Heath found a 'good Samaritan' in the driver of a lorry, who, seeing that he was badly hurt and bleeding, took him to hospital.

A more serious assault was made on Alfie Solomon, who was bookmaking that day, and his clerk, Charles Bild. Shortly after arriving in Bath, Bild left a shop when 'a big man came up and seized the lapel of his coat, and then hit him a violent blow on the head with a hammer'. Others struck him with sticks and, finally, someone else pushed a sandbag into his face and hit him down. Terrified of the large crowd of attackers, somehow he managed to get up and rush through them into a hotel. One of the maids tore a sheet and bandaged his head, which was bleeding streams. Bild named two of those who assaulted him, as he knew them well. They belonged to 'a gang of Birmingham roughs who are out to blackmail and damage London bookmakers and their assistants', and were of the same party that had set upon the Jewish bookmakers at Ewell. As for Solomon, he could remember very little except that he was felled by a heavy, hard weapon. Lying bleeding, he was hit with other weapons and kicked violently. After the assailants cleared off, Solomon was taken to the hospital by the police. Nobody would be arrested for the attack on him but three men would later be charged with the vicious beating of Bild. One of them was Kimber.

A large party of rough-looking men also attacked three or four other Jewish bookmakers. One them bolted from the crowd and took refuge in a shop. Very much shaken and scared, he said that those who assaulted him and his friends were 'a lot of Birmingham roughs'. About an hour later, trouble erupted in the cheap ring on the racecourse itself. A sudden rush was made for a man who was being assaulted by a crowd.[233] In self-defence, he drew a small six-chambered revolver from his pocket. Knocked out of his hand, it was picked up by one of the assailants, who was disarmed by a constable. Then the lone man was knocked to the ground and hit on the head with a hammer. The policeman grabbed the attacker but was forced to release him by four or five men from a crowd that was estimated at between 100 and 150.[234] At last, the police managed to get the victim away to be treated for a severe scalp wound inflicted by a heavy bludgeon or hammer. Of 'Jewish appearance', he spoke with a Cockney accent. His revolver was loaded and he also had a razor and a life-preserver (cosh).

During this disturbance, another man piteously appealed to the police to lift him over the rails, saying, 'I shall be killed.' The police did so, and 'once over the rails, he ran, as if pursued by demons, right off the course'. While this was happening, 200 or 300 men attempted to rush the entrance to the ring, but were stopped by the police. Other 'hooligans' were in three charabancs on the way to the races. They forced their drivers to stop and, swarming out, they 'set about' some of those walking to the meeting.[235] An Italian man from London was another badly injured victim after he was hit on the head with a hammer, and as soon as racing was over, several other Italians sought police protection.

Tom Divall, 'the respected custodian of the Ring', was there when the East End Jewish bookmakers were mauled. Several of them looked to him for help and he managed to put them temporarily in a safe space. Then he ran over to Billy Kimber and asked him and a few of his leaders to see the secretary of the course to tell him the cause of the awful trouble. Kimber went and, 'speaking in his usual soothing and tactful way, soon calmed the troubled waters, and that battle was at an end.'[236] As Kimber had actually been the chief instigator of the 'wild scenes', he was probably the only man who could rein in the Birmingham Gang – but by the time he did so, the Jewish bookies had already had been attacked or else had fled in panic. Divall's account also reinforces the suggestions that there was a close relationship between him and Kimber.

Kimber had now avenged himself on Alfie Solomon, whilst the 'Cockney' with the gun who had also been attacked was his brother, Harry Solomon. Three days after the races, looking ill and with a bandage around his head, he appeared in court charged with carrying a revolver and ammunition without a licence and with intent to endanger life.[237] His defence stressed that he was not the aggressor and that he would have been killed if the police had not intervened. The magistrates ignored these appeals and sentenced Solomon to one month in prison. His lawyer had also been concerned that two of the witnesses against him came from Birmingham. Attempts were made to get them to divulge the identities of Solomon's assailants but they denied any knowledge of the people taking part in the row.[238]

One of them said that he had been terrified when Solomon drew his revolver and that after the arrest he had picked up a life preserver and razor that had been dropped on the ground. The other was 'Cunny' Cunnington, a key figure in the Epsom Road Battle. Described as a dealer in oil-polishing mops, he informed the court that he had not been at a race meeting for years until he went to Bath. Of course, that was a lie. He then gave a stirring account of the chase of Solomon, who, 'when the crowd pursued him made a leap for liberty over a paling but tripped over an overcoat he was carrying'. There was also a witness for the prosecution from Brighton. A seller of racing lists, he feared that his life was at risk because he was giving evidence against Harry Solomon. Recently, he had been chased off Waterloo Station by fifty men, after which he had approached Scotland Yard for protection. His sixty-five-year-old father had also been targeted and his jaw broken at Goodwood races. Under severe pressure of questioning, the frightened witness mentioned that one of the attackers was Alfred White, a key figure in the Sabini Gang.[239]

It was obvious that Kimber was able to call upon tough and terrifying men from across Birmingham, and some of the Elephant Boys and Newcastle Boys had also turned up at Bath. Yet this demonstration of power backfired. Alfie 'Bottle' Bottrell, had been one of the Birmingham Boys but had become a bookmaker.[240] Small but tough, in the early 1920s, he used to take his son, Horace, racing with him and he maintained that after the Battle of Bath, very few Birmingham bookmakers were allowed to go down south because their pitches were wanted by London bookies.[241] Any Birmingham bookies who did so faced the vengeful Sabinis, as at Hurst Park on 19 August.

Just two days after the Battle of Bath, a considerable number of 'the Boys' turned up and they targeted a motor car owned by a Birmingham bookmaker who travelled all over the country. It looked like the vehicle was going to be demolished, but fortunately the damage was small as the police were quickly on the spot. Mounted officers then cleared the course at a gallop.[242] One man was arrested for carrying a hatchet. He was Aaron Jacobs, a thirty-six-year-old bookmaker's clerk, but in reality a minder. Accompanied by other men, as he passed through the turnstiles he declared that, 'If any of the ——s are here today they will catch it.' A terror of the East End, Jacobs had a long list of convictions dating back to 1901. He was found guilty and sentenced to three months' hard labour. Three other men who had been carrying weapons escaped.[243] A few days later, it was reported that several Birmingham bookmakers had received anonymous postcards printed in black ink and warning, 'Beware, your time draws near. This is not bluff.'[244] Their problems were further exacerbated by the formation of a strong association by London bookies, an association which legitimised the power of the Sabini Gang.

A TRUCE IN THE TURF WAR

On 24 August 1921, a number of newspapers reported that 'owing to the recent very serious racecourse ruffianism there has been formed a 'Bookmakers' and Backers' Racecourse

Protection Association'. Its main objective was simple: 'to take all necessary steps to prevent molestation of bookmakers and backers on all racecourses, to protect bookmakers from blackmailers and defaulters, and generally promote the welfare and safety of the bookmaking profession, so that they will [be] enabled to carry on their calling the same way, and with the same safety, as any other profession'. The Association was to be governed by a president, vice-president, and a committee of twelve, and all members were to be provided with distinctive badges so that racegoers would know they were not welchers. Crucially, it would employ not only a secretary but also stewards who would be represented at all race meetings in and around London.[245]

Walter Beresford was the chief mover of the new Association. A prominent and respected racecourse bookmaker, he was distinguished as the first to start betting at a meeting and from whom the other bookies took their prices.[246] But he had gained that admirable position through money made illegally. The son of a prosperous publican, in May 1902, he and others were charged with using the New Savoy Club in the Strand for unlawful gaming and betting, the magnitude of these transactions having been noted in the books. They recorded that on fifteen racing days, £1,548 had been taken and a net profit of £223 had been made. As the proprietor, Beresford was fined £200 under the Gaming Act and £50 under the Betting House Act.[247] The total sum was over four years' wages for an unskilled worker.

Beresford's vice-president in the new Association was Edward Emanuel, the powerful guv'nor of the Jewish East End underworld who had brought in the Sabinis to defend the Jewish bookmakers. Emanuel was in the throes of transforming himself from criminality into respectability, and the attack on Solomon had given him the chance to do so. Born in 1880 to an Anglo-Jewish family, he had the reputation as a terror of the East End, and in 1904 was named in court as 'a dangerous fellow'.[248] A market porter, his earnings would have been less than the poverty line of about a pound a week, yet within seven years he had become a retail fruit salesman and he and his wife were living in a five-roomed house in Bethnal Green. His main income, though, was made as a proprietor of spielers and in January 1912, he and two other men were convicted of keeping one in Whitechapel.[249] Five years later, he incurred the heavy fine of £300 following a raid on another spieler in Whitechapel in which over a hundred men were arrested. As well as a gaming-house keeper, Emanuel was an illegal bookmaker, for in addition to eighty-four packs of cards discovered in the 'gambling den' there was also a large number of betting slips and racing cards.[250]

When this club had been raided, it was disclosed that behind Emanuel was a man of means, but that it had not been possible for the police to charge him.[251] There can be little doubt that this person was Beresford, whom Emanuel wished to emulate by becoming a legitimate businessman. Bookie Lou Prince explained that Emanuel planned to set up the Portsea Press printing company to provide bookmakers with the lists of runners for each race and with other printed material.[252] But in order for his business to succeed, he had to oust Kimber from the southern racecourses. The first brutal attack on Alfie Solomon, at Sandown Park in March 1921, gave Emanuel the opportunity to do so by bringing in Darby Sabini, whom he would have met through their mutual interest in gaming houses.[253] Through Emanuel and going racing, Sabini was then introduced to Beresford, who took on his brother, Harry Sabini, as a minder in 1921. The strength of these connections was confirmed by the writer and conman, Netley Lucas. In 1926, he wrote that the Sabini Gang was 'backed and upheld by one of the best-known and most powerful bookmakers on the turf. A member of all the racing clubs, a man who pays out thousands after each big race, and retains twice as much, he has a smart flat in the West End, several expensive cars and a still more expensive wife.'[254]

The Sabini Gang would provide the muscle to stop the Birmingham Gang intimidating London bookies, gaining Beresford status and popularity, and in so doing, Emanuel would have a free hand to sell his racing lists. And it would all be done above board. At its inaugural meeting at the end of August 1921, the new Bookmakers' Association agreed to put up and pay for a special force of stewards to travel to race meetings. The expense would be considerable, but it was confidently expected that it could be met through subscriptions.[255] Within a month, eight stewards had been appointed at the high wage of £6 a week. Among them were Darby Sabini and Philip Emanuel, a nephew of Edward Emanuel.[256] Others included Augustus 'Gus' Cortesi and Alf White, and like them the rest also belonged to the Sabini Gang.[257] The police observed that the stewards were 'mostly well-known race course frequenters and of a pugilistic tendency, and their duties were to look after the bookmakers generally and to see that they were not blackmailed by the roughs who habitually frequent race courses for this purpose.'[258] Ron Whytock, a later secretary of the Southern Bookmakers' Association, emphasised that 'of necessity it was a question of fighting fire with fire in the early stages, and "strong-arm" men were recruited to defend the members of the new Association'.[259]

Importantly, the Jockey Club affirmed its entire sympathy for the aims of the Association, recognising 'its importance for the comfort and security of the followers of the turf, whom the Association represents'. In return for this crucial support, the bookmakers' organisation pledged to work with the police and racecourse executives and to prosecute bad characters who committed offences. By the end of 1921, the new body was recognised by the management of eight southern racecourses, whilst the Racecourse Association was issuing free passes to its stewards.[260] The police were as supportive. Previously, as they had noted, they had 'great difficulty in dealing with mobs of roughs on racecourses, and they could not impress upon the bookmakers that they would be given adequate protection'. That problem was now solved by the stewards.[261] And the Sabinis benefitted greatly from the legitimacy bestowed upon them, making it all but impossible for them to be challenged on southern racecourses by the Birmingham Gang and the Elephant Boys. Beresford and Emanuel had made a shrewd and successful move.

Now in the ascendancy, the Sabinis could make good their threats of warning off Birmingham bookmakers from southern racecourses. In turn, the Birmingham Gang announced that no London bookmakers or their employees would be allowed to attend the St Leger week at Doncaster beginning on 6 September. In what was probably a pre-arranged meeting, however, Beresford decided to go. The Sabinis escorted him and his staff to King's Cross station and, as expressed by Divall, 'the Italians, armed to the teeth, warned the enemy that, if they interfered in any way with that gentleman and his subordinates, they would slaughter the first man that placed a hand on them'. After searching the train, they found no opponents, but when it arrived at Doncaster 'it was met by an infuriated mob of the enemy'. Some searched Beresford and other London bookmakers, 'whilst others were hiding behind the iron pillars supporting the roof, behind taxis and in other places where they could be easily seen – all waiting to attack the Italians etc. They too were armed with razors and other murderous-looking weapons.' Finding none of their enemies, the Birmingham Gang ordered all of the London bookies back to the capital, accompanying their commands with the most terrible threats. Only Beresford and his workers were allowed to remain, and with the whole 'Brum' gang they adjourned to the station refreshment room, where, as Divall dramatically expressed it, there 'took place the most awful and threatening conference in the history of racing'.

There is no record of what happened except that arrangements were made for a follow-up meeting. However, a few days later and before it could take place, 'the Italians' turned up in force at the Yarmouth meeting, which they claimed was in their territory. Divall noticed that they watched the railway station and the principal roads leading into the town, and searched the public houses and other likely places where they might find their enemy. Armed with revolvers and other weapons, they were 'eager to avenge themselves on their adversaries and compete with them for superiority on the race-course'. Divall had an anxious time, especially as he had 'experienced some good turns done me by a few of the Birmingham lot, and these I had found to be really good fellows'. If he had come across any of them, he would have got them out of the way to prevent violence. Late on the evening, Divall met some of 'the Italians' opposite the pier, and to his relief he was informed that none of the opposition had turned up. As it was the racecourse war between the Birmingham Gang and the Sabini Gang would soon be over.

After the 'discussions' at Doncaster, the follow-up meeting was held at Beresford's house. Sixteen of both parties arrived, all armed with revolvers and razors. According to Divall, Beresford then succeeded in inducing the two gangs to make peace with each other and become friends.[262] He was unduly optimistic. They did not become friends but, out of necessity, they did come to an agreement. Beresford himself related a less dramatic but self-praising account of the meeting, emphasising both his superiority and his victorious approach.

> I went to Doncaster to interview the 'terrorists', and I had an appointment with them after the racing. Some people might have thought it risky, but those men said: 'Will you give us an appointment to meet our representatives in London?' I said we would be delighted. We met them here and lengthily discussed the whole matter, and they promised there would be no more trouble. [263]

It is highly unlikely that these meetings were as friendly as suggested and Beresford himself received anonymous letters, some of which threatened that awful things would be done to him. Still, in calling a truce both sides had realised that 'inter-tribal warfare was not a paying game'.[264] The extensive reporting of their feud had been bad for business, pulling in too much attention from the police and pushing away racegoers. An agreement was essential and the gangs agreed to divide the country into spheres of control for the racecourse protection rackets. The Birmingham Gang would work the Northern and

Midland meetings and 'an amalgamation of the Sabini and the Jew gangs', as one newspaper put it, would control the southern meetings. Any other gang operating in either territory would be deemed enemies.[265]

This agreement greatly benefitted Emanuel, allowing him to sell his racing lists freely in the South with the support of the Bookmakers' Association. Ex-policeman Greeno made clear the profitability of this enterprise: 'For every race the bookmaker needed a printed list of runners to pin on his blackboard with the fluctuating odds chalked alongside. They were printed by a Mr. Edward Emmanuel for maybe a farthing apiece. To the bookies they were half a crown a set.'[266]

The news of the truce made its way into the papers. On 20 September, it was reported that 'the feud between the two London and Birmingham gangs had been settled, and there is no fear of any repetition of the undesirable proceedings which recently occurred in the south'.[267] Ten days later, in a tongue-in-cheek piece belying the previous seven months of violence, *The Sporting Times* headlined 'The Bubbly Armistice in the Great Turf War!' Mr Basham of Birmingham and Signor Stiletti of King's Cross had ended temporarily their conflict because 'the Birmingham, Italian and other gangs of thugs know very well which side their bread is buttered, and that it was not really profitable to hammer and bottle each other frequently on racecourses'. A code of terms was finalised at Newbury races, where 'the wildest and woolliest of film dramas could not have flickered a more tensely-dramatic and restrained scene. No pens or ink were produced. Half-a-dozen bull-necked or swarthy-featured accredited agents of the rival factions stood near a racecourse bar, half-a-dozen champagne corks popped, and a silent bond was drunk.'

Beresford and the sturdy stewards of the newly formed Bookmakers' Association occupied a sound defensive position between the 'boys' and the public, but the outlook was still rather interesting.[268]

Less than a week after the publication of this piece, confirmation of the truce came from an unexpected source – the Birmingham Gang itself. On 5 October, three of them appeared in court charged with the unlawful and malicious wounding of Charles Bild at the Bath races in August. They were Phillip Thomas, Edward Joyce and Kimber.[269] Aged twenty-seven, Thomas gave his address as in the Summer Lane neighbourhood, but ten years before, he was recorded as living with his parents off Garrison Lane. Like Kimber, he was another prominent member of the Birmingham Gang who became involved with the Elephant Boys.[270] So too was Joyce, who was living in the New Cut in the bastion of the Elephant Boys.[271] He was the eldest son of an Irish couple who settled in the poor neighbourhood of Deritend, Birmingham. In March 1891, they were summoned for neglecting their four children, all aged under nine. When an inspector of the Society for the Prevention of Cruelty to Children visited their home, they were in a very neglected condition although fairly well nourished. Practically naked, they were 'covered with vermin. There was no fire or food in the house, which was almost devoid of furniture. In one upstairs bedroom there was a mattress, which was very filthy, whilst in the other was a heap of straw, which was sodden and filthy.' It was contended that their fifty-six-year-old father could earn good money, but was lazy, whilst their twenty-five-year-old mother went to work. The magistrates did not want to take the children away from her, but ordered the inspector to check on the children's welfare.[272] Two years later, the father was sentenced to two months' hard labour for stealing lead from a church, and in 1895, he and his brother were involved in a violent confrontation with another family.[273]

The eldest son, Edward, was named as one of the 'Boys' in March 1907 when he and four other Birmingham men were charged with frequenting Rugby races. Saying he was a race card hawker, he was imprisoned for two months.[274] Later that year, he was one of six men arrested for not paying for their railway tickets on their way home from the Cheltenham races.[275] By 1911, he was still living at home with his parents but now described himself as a bookmaker. Within eight years, he was recorded as a commission agent living in Lambeth, South London, when he was charged with maliciously cutting and wounding Joseph Palmer, the well-known boxing referee and journalist, at a boxing tournament. Suspiciously, after 'friends intervened', both parties agreed to reduce the charge to common assault, with Joyce paying compensation of £25 and costs.[276]

As for Kimber, of course, he was the main leader of the Birmingham Gang. However, the case against him, Joyce and Thomas for attacking Bild, Solomon's clerk, collapsed in a curious way. The previous week it had been adjourned, as Bild was unwell, according to his solicitor. Now neither he nor his solicitor turned up, whereupon the Chief Constable of Somerset had no further evidence to offer with the result that the charges against all three men were dismissed. The defence counsel then made a startling statement that: 'There would no more trouble of this kind. There had been a feud between certain sections of race-going fraternity, but it had been amicably settled. Both public and police might rest assured that no breach of the peace would occur again.'[277]

The truce between the Birmingham Gang and Sabini Gang held and there was no more trouble between them, leading Beresford to give a triumphant speech at the inaugural banquet of the Bookmakers' Association on 6 December 1921. To a cheering audience, he related that at the most recent Newmarket meeting, the superintendent of police had been asked how things had gone over the eight days of racing. He replied, 'We have not had a charge, and we have not had a complaint.' Four months previously, Beresford averred, racing had been in a very bad state, 'and if we had not started this Association, racing, no doubt in this part of the world would have been stopped on account of the various feuds, we will say, between the Midlands and the south of England'. To more cheering from the large gathering at the Holborn Restaurant, he announced that there would be no more feuds and no more trouble. He tendered his thanks to the best of the Birmingham people, 'but the low-down Birmingham people who were the cause of the trouble, we do not want anything to do with'. The leading Birmingham bookmakers had done a lot to help the Association and their hearts were with it. Regrettably, they had not been able to make the banquet but sent their best wishes. They had told the Association that, 'If any of their members went to the Midlands or North of England, they would be well looked after by the leading Birmingham men, and on behalf of the Association an assurance has been given that if any of the Midland or Northern people come to the South, they would be protected in the same way'. Beresford affirmed that there was no antagonism on the part of these Birmingham bookmakers, who had helped to bring their people to book.

Despite these assurances, it was obvious that bookies from both Birmingham and London were staying within their own regions and were apprehensive about travelling 'away'. The unease of those from Birmingham in particular must have been heightened due to the Association's stewards, but Beresford revelled at having some of them at the banquet. He praised them as 'very good fellows' and without any trace of self-delusion, he announced that 'practically they say: "Do not trouble about OUR wages, but let us be in it."'

They were in it – in it for the money they could make. Returning to reality, because of the 'muscle' of the stewards, Beresford was able to make a veiled threat to anyone seeking to challenge the new Association: 'We want to try and do things amicably, and if we cannot do that, we shall have to do the other thing.' Emanuel was as exultant in his speech. With no hint of hypocrisy, given his own violent and criminal background, he proclaimed that, 'With regard to the terrorists and blackmailers they are now nothing to worry about. We have beaten them and consider them a back number.'[278] He was wrong. They were not a back number. The blackmailing of bookmakers carried on unabated, only now from the 'legitimate' stewards, and a new gang war would soon break out in the capital.

Chapter 4

THE CAMDEN TOWN GANG AND HOXTON'S TITANICS

RAZOR SLASHINGS AND THE CAMDEN TOWN GANG

A cut-throat razor was the favourite weapon of the London racecourse gangs. It inflicted terrible wounds, as Ralph L. Finn saw when two gangs clashed with razors at Aldgate East Station. The station's forecourt dripped with blood and bodies were intertwined all over the floor as if in all-in wrestling poses. Razors were wielded like floor mops, men screamed in their agony, curses filled the air, and terrified passengers huddled in corners for safety. The jackets and coats of the gangsters were ripped, and pieces of material and human skin lay all over the place. As the fight raged, the police just watched, and the eleven-year-old Finn saw the lobe of an ear at the toe of a copper's boot. Eventually, though, the police waded in with truncheons, battering everyone into insensibility and carrying them away in Black Marias. Not many days later, a few of the gangsters were back, 'their scars incandescent, their eyes swollen, their noses bulbously hideous, bright as prize beetroots'.[279]

In his fascinating memoir of his Hoxton childhood, *Clouds of Glory*, Bryan Magee stressed that open razors were favoured by gangsters because they caused grievous bodily harm without killing. Stabbing with them was not possible, and however wildly 'you slashed at someone it was only by the most outside and unlucky chance that you could kill him, or even blind him, whereas you could hardly fail to slash his face, or his hands, and had a good chance of lopping off a piece of ear, or nose, or a bit of finger'. Slashing inflicted just about the maximum nastiness with the minimum risk of killing, and that was the point – making a mess of another man's face. The razor had another great advantage as a weapon: it was terrifying, more so than a cosh, for example, and it could be used for graded punishments to rivals. On the first occasion, a victim might be beaten up; the second time, he would be battered and could also be cut; and the third time, cutting was certain. Held down by several men, the victim's face would be elaborately carved by the 'cutter'. An informant would have an 'especially long cut deep down to the upper lip which, when the scar tissue formed and pulled the lip upward, had the effect of leaving the mouth permanently open'.

Once a victim had been got hold off, he knew the cutting would be worse if he struggled violently so it was best to let them get on with it. Magee observed that there was scarcely a significant figure in any of the racecourse gangs who didn't have razor scars on his face, but even this disfigurement had its uses, as it showed they were seriously in the business of extortion. Because a razor was frightening and was meant to be, a gangster carried it folded into the outside breast pocket of his suit, with the tip of the metal hinge showing to ensure that it was slightly visible. Crucially, if he were stopped by the police, he could explain that he was carrying a razor as he expected to stay away from home that night.[280]

In the spring and summer of 1921, razor slashings scarred a number of men in a renewed racecourse war but, as the *Daily Mail* noted, the 'Birmingham or hammers gang' was not involved.[281] Instead, it was a fight between the Sabini Gang and former associates of the Birmingham Gang, most of whom the police regarded as 'London thieves of the worst type' They were, having been brought together by their joint leaders, Fred Gilbert and George 'Brummy' Sage, into the Camden Town Gang or Sage's Mob. Sage was 'an oft-convicted criminal' and was accused by Sabini as having led the attack on him at Greenford Trotting Track.[282] Born in 1878, Sage's father was a labourer in the brickfields and his mother was a laundress. Both jobs would have been strenuous and poorly paid. In 1896, their son was also labouring when he was imprisoned for nine months for burglary at the house of his cousin, where he was lodging. With no apparent connections to Birmingham, he was already nicknamed 'Brummy', whilst his inclination to violence was obvious as he told the police that he would smash the nose of an accomplice.[283] His prison record indicated that he was just under 5 foot 6 inches, had light-brown hair and blue eyes and was distinguished by several tattoos on his arms and the name Elizabeth Allen in capital letters across his chest.

Although living in Enfield on the outskirts of London, two years previously Sage had been convicted in Clerkenwell, suggesting that he had links there.[284] Following his release, he moved to Holloway in North London, working as a coal porter, and married Lilian Bussey. The previous year, they had fought each other in the street, and after Sage refused to stop when ordered by a policeman, he was fined.[285] It is most likely that he was also the 'Brummy (Holloway)' who boxed professionally for seven years from 1898. An erratic but determined and hard-hitting fighter, he had numerous contests at around nine stone. In 1901, he joined a troupe of boxers travelling across the country putting on exhibitions, but his tendency to street fighting was shown when one of his bouts was stopped and called a no contest because neither he nor his opponent boxed strictly under the Queensberry Rules.[286] Sage's boxing career ended soon after. He returned to criminality and, in 1910, when a young woman and man from Islington were arrested for uttering false coins, Brummy was blamed for inducing them to commit the crime.[287]

How and when he met Billy Kimber is not known, although it's likely that they'd done so on the racecourses in the years immediately before the First World War. They also came to live near to each other. The birth certificate of Sage's eldest child in 1911 recorded the family's address as Comyn Road, Clapham in South London. By then, he had left his wife and set up home with Ellen Brookes, who was calling herself Mrs Sage.[288] The house itself was an impressive three-storey terraced structure with a small front garden and bay windows – both symbols of a respectable upper working-class or lower middle-class road. Kimber was living not too far way in York Road, Lambeth, as were the McDonalds of the Elephant Boys.[289] By 1913, Sage and Kimber were close associates and both were arrested for stabbing a man in the face and neck in an East End pub. They were discharged but Sage was noted as well known on racecourses and in the boxing ring.[290]

He joined the Army Service Corps in September 1915, stating that he was a foreman porter, although on the death certificate of his youngest son, it indicated that he had been a commission agent. Aged just under two, the toddler died tragically in July 1916 after having been given a poison mistaken for syrup of senna. By then, Sage, Ellen Brookes and their children were living at 3 Mornington Crescent in Primrose Hill. Four storeys high, including the basement, it was part of a splendid Georgian terrace of thirty-six houses. Sage's criminal earnings must have been exceptionally high to enable him to live in such an expensive property. Posted to France for several months, he was discharged in September 1916 as no longer physically fit for war service. He had exposed varicose veins and multiple lipomata, non-cancerous growths of fatty tissue cells, which had to be operated on. Having been promoted to sergeant, his character was given 'as a good supervisor of military labour'. Two months later, he wrote to the Army asking to be sent his Silver War Badge, saying he needed it as he met with a lot of insults. Many other men had to do the same, as if they were seen as fit and healthy it was thought that they were shirkers avoiding active service. In April 1917, Sage then applied for a gratuity instead of an Army pension so that he could go to Ireland on business.[291] Undoubtedly, that business was joining Kimber in pickpocketing in Dublin and the nearby racecourses. By then, Kimber had deserted from the Army and was already in Ireland, and he would be arrested for pickpocketing a month after Sage's application.[292]

With the resumption of racing after the end of the war, Sage joined Kimber in the Birmingham Gang's takeover on the southern racecourses. The former policeman Divall had a respectful, if not closer, relationship with both of them, praising them as 'generous and brave fellows'. At one particular meeting at Hurst Park in 1921, at the height of power of the Birmingham

Gang, he approached Sage for help. The Jockey Club wanted bookmakers to stop displaying large flags and advertising boards but they were carrying on regardless. Fearing that he would lose his licence, the secretary of the course requested Divall to take strong measures to end the practice. In turn, he sought out Sage, who went along saying, 'I'll ensure every one of them comes down!' He did so in less than an hour. Divall was delighted that Sage and his friend, Gandley, had managed the business so well, exclaiming that, 'I should like to know who could have done that work more satisfactorily than these two men!'[293] They did so satisfactorily because they were feared.

The mention of Gandley underlines the close bond between Sage and the Birmingham Gang. Born in 1894, Gandley grew up close to the Bull Ring markets. When he was thirteen, he was sent to a reformatory for Roman Catholic boys in Yorkshire for stealing six packets of biscuits. Then, in 1913, he was imprisoned for three months for theft. Both offences were carried out in his real name of Joseph Brueton. A year later, calling himself Joseph Gandley and of no fixed abode, he was discharged from stealing a horse. It is likely that he adapted the name of his mother, Margaret Gandley, who had also been a petty thief as well as a streetwalker. At just over 5 foot 1 inches, Gandley was a small man but he must have been able to handle himself to be associated with Sage, who was admired by Wal McDonald 'as a stand-up, toe-to-toe fist fighter', with both revelling in their reputations as 'top men'.[294]

The agreement between the Birmingham Gang and the Sabinis dividing England's racecourses between them left no place for Sage. Not a man to accept a loss of power and income, he quickly strove to challenge the Sabini Gang. But because of the agreement with the Birmingham Gang, he could not turn for support to his close friend, Kimber, even though he was living in London in Warren Street (now Grant Street), Islington, in the family home of his friends, the Garnhams.[295] Seeking a new ally, Sage found an unexpected one in Fred Gilbert, formerly a leading figure in the Sabinis, and in the spring of 1922 they formed the Camden Town Gang. Although still sometimes called the Birmingham Gang, none of its members were Brummies as it included men from North London and Elephant Boys from South London, whilst being allied to the Titanics from Hoxton.

Gilbert was as tough as Sage. In 1911, and aged eighteen, he was lodging with a friend's family in Clerkenwell and was a boxer/pugilist. Though born in London, he did not know where, and it is obvious that he had an unsettled childhood. Christened Frederick Thomas Gilbert in 1893 in Hoxton, his father was a printer's labourer.[296] Six years later, when he was only six, Gilbert was charged with wandering the streets and taken by the police to the casual ward of the City of London Union Workhouse in Holborn. He was only in overnight, but his eight-year-old brother, John, was there for several days when he was admitted on a separate occasion that year. Both would have endured unhappy and difficult experiences, sleeping in dormitories with strangers in a prison-like structure.[297] It is clear that the family was transient and dysfunctional, as in 1911, when Fred Gilbert was lodging with his friend's family, his mother, Mary, was living separately in nearby Clerkenwell. There was no mention of her husband, although she did not record herself as a widow. She was getting by in poorly paid work as a book folder, supplemented by the earnings of Gilbert's brother, John, who was living with her along with two much younger siblings.

Fred Gilbert fought professionally between 1910 and 1913, sometimes on the same bills as Darby Sabini, and he was noted for his skill and good straight left. However, one of his fights suggests that he was involved in betting against himself. In April 1912, he was on top and going well in a six-round contest, but unexpectedly he gave in without any reason and was disqualified.[298] Using the name of Fred Clancy (Clerkenwell), he continued boxing after he joined the Royal Welsh Fusiliers in 1916.[299] He was not in the Army for long, and his last fight was three years later, when he was giving himself variously as a bookmaker's clerk and commission agent living in Moreland Street, Finsbury, between Hoxton and Clerkenwell. Like Sage, Gilbert was also a street fighter. He was fined in October 1919 for having been drunk and riotous in Farringdon Road, and the next year he was convicted of assaulting a policeman. Yet, as with other gangsters, despite his strength as a one-to-one scrapper, he was ever ready 'to do someone in' mob-handed. On Christmas Eve 1921, he was one of three men who assaulted another in Clerkenwell. The victim was punched and, after falling, kicked about the head. He suffered a jagged wound on his upper lip, a contusion on the back of his scalp and considerable haemorrhaging. Probably fearful of repercussions, he withdrew his charge on payment of his doctor's fees.

By now, Gilbert was a leading light in the Sabinis, unsurprisingly given his fighting abilities and the fact that he had grown up in Clerkenwell.[300] His high status within the gang was emphasised by his appointment as a steward of the Bookmakers' Association alongside Darby, Joe and Harry Sabini and Alf White, and Gilbert later admitted that he was one of the roughs paid to report anybody who was blackmailing bookmakers and to assist the police.[301] Yet it was not long before Gilbert was 'at daggers drawn with his erstwhile companions'. The 'commissioner' of the *Empire News* believed that the split arose over money.

> It is a strict rule of the S– Gang that the proceeds of any outrage must be handed over to the leaders, who, after helping themselves to a lion's share, distribute the rest. It is, too, a rule that is obeyed because failure to do so brings swift and condign punishment – probably a slash across the face with a razor.

Gilbert aroused the suspicions of his fellow gangsters because he had accumulated enough cash to contemplate buying a public house. He had won the money, but his jealous colleagues believed that he had not handed over all of his takings to the gang. One night at their headquarters, other members of the Sabini Gang attacked him. It was obviously pre-planned but he didn't expect it. Someone smashed a bottle over his head and then, while he lay unconscious, savagely slashed his thigh with a razor. He received five gashes, each nine to ten inches long, which penetrated to the muscle and left him lame in the right leg.

> Men of his stamp are wonderfully tough, however, and after lying bleeding for an hour he managed to clamber to his feet and offer battle to the man responsible for his injuries. After landing a knock-out blow he again fell unconscious, and this time the ever-ready razor nearly removed his left eye.[302]

The wounds were made carefully so that they would maim and not be fatal.[303] This attack happened on the evening of Good Friday, 14 April 1922, at the Raleigh Club in a turning off Jermyn Street. Gilbert was slashed so severely across the leg that he had to have sixty-two stitches, including five in his eye and four in the back of his head. Alfie Solomon was the Sabini Gang member arrested for this ruthless assault, but true to the underworld code of not grassing to the police, Gilbert gave inaccurate information about his assailants, saying that he had received his injuries in Drury Lane from men whom he did not know. Called 'a spiteful little bastard' by racing man Maskey, Solomon was freed and no further proceedings were taken.[304] However, at a later date Gilbert named his attackers as Solomon, Alf White and George West, alias Dai Thomas, telling a court 'that you must call it carving when they cut a man up as they did me'.[305]

Gilbert was in hospital for five weeks and, when he recovered, his former pals in the Sabini Gang warned him that his life was in danger and that he should stay off racecourses.[306] The Bookmakers' Association also discharged him from his duties as a steward.[307] Having lost all sources of income and seeking vengeance, Gilbert teamed up with Brummy Sage, who had begun pulling together a gang of toughs. Two of them, Michael Sullivan and Archie Douglas, had already been slashed across their faces in London's West End, allegedly by the Italian or Sabini Gang. Five men were arrested, including Alfie and Harry Solomon and Alf White, but the victims declined to prosecute. A police source remarked that both men were convicted thieves and members of the so-called Birmingham Gang. In reality, they were part of the emerging Camden Town Gang, but Gilbert did not only look to Sage and North London for allies; he also looked east to Hoxton and the Titanics.

Birmingham Bookmaker Bill Ashby stands on the left, taking bets for the
Portland Handicap at Doncaster soon after the end of the First World War. Ashby
would have had to pay the Birmingham Gang for the stool he is standing on, the
chalk to write up the names of the horses and their odds on his blackboard, and
the bucket of water and sponge with which to rub them off. The man with the
sheaves of paper is the clerk, who wrote down the bets, and behind him is a tic-tac,
who would transmit betting information to other bookies with hand signals.

Above: A scene from Bromford Bridge Racecourse on the outskirts of Birmingham in September 1923. Local bookmaker Edward John Guy is in the centre and counting his money. Respectable bookies like him would have welcomed the truce called between the Birmingham Gang and the Sabinis and their allies in late 1921.

Below: Birmingham bookmaker Alfie Bottrell, known as Bottle, bookmaking as Joe White The Silver King in about 1924. Many bookmakers dressed in uniform immediately after the First World War. Alf's son, Horace, is front left.

Alf Prince, a London Bookmaker with a racing list on his board printed by
Edward Emanuel's Portsea Press and probably sold by associates of Darby
Sabini.

Top right: Henry Tuckey in 1906, one of the Birmingham Gang imprisoned after the Epsom Road Ambush of 1921. He had been a slogger, a forerunner of the peaky blinders.

Middle: William Darby in the early twentieth century with three of his children. In June 1921, he was arrested at Epsom with two other Birmingham men for threatening bookmakers. This photo was given to me by his niece, the late Ann Middleton née Darby, a wonderful woman who generously shared with me her vivid memories of back-to-back life in Birmingham.

Below: The Emily Street neighbourhood in Birmingham before it was cleared in the 1930s, with the spire of St Martin's in the Bull Ring in the background. This area was dominated by back-to-back housing and small workshops, and it was home to several members of Banks's Mob.

Above: Moses Kimberley in 1907, one of the leaders of the Birmingham Gang who escaped capture after the Epsom Road Ambush. He was involved in the slashing of Thomas Macdonald in 1925. © *West Midlands Police Museum*

Below: Thomas MacDonald, a peaky blinder who became one of the Birmingham Boys and a leading racecourse rough. This photo was taken in 1910, fifteen years prior to his clash with Kimberly. © *West Midlands Police Museum*

Meet the Kimbers: Billy Kimber himself (*above* © *Brian MacDonald*) with his two daughters from his first marriage in Birmingham. His eldest Maude aged sixteen in 1917 (*below right* © *Juliet Banyard*) and Annie (*below left*, © *Juliet Banyard*) who was twenty-four when this photograph was taken in 1927. Kimber abandoned them both to live in poverty when he left their mother in 1910.

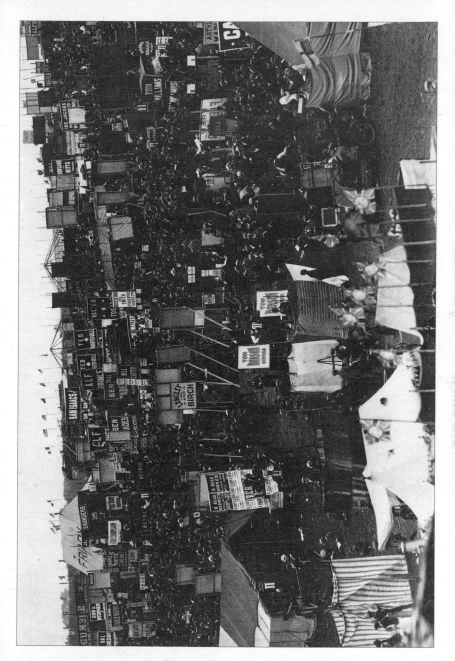

Immense crowds of racegoers at the Epsom Derby in 1920 packing out
the spaces between the bookmakers. In the middle is the white banner of
Beresford and Smith – Walter Beresford was the leading figure in forming the
Bookmakers' and Backers' Racecourse Protection Association.

© Alamy

Above: A rare photograph of the first annual dinner of the Bookmakers' and Backers' Racecourse Protection Association at the Holborn Restaurant on 6 December 1921. It includes Edward Emanuel, regarded as the guvnor of the Jewish underworld in the East End, and Walter Beresford, president of the Association, on the top table.

© Carl Chinn Bookmaking Archive

Right: The National Committee of the Bookmakers' Protection Association at their dinner in Birmingham 18 March 1925.

© Birmingham Daily Gazette/ Reach Licensing

BIRMINGHAM GAZETTE. WEDNESDAY, 18 MARCH, 1925.

D CHANGE : BILLIARDS CHAMPION IM

GOLFING GOSSIP.

FORTHCOMING EXHIBITION MATCHES AT MOSELEY.

IN AID OF W. H. ADWICK

BY A MIDLAND GOLFER.

LAWN TENNIS AFFAIRS.

ANOTHER RULING CONCERNING AMATEUR STATUS.

HOTEL EXPENSES.

'NATIONAL HOCKEY IN BIRMINGHAM.

Next Saturday's Big Match At Edgbaston.

ENGLAND V. IRELAND

BY BULLY-OFF.

BOOKMAKERS' PROTECTION ASSOCIATION.

The National Committee of the Bookmakers' Protection Association held their dinner and meeting at the Central Hotel, Birmingham. Picture shows the delegates.

HOXTON'S TITANICS AND SABINIS WARRING

A gang of pickpockets, the Titanics worked anywhere large numbers of people were gathered. Arthur Harding recollected first noticing them in 1902:

> They were all very well dressed fellows. I think they were named after the liner because they were so well dressed . . . They had plenty of money and they used to straighten everybody up. They were a very good proposition from a police point of view. Very specialist. They used to rob men only. A crowd of six of them went up – at the theatre or the railway stations or going away to the races. They were whizzers (pickpockets) but they would also take part in burglaries.[308]

Their name, though, did not come from the ill-fated liner. In his landmark book of 1923, *The Underworld of London*, Sidney Theodore Felstead explained that the Hoxton whizz mob were called Titanic because of their size and supposed invulnerability. Indeed, 'their prowess became a byword among the criminal fraternity of London; stories were legion of their wonderful successes, while the ease with which they dodged the police made them admired by all the lesser fry of the profession'.[309]

Detective Inspector Grosse was the first head of Scotland Yard's Flying Squad, a motorised unit formed to tackle the burglary gangs that were now using cars, and he agreed that the Titanics were so named because they were extremely strong and a very dangerous gang.[310] But unlike their reputation seemed to suggest, they were not invincible. Grosse led a relentless pursuit of the gang, which had between twenty and twenty-five members. With something like twelve hefty young detectives, he chased them from one end of London to another and never gave them peace.[311] In 1921 alone, at least eight of the Titanics were imprisoned.[312] The police crackdown continued into 1922 and, under pressure, that summer some of the gang unwisely turned their attention to working racecourses.[313] Unwise, as the correspondent to the *Empire News* pointed out, because it was 'generally accepted in the underworld that the notorious S– gang have the monopoly of the racecourses in the South of England for all pickpocketing, blackmail, and the more violent forms of robbery'.

Angered, the Sabinis descended upon some of the Titanics at one meeting, threatening them that a repetition of their 'offence' would have serious consequences. The warning was ignored and now the Titanics were followed around London at night and attacked with razors wielded by the Italian and Jewish members of the S– gang. Keen to return to the rich pickings on the racecourses, the leader of the Titanics welcomed Gilbert's approach to join him and Sage in wresting control of the rackets from the Sabinis.[314] This leader was hailed as 'a handsome, keen-faced young man with a positive genius for organising and a capacity as a fighter that has made his name a terror in the East End'. There is no firm evidence to identify him, but he was on very friendly terms with Gilbert and agreed for the Titanics to join in a fight that would be 'waged with a merciless fury that makes one wonder if this is a civilised country at all'.[315]

The Titanics came from Hoxton and, as Magee pointed out, its people 'always had a sense of their own identity and of Hoxton's being a distinctive place; and I have to say that I grew up thinking that there was an East End and a West End and that Hoxton was different from either of them, being on the northern edge of the City'. A poverty-stricken area, its name became used in speech and writing 'to represent the ultimate in social degradation, the poorest, most criminal, most uncivilised corner of Britain'.[316] Yet, it is essential to bear in mind that the negative labelling of poor districts like Hoxton arose from middle-class outsiders who 'explored' them in the late nineteenth century. They brought back tales about the 'physical inefficiency' of the 'street people', as they were termed, and their un-Englishness – that is, according to bourgeois notions of Englishness. And whilst the peaky blinders of Birmingham and the gangsters of London did overwhelmingly come from the poorest localities that were denigrated as 'the blackest' in their cities, it would be a calumny to demean all the poor as criminal and debase their neighbourhoods as 'nether worlds'.

Magee stressed that within a generally poor neighbourhood like Hoxton, there were distinctions between respectable and 'rough' families and between respectable and 'rough' parts of a street. Yet some streets, like Wilmer Gardens, were seen as wholly rough, as was the whole district of Nile Street and its surroundings.[317] The Nile was the stronghold of the Titanics and was regarded by the police as 'a very rough and dangerous quarter'.[318] Such a critical, indiscriminate generalisation was ignorant of the diversity within such neighbourhoods, where differing concepts of rough and respectable held sway.

Charles Maskey was born in 1905 and grew up in Custance Street, a short turning off Nile Street. In 1898, in notes for the monumental study of *Life and Labour in London* by Charles Booth, it was stamped as 'rough, convicts, windows broken, mess in the street'. It had been a cul-de-sac, but recently an opening had been made at the closed end, which 'was a great convenience to the police, as they can now work the street from both ends'.[319]

Maskey's memories contrasted with this bleak description. He remembered that after the First World War, there was a Victory party organised by the local illegal street bookmaker, Billy Chandler, who 'used to have races up and down the street for the kids'. He also lived in Custance Street, and he would often pay for the local youngsters to be taken on a day-trip.

> They'd say to him, 'Well they aint been out' and he'd say, 'Well alright. We'll have 'em down Friday. Tell them how many of 'em.' They'd say, 'We want eight coaches'. 'Alright, they're going out Friday.' And he used to take them all. Oh, a hell of a man.

A terrific gambler, Chandler would play cards all night and used to eat a tin of condensed milk, 'that was his grub. Never drunk, never had a drink in his life. Smoked on a bad night but never had a drink in his life.'[320]

Chandler was also a bookie and was at Greenford when Sabini was attacked. He gave evidence in support of Fred Gilbert on that occasion, explaining that he had only intervened in the melee to assist Sabini.[321] Chandler was not to be messed with himself, and had been fined for possessing a loaded revolver, which he protested was to protect his street bookmaking pitch from blackmailers. He had also been one of the Titanics, as in 1909, when he was nineteen, he was arrested for pickpocketing.[322] Despite this background, and even though he was seen by many as the 'guv'nor' of Hoxton, as Maskey made clear, Chandler was not the leader of the Titanics.[323] A highly intelligent and motivated man, he was determined to move away from criminality. He would soon have offices for legal credit betting in the West End, with a business turning over the phenomenal sums of between £30,000 to £40,000 a week; he would go on to start up Walthamstow Greyhound Stadium, and he would become a major racecourse bookmaker.[324] Moving towards business legitimacy and respectability as he was, Chandler did not need to become embroiled in the war between the Sabinis and the Camden Town/Titanic alliance. The identity of the leader of the Titanics, then, is a mystery, but there is no doubt that many of them followed him in supporting Gilbert in what became known as the Racecourse Feud.

Darby Sabini himself acknowledged that peace did not last long following the truce with the Birmingham Gang. He explained that when many of the leading bookmakers joined the Association, members of a gang who had been employed as protectors were discharged from their jobs. These would have been the Londoners associated with the Birmingham Gang, and some of them became so 'furious and enraged that they formed a counter organisation to defeat us'.[325] That rival body was set up by Gilbert after his slashing and after he palled up with Sage. Ironically, it was called the Bookmakers' Protection Society. As exposed by the *Daily Mail*, it guaranteed 'to offer immunity from molestation to any bookmaker who will pay them the price demanded for the day's service'. All bookies knew that once offered, they had to take the 'protection' because if it were refused, then after racing finished, the gangsters would rob those who had defied them. They might use threats or do so by force with a slash across the face or a stab in the back. Unhappily, the bookmakers were exposed to a dual danger as the different gangs worked against one another, as the 'protectors' themselves were often molested by rival gangs.[326]

Bookmakers had to pay up to £30 a week for protection. A Scotland Yard detective knew of one bookmaker who, having to pay the piper to three separate gangs, had now backed out of business. If a victim dared to divulge the names of the desperadoes, they knew they were in for something far worse.[327] Punters who enjoyed a good day were also prey to the 'Protection Society'. If they did not hand over 'ten of the best' (£10), they would be slashed or stabbed. And women were employed by Gilbert's gang and others 'for special investigation work' – the finding of 'mugs'.[328] Once found, the male gangsters made plans to rob the 'mugs'. One case involved a pair of Americans, who were drawn into conversation by two women at Goodwood. After the races, they all went to a nightclub and, later, the Americans 'discovered themselves penniless in a taxicab. The driver remembers they seemed intoxicated on entering the cab, hardly able to walk. The fact was, as afterwards discovered, they were half-intoxicated, half-drugged, and were practically dragged into the taxi.' Another American victim was relieved of £350 and valuable jewellery. The spoils were so rich, that a detective was certain that the gangs had made thousands of pounds.[329] Even if exaggerated, the sums involved were huge, given that the average wage for a working man in 1924 was £2 10 shillings and that unskilled men such as labourers and porters would have earned less.[330] It is little wonder that Gilbert, Sage and the Titanics were resolved to fight the Sabinis for control of the racecourse rackets.

Greeno was policing when the new gang war broke out. In his memoirs, he wrote that in April 1922, the month that Gilbert was slashed, four other men were stabbed in the back and another clubbed in the West End. They were all strangers to each other but they had two things in common: they were all racing men and they all refused to talk. Greeno recollected that trouble was then expected at the Epsom Derby meeting in June, but there was only one little fracas when a bookmaker who was an ex-boxer 'tangled with some Sabini boys over a pitch and they beat him up and, he said, threatened to stick a knife in his eyes'.[331] But violence was not long in erupting. Five of the Sabini Gang went into a pub in the East End to 'do' another enemy. The intended victim was alone, but before he could be cut up, the leader of the Titanics walked in. Deciding that discretion was the better part of valour, the head of the 'raiding party' assured the guv'nor of the Titanics that he was on a peaceful mission and asked if he could he buy the drinks. After paying for three rounds and leaving a pound on the counter, the Sabinis went to leave. As they did so, the Titanics' head man called out, 'I think you are very lucky men to get out of here alive.'[332]

After this loss of face, Darby Sabini needed little persuasion to order a full-scale demonstration of his gang's power in enemy territory.[333] Now dominant on the racecourses of southern England, he particularly wanted to assert his supremacy over the Titanics, the Sabini's main rival in North London. The attack by the Sabini Gang took place in late June 1922 and entered into folklore, with the *Empire News* dramatically drawing the picture:

A strong party of them marched down the 'Nile', firing revolvers and threatening death to all and sundry. Many of the Titanic gang were away from home at the time, but such of them as were present, reinforced by certain of their women-folk, turned out with anything they could lay their hands on to do battle.

After a fierce fight they drove the S—s off. One of the

attacking party was left behind, and as he lay helpless in the road a Titanic walked over with the expressed intention of 'taking half his face off' with a piece of broken glass. But the man in charge, magnanimous in victory, gave orders that he was to be released, and he was merely driven from the scene bruised and bleeding.[334]

Maskey had striking memories of this violent episode: 'The Sabini mob, they come round there once, yeah, to sort them out, yeah, what you call 'em, the, Titanic mob they called 'em. They give 'em a fuckin' belting, they give 'em. They come right out. I thought they was gonna shoot them out.'[335]

The Titanics were ready to shoot again the next night as the Sabinis had threatened to return. Once more they were joined by many women, who 'were in ambush behind their doors, armed with choppers'. Having got wind of the preparations, the Sabinis abandoned their attack. Usually preferring to gain his victories by stratagems rather than hand-to-hand fighting, Darby Sabini then devised a plan to undo the Titanics. At the Alexandra Park meeting in early July, one of his men approached a leading Titanic and 'with many lurid adjectives' told him that the Sabinis were going to Hoxton that evening 'to pull his friends out their beds and slit their throats'. Thus alerted, the Titanic missed the last two races and rushed back to the Nile, where he gathered the local forces. But at the time the Sabini Gang was expected to arrive, two vanloads of Scotland Yard officers drove up. If it had not been for a timely warning, the armed Titanics would have been rounded up – just as Sabini had connived.[336]

Soon after, on the evening of 24 July, John Thomas Phillips, was razor slashed. He was one of the Titanics, as had been his parents, Arthur and Annie, and as was his brother, Arthur 'Toddy' Phillips.[337] The evening before the Goodwood races, Johnny Phillips had gone into a hotel in Brighton, where he was asked to have a drink with George Langham, Jim Ford and Alf White, three of Darby Sabini's closest associates. Later on, Phillips declined to lend Ford £2, who angrily brought this up when they left the hotel. Drawing some loose notes from his pocket to offer them, Phillips was punched on the jaw by Ford. The two men fell and the next thing Phillips knew, Ford was leaning over him with a bright instrument, either a razor or a knife, in his hand, and he felt a slash across his face. The cut went across the right side, just below the eye, nearly severing the top of his ear and needing fourteen stitches. Struggling, Phillips got up and tried to escape, but Langham ran after him, knocked him down, and kicked him in the head and body. In court, when he was asked why he had been friendly to the men, Phillips replied that they had stabbed him before and that, 'I am in fear of my life. It is more than I dare do to refuse their drinks.'[338] Phillips was fearful not only because of his association with Gilbert but also because he had run away with the wife of an Italian called 'Johnny the Barber', who was friends with Ford and Langham. Both were charged with malicious wounding.

At the magistrates' hearing in September, their counsel emphasised that Ford and Langham were employed by the Bookmakers' Association, 'a perfectly respectable body', and that it was 'absolutely untrue that they were in anyway connected with a race gang or a gang roughs'. A bookmaker called Harry Cohen supported the accused, explaining that the Bookmakers' Association had been formed by responsible people and that they employed stewards who could use their fists to stop bad characters blackmailing bookmakers. He himself had suffered a broken nose from roughs, but now they were kept off the racecourse and racing was 'a garden party compared with what it used to be years ago'.[339] Cohen did not mention that he was a friend not only of Langham and Ford but also of Darby Sabini, who had a share in Cohen's bookmaking. Langham agreed that he and his two friends had been stood drinks by Phillips, but insisted that he had left before them. When they went outside, they saw Phillips on the ground with a crowd round him. They did not go near and went up the street, because 'they did not want to get a hiding like Phillips had'. The prosecuting counsel suggested a different story: that Langham had drunk with Phillips and then 'Judas-like, betrayed him afterwards'.

Ford also denied that he had anything do with the assault, declaring that, 'A friend of Phillips named Gilbert is an enemy of mine, and he got Phillips to frame the case up against me and Langham.'[340] Gilbert was a friend of Phillips and was a material witness in the case, as one of the attackers had supposedly confessed to him. However, Gilbert did not give evidence at the first magistrates' hearing as, when he arrived in the court building, he was threatened with a revolver by Harry and Darby Sabini. A police constable who had tried to help Phillips did testify but could not identify the assailants as they ran off when he approached and it was dark. By contrast, Phillips had not a shadow of doubt that it was Ford who had slashed him, but when the case came to the higher court in December, his identification of his attackers was 'vague and uncertain'.[341] The judge confirmed that it was clear he had changed his mind 'under what influence we can guess'. Consequently, the jury was instructed to return verdicts of not guilty.[342] However, the friends of Johnny Phillips did not wait for the conclusion of the court case to seek revenge, and his slashing was the signal for a summer of shootings between the Camden Town Gang and the Sabini Gang.

CAMDEN TOWN GANG DESPERADOES

The tensions between the two gangs had been heating up and now they boiled over. Emboldened by the alliance with the Titanics, Gilbert and Brummy Sage acted. On the evening of 29 July, five days after the slashing of Phillips, 'a number of roughs' from the Camden Town Gang went to the Red Bull public house in Gray's Inn Road, where members of the Sabini Gang were drinking. A shooting affray ensued.[343] Given their animosity, it's not surprising that those involved gave conflicting versions, but what seems to have happened is that when the 'band of desperadoes' from the Camden Town Gang went into the bar they were forced outside when the Sabinis made a move for them. An off-duty policeman followed and was shot at. Others joined the Camden Town Gang and there was more shooting, after which several of them were arrested.[344]

George Langham was one of the Sabini Gang who was targeted. He told the police that about 10.30pm five men came into the pub, including Arthur 'Toddy' Phillips, the brother of Johnny Phillips. He held a revolver in his right hand:

> I was terrified and hid against the counter. The man who followed behind Phillips also had a revolver in his right hand – I know him as a man called Jackson – I saw him in custody that night when he was on the way to the Police Station. I saw his photo in the 'News of the World' the following Sunday (6th August). When Phillips and the other man came into the Public House

some of the customers ran out followed by Phillips and the other man.[345]

Alf White was also at the pub, arriving by car with Darby Sabini at about 10.25pm after having been at Goodwood races. The bar was full, but contradicting Langham, he did not notice any person in particular. Going through the passage towards the street door, someone warned him that, 'You had better keep inside.' He returned to the bar and remained there for a few minutes until he left with Sabini. There was a crowd outside and they got into a car that was waiting for them. White added that he did not know Phillips and could not say if he was in the pub.[346] This account was corroborated by Sabini in almost every detail, suggesting that they had agreed between them exactly what to tell the police.

The off-duty officer who was in the packed bar was Detective Constable John Rutherford. He recognised three of the Camden Town Gang who entered the bar as Laurence Tobin, William Edwards and Arthur Phillips. Almost immediately after they were forced outside by the Sabinis, Rutherford heard a shot. Running outside, he saw Tobin and his men flourishing revolvers. He heard Tobin shout, 'Shoot the bastards', and saw him fire at the men who had chased him out of the bar. Noticing Rutherford, Tobin called out to his gang, now having increased to twelve, 'There is Rutherford, let the bastard have one.' From about fifteen yards, Tobin fired but the bullet missed. The gutsy Rutherford followed the men as they backed off. He was then shot at by Joseph Jackson, who shouted, 'Take that, you bastard.'

Several more shots were fired, but fortunately Rutherford escaped injury by hiding in a doorway. Once more, he followed the men as they ran off:

And upon reaching within 10 yards of two of the leaders, one turned and said 'Go back Rutherford'; both of these men then fired at the officer, but fortunately again missed. He still persisted in his pursuit, however, and when in Hatton Garden, came up with a man named Jackson who pointed a revolver at him and said 'Go away or I'll do you in'. The Constable knocked him down with his fist and took the weapon from him, which when examined was found to contain four empty cartridge cases. A uniform officer then came upon the scene, and after handing Jackson over to him, Rutherford searched the district to find the other men, but without success.

On his way to the station, Jackson told one of the officers escorting him, 'I was fucking well glassed and that started the barney.' The Commissioner of the Metropolitan Police noted that Rutherford and other officers had been concerned for some time 'on the extermination of these pests'. Justifiably, he acclaimed Rutherford for his exceptional courage and held him up 'as a splendid example to all ranks of the Force of a devotion to duty, which in the face of the most perilous risks, is beyond all praise'.[347] Rutherford was indeed courageous, as he had tackled very dangerous men.

Joseph Jackson, thirty-four years old and an Elephant Boy from Bermondsey, was a confirmed thief and blackmailer with nineteen previous convictions. These included six for assault; one for causing grievous bodily harm to a policeman; three for larceny; and nine for drunkenness and disorderly conduct. At 5 foot 6 inches, he had scars on his right eye, second left finger and nose, as well as a wound on his right side. Having joined the

Rifle Brigade in the First World War, he served only twelve days in France and was discharged as unfit in November 1917, after which he received an Army pension. This was supplemented by £2 a week from Parish Relief, handed over by the local Board of Guardians from money raised from a property rate. A married man with five children under five, for three or four months after his discharge, Jackson worked casually on linoleum laying, but apart from that had done no other work. In his neighbourhood, he was 'regarded as a notorious blackmailer and terror and great relief was expressed when he was arrested'. He had blackmailed costermongers, shopkeepers and bookmakers, usually demanding subscriptions for some fictitious person in trouble. He had even done so whilst under treatment in a military hospital.

In one case, he and his associates had badly injured a street bookmaker at Walworth because he refused to give them money. As in other instances, the victim feared to lodge a complaint with the police. And when he was arrested, Jackson had upon him a subscription list headed: 'On behalf of W. Jackson who needs your assistance in consequence of having fallen into trouble through no fault of his own'. Two subscriptions were entered – one for ten shillings and another for five shillings.[348]

Four other men from the Camden Town Gang were later arrested, including Lawrence Tobin, who had fled to Birmingham immediately after the shooting, indicating an ongoing bond with the Birmingham Gang. Tobin was an alias of George Baker, also known as George Martin and George Hillier. Having tattoos of a flag and a woman on his right arm and clasped hands and a flower on his left forearm, he stood at 5 foot 6 inches. Supposedly a bookbinder, he was another pickpocket to be found in the company of racecourse thieves, having convictions for loitering, frequenting and breaking and entering. From Sydney Street, Clerkenwell, he was probably connected to the Titanics, whilst William Edwards from Hoxton was one of their leading figures. Edwards was another persistent criminal and incorrigible rogue with eighteen convictions for larceny and assault on the police. Having joined the Royal Fusiliers in 1915, he was arrested for attempting to pick pockets in April 1918 and sentenced to twelve months in prison. Upon his release, he was handed over to a military escort, from which he escaped the same day and was thence classified as a deserter.

The involvement of Jackson, Baker (Tobin) and Edwards in this disturbance flags up the Camden Town Gang's anti-Sabini alliance with the Elephant Boys and the Titanics, to which Toddy Phillips also belonged. He was the fourth man arrested and had been convicted three times for unlawful possession, larceny and as a suspected person. Last released from prison in June 1921, when asked by the police what he had been doing since, he replied that he had done some work for his aunt, a tallywoman selling goods on credit to poor people at a high interest rate. She agreed that Phillips helped her occasionally, for which she gave him his food and a couple of shillings. When questioned by the police, Phillips admitted that he had been in the Red Bull on the night of the shooting with two young women. He said that he had seen Darby Sabini, Alf White and another man outside with razors in their hands, and when the Camden Town Gang came inside he knew that trouble was sure to take place. When asked if he knew any of the names of the Camden Town gang, Phillips answered:

> Long Jim is the only one of that mob I know by name,
> there were about 20 to 30 of the two mobs there. When

the shooting commenced the two girls ran away and I went across the road and stood by myself all the time. All this trouble has been brought about through my brother Johnny being slashed at Brighton. They tried to do him in and now they are trying to put it on me.[349]

Phillips, Jackson, Baker (Tobin) and Edwards were charged with shooting at detective constable Rutherford with intent to kill and with possessing firearms with intent to endanger life. Another man, George Fagioli, aged twenty-one and single, was also charged with the latter offence. His father, the son of a Frenchman and Englishwoman, was a groom with a cab company and his family was well established in Holborn and Clerkenwell and was law abiding. George Fagioli was not, and aged eleven he was convicted of office breaking and sent to an industrial school in Staffordshire as 'one of the worst of a gang of young thieves'. He stayed there until he was sixteen and his conduct was given as satisfactory. Returning home to his parents, he worked at a carrying company, but was let go because of slackness of trade. He had a good reference from that job and from two others, which also discharged him through lack of work. However, another employer stated that 'he had been associating with undesirables and frequenting their company at evenings'.[350]

One man escaped arrest for the Red Bull affray. He was Fred Gilbert, one of the leaders of the Camden Town Gang, who was spotted at the scene by a James Edwards. He told the police that he and a man called William Beland had been nearby on the evening of 29 July when they heard shots fired from the vicinity of the pub.

We immediately walked towards the sound of the firing but before getting there we were stopped by a man named Fred Gilbert, age about 30 who gets his living on the racecourse. I heard Gilbert say to Beland, 'You go the other way or I shall blow your f . . . . . g brains out', and I saw him put his hand in his right hand pocket as if to pull out a revolver. Beland said to him 'You don't want to go mad to me'. Gilbert said to Beland 'Well f . . k off'. We then walked on towards the 'Yorkshire Grey' public house. We did not see Gilbert before this meeting and I cannot say whether he was in the shooting affray in Grays Inn Road or whether he was in possession of a revolver. I know him to be a dangerous character and in my mind he had taken some part in the shooting affray in Grays Inn Road just before meeting us.

It may be wondered why Edwards and Beland walked towards the shooting rather than away from it. Both men, however, lived in Clerkenwell and may have been associated with the Sabinis. Be that as it may, from first-hand experience Beland knew that Gilbert was a most violent and dangerous man. Eighteen months previously, in early 1921, the two of them had been with others gambling on the canal bank by the Caledonian Road when Gilbert began quarrelling with a man named George Droy. A fight started, and with Gilbert getting the worst of it, he drew a razor from his pocket and slashed Droy across the left shoulder. Frank 'Trixie' Droy went to help his brother and Gilbert then pulled out a gun and fired at him point blank. Fortunately, the bullet passed through Droy's left shoulder.[351]

The attack on the Sabinis at the Red Bull had failed, so Gilbert and Sage now decided to target Jewish bookmakers, one of whom was Harry Margulas. On 1 August he claimed to have been stopped in Clerkenwell by two men. They were Fred Brett (also calling himself Jim Stevens) and Fred Gilbert, who took a revolver from his pocket vowing that, 'I am going to blow your brains out'. After making more threats, he demanded £10 and pressed the revolver to Margulas's face. Brett then encouraged Gilbert to, 'Let the bastard have one.' Margulas managed to run away, but though he reported this incident to the police, he refused to take action. Two weeks later, he went to Nottingham Races and, whilst at the station, he was again approached by Gilbert and Brett. They were with five other men. Tellingly, one of them was Andrew Towey, a leader of the Birmingham Gang. Gilbert warned Margulas that, 'We have got you on our manor now.' Again demanding £10, Gilbert waved a revolver, saying, 'Come on, let's have it, or you'll have this.' After a time, the bookie managed to pacify things by promising that he would give them something later. He was allowed to go on but did not report anything to the Nottingham Police. [352]

Brett was from Camberwell, South London, and his involvement was another pointer to the support of the Elephant Boys for the Camden Town Gang. He and Gilbert were together again late on the afternoon of 19 August along with George 'Brummy' Sage. After a day's racing at Hurst Park, they threatened a number of Jewish bookies, including Margulas. He and another bookmaker, Jack Delew, went into the Rising Sun pub near Waterloo Station. They were followed by Sage, who caught hold of the lapels of Margulas's coat saying, 'You're one of the bastards, do him Fred, through the guts.' Complying, Gilbert pressed a large service revolver into Margulas's body and demanded, 'Give us a tenner, and we'll let you go. I would have done you at Nottingham if I had not won seventy quid.'

Brett then turned to Delew, who was moving towards the door, and called out, 'Here's another one of them.' Sage let go of Margulas and urged Brett to 'Give him one'.[353] According to Delew, Brett pulled a large butcher's knife from his sleeve and pointed it towards him saying, 'Shall I do him, George?' With vehemence, Sage then told Delew: 'We want you bastards to understand that we're going to be top dogs, there's fifty of us tonight and it's going to finish. Alf White and the Sabinis will be done in for certain.' Pulling out a revolver, Gilbert warned that it was something for White.

Another man had arrived and, after he urged Sage to leave Delew and Margulis alone, they immediately went off to Waterloo Station to alert other Jewish bookmakers who had been at Hurst Park of the danger they were in.[354] One of them was Alfie Solomon, who had been racing with some of his brothers. Another of them, Simmy Solomon, was in Piccadilly when someone urged him to go over to Waterloo, as Gilbert and a mob were waiting there for his brothers. Simmy Solomon swiftly got into a cab, but when he arrived at the station he was confronted by Gilbert and another man whose face was much scarred. After demanding money, Gilbert said, 'I suppose you are looking for your sheeney brother of a bastard, Alf. The lot of you are only a lot of Jew ponces, you are frightened to have a go. I hope to see him first, I'll shoot his fucking brains out.' Told to 'piss off out of it as quick as you can', the frightened Simmy Solomon went home.[355] Samuel Samuels from Aldgate was also pulled up at Waterloo Station, this time by Sage, who had the butt of a revolver sticking out of his jacket pocket. He cursed Samuels as: 'You Jew bastard, you're one of the c . . . s we're going to do. You're a f . . . . . g bastard Jew and we are going do you and the Italians in, and stop you going racing. I want to be governor there.' Fortunately, another man came along and allowed Samuels to escape.[356]

SHOOTINGS AND BLACKMAIL

Sage's local pub was the Southampton Arms, near to his home in Mornington Crescent, and after making these threats, he and Gilbert met up there with other members of their gang. At about 10pm, just after closing time, a group of them were standing outside with Ellen Brookes and her sister. Suddenly, three taxi-cabs drove up and a crowd of men got out. Some of them were armed with revolvers and other weapons. They included Alf White, who was holding a coat over his left arm. From underneath it, he drew a pistol and, taking deliberate aim, fired at Sage from only a few yards away, shouting, 'Take that you –.' George West, alias Dai Thomas, drew another revolver and also fired at Sage, saying, 'Take that and all.' Joe Sabini was with them and was later named as a principal member of the gang. He too had a pistol and, shooting at Gilbert, called out, 'That's for you, you English –.'[357] When asked in court if he was hit, Gilbert answered, 'No, I have been wounded by these men before, though, and had to have seventy stitches.'[358]

After firing, the shooters scattered in different directions. Having been alerted to a possible confrontation, several police officers were close by and witnessed the event.[359] One of them saw Joe Sabini pull out a pistol with a handle resembling a walking-stick. When exhibited in court, the prosecuting counsel pronounced that, 'In the whole of my experience dealing with matters of this kind I have never seen a more dangerous weapon. I do not know whether it is German or not, but it is half six-chambered revolver and half stiletto, and can be housed in an innocent-looking walking-stick. It still bears on its point the marks of blood it got on it that night.' [360] A pistol and a life preserver were found in other directions in which the assailants ran after shooting. With the swift arrival of more policemen, Sabini Gang member Paul Boffa was quickly caught. He was believed to be the man saved from maiming in the Battle of the Nile with the Titanics.

Sage and Gilbert had many of their gang with them, and its mixed make-up was highlighted by some newspapers reporting the affray as 'Titanic versus Sabini', with the Camden Town Gang using the pseudonym of the Titanics. Because of this extremely hostile crowd, the police had great difficulty in arresting the offenders. [361] A Jewish associate of the Sabinis called Simon Nyberg had also shot at Gilbert but was actually caught by one of the Camden Town Gang. Nyberg managed to trip up the man and, running on, threw away a hammer that was later described as heavy enough to have killed a person if dropped upon them. [362] Someone else then knocked him down and secured him until a policeman arrived. Aged twenty-eight and supposedly a clerk, Nyberg came from Whitechapel and was the son of immigrants from the Polish part of the Russian Empire. His father was an interpreter, but Nyberg went on to have a bad record as a thief using several aliases. He was scarred on his forehead and the back of each hand and had been imprisoned for nine months in 1920 for larceny. A year later, he was fined for illegal gambling on the Surrey Downs, which was regarded as 'a great week-end resort for East-End Jews'. In another report, imbued with anti-Semitism and headlined 'The Invasion of Jews', it was revealed that in July 1921 Nyberg had attracted about forty Jewish men to a spot for gambling with dice. [363]

However, he had no convictions for violence and his involvement with the Sabinis at the shooting at Mornington Crescent is puzzling. That of Thomas Mack was not. A number caller on racecourses, he was deeply involved with the Sabini Gang and, after the shooting, he jumped onto a tramcar. As he did so, he knocked down a young woman called Amy Kent, cutting through her coat and blouse with an object gripped in his hand.[364] A closed knife was later found in his pocket. Hearing police whistles, PC Archer noticed a tram with a large crowd beside it. He pushed his way through and, boarding the vehicle, saw Mack struggling with Amy Kent. As he separated them, several men rushed onto the tram, now at a standstill. One of them was Fred Gilbert, who would later deny that he pointed a revolver at Mack, who was charged at by other men. So infuriated were they that the constable had to strike down two of them with his fist, before drawing his truncheon. Mack was then escorted off the tram by two officers to protect him from the enraged crowd of about fifty to sixty, some of whom were waving sticks and shouting, 'There he is. Let's kill him.'[365] As for Amy Kent, she fainted half an hour later when she found that the penknife Mack had been carrying had cut her arm.[366]

Alf White was named by the police as 'the ring leader' in what became known as the 'Shooting Affray' in the 'Racing Feud'.[367] He ran off with three other men. They were spotted by an off-duty policeman who was in civilian clothes and out with his wife. He had heard the shooting and, realising that the men running were involved, he followed them. When they separated, White got into a passing taxi-cab. Without hesitation, the constable stopped it and ordered the driver to go directly to Albany Street Police Station. White, West (Thomas), Nyberg, Mack, Boffa and Sabini were charged with maliciously shooting at Sage and Gilbert with intent to murder, with riotous assembly and with having loaded revolvers in their possession. Mack was also charged with wounding.[368] Their appearance on Monday 21 August at Marylebone Police Court was headlined on the front page of the *Pall Mall Gazette* as the 'Racing Feud Sensation'.[369] An hour beforehand, 'the vast space in front of the entrance doors was packed by a surging seething mob of men and women, who fought eagerly for places of vantage near the entrance'. When the doors were finally opened, there was such a rush to get inside that the police were almost overwhelmed. Bail was opposed for the safety of the prisoners, as if they were liberated it was feared that they would be in danger.[370]

Events were moving rapidly. Two days later, on 23 August, there was a confrontation at Paddington Station on the morning of the Bath races. Gilbert alleged that Harry Sabini had pointed an automatic gun at him and threatened to blow out his brains, after which he left the train to find a policeman. The officer supported this story, adding that he saw several men running to get on the train and that one of them dropped an automatic pistol, which he picked up.[371] Aged twenty-two, Sabini usually claimed to be a fruit dealer in Clerkenwell, and when charged, he exclaimed, 'What a liar! I never said a word to him.' He maintained that Gilbert had turned up at Paddington in a crowd and that:

Alfie Solomon asked him why he was going and whether he was going to make trouble. He told him to mind his own business. The train started and we rushed to get in. We only got out in case Gilbert's crowd set about Alfie. I never carry a gun or anything. I don't like trouble of that kind.[372]

On 22 September at Marylebone Police Court, however, Harry Sabini was found guilty, called a dangerous man, and bound over to keep the peace in the large surety of £200.[373] It was paid by Edward Emanuel.[374] The same day, Sabini's brother Joe also appeared at the same court for another hearing in the Shooting Affray. The two of them came up with a rather desperate scheme to discredit a police witness in that case. Harry stated that he had seen Joe Sabini draw a pistol from inside his jacket pocket, similar to the one that he was now wearing in court. Sabini's counsel challenged the officer to examine the coat to determine whether there was room under the coat for such a weapon. After doing so, he informed the court that the coat was not the same one that Sabini had been wearing when arrested. In response, Sabini insisted that he had not changed his clothing since then. Detective Inspector Hambrook decided to make enquiries. Harry Sabini was still at the court awaiting his surety, and it was noticed that his coat and waistcoat were of the same material as the trousers worn by his brother – and the coat had a pocket such as that described by the officer. When challenged, Harry Sabini apologised and admitted that he and his brother had changed clothes in the lavatory.[375]

Throughout the hearings, it was made clear how difficult it was to get information about the assaults, so greatly was the Sabini Gang feared.[376] Gilbert stuck to his original statement: Sabini had fired at him; West and White had run towards Sage; and he had heard two shots. Contrarily, Sage changed his mind, saying that he must have been mistaken in seeing West and White shoot at himself and Gilbert. His wife, Ellen, and a fellow gang member followed on the same lines. The police believed that 'there was every indication, by the demeanour of these witnesses, that they were either afraid to give evidence according to their voluntary statements or had been "got at" – the alternative seeming the more probable'.

Of the accused men, Boffa, who had only been seen running away with Sabini, was discharged due to insufficient evidence against him. The other prisoners were committed to trial at the Old Bailey, where they pleaded not guilty on 23 October.

When the day of the trial arrived, one of the key witnesses was due to be a man named William Roberts. Previously he had given important evidence against Joe Sabini, having found the stiletto-revolver combination where Sabini had run in trying to escape. Now, though, Roberts had disappeared from his lodgings and was nowhere to be found. Of course, immediately there was grave suspicion that he had been approached by Sabini's associates and induced to leave the district.[377]

Fortunately, unlike him, a witness called James Camp did turn up to corroborate Gilbert's account that White had been present at the shooting, that he had something in his hand, and that he had definitely taken part in the riot. Camp spoke nervously and, when asked if he had been threatened and was afraid, he replied that he was not comfortable. This aroused laughter in the court, which irritated the judge who pronounced that it was 'not a laughing matter. It is a matter of the gravest possible import when witness after witness comes in here obviously afraid, obviously uncomfortable'.[378]

It is little wonder that Camp was nervous, as the police later confirmed that he'd been in fear of the Sabini Gang since he had come forward to give evidence. It seems he had known White and his associates for several years, and had been a valuable informant to the police. But despite any reservations Camp may have had, he acted with 'conspicuous courage and determination in following up the prisoners some of whom were known to be in possession of firearms'. The arresting police officers were also commended for their bravery. [379]

The case was watched carefully by Edward Davis, the solicitor of the Bookmakers' Association, which employed White and Joe Sabini as stewards. White's defence emphasised this connection with what was regarded as a legitimate organisation, explaining that he was a senior steward and was disliked by Gilbert because he had been dismissed from his position with the Association.[380] In his summing up, the judge made it clear that no suggestion had been made by the witnesses or the Crown that they had been threatened or interfered with by the prisoners or their friends, yet it was quite obvious 'that with an organisation like the one White was a member of – the Bookmakers' Protection Association – which defending counsel had described as both "reputable and powerful", people would be rendered uncomfortable and fearful of giving evidence which might lead to conviction'. The jury found Sabini and White guilty of shooting with intent to cause grievous bodily harm, the unlawful possession of firearms, and riotous assembly – for the latter of which Nyberg was also found guilty. Mack was found guilty of both riotous assembly and unlawfully wounding Amy Kent; and, on the instruction of the judge, West was found not guilty on all counts – this being rather fortunate considering his influence and status within the Sabini Gang.[381]

Before sentencing on 3 November 1922, White's counsel affirmed that he was a man of perfectly upright character and intimated that he was going to call various eminent bookmakers as character witnesses. He added that on racecourses, White had given information to the police. The judge interposed: 'That should be something in the man's favour but I am going to teach people to act through the police for their protection and try, so far as I can, to prevent people from taking the law into their own hands, with pistols, knives and other weapons for their remedies.' He made it clear that he was not going to investigate the merits of the Bookmakers' Association but declared that the sooner it was dissolved the better. The judge, though, did allow some evidence in White's favour, including from racecourse official, Divall. With the expulsion of the Birmingham Gang from the South, it is obvious that he had no option but to accommodate the takeover by the Sabinis, given the legitimacy conferred on them through their role as stewards. [382]

The counsel for Joe Sabini stressed that he had also given information to the police, that he had no previous convictions, and that he had served his country loyally. The judge, however, was unaffected by such considerations, but before he could pass sentence, a woman came to the front of the dock and pleaded for White, 'Have mercy on him, my lord!' After she was moved away, he was imprisoned for five years and told that he was fortunate not to have faced a capital charge. At that, he put his hands to his head, exclaiming 'My God!' [383] After the trial, White quickly appealed against his conviction and, in December 1922, it was quashed, the appeal judge doing so with the greatest reluctance on a point of law. As for the other guilty men, Joe Sabini was sent to prison for three years; Nyberg for twenty-one months' hard labour; and Mack for eighteen months. After Mack's release, he would rejoin the Sabini Gang along with White. Both of them highlight the significance of 'Englishmen' in the Sabinis, whilst Nyberg's participation was a further indication of the important role of Anglo-Jewish criminals. He also appealed against his sentence but was turned down. Obviously not as hardened a criminal as White and Mack, neither was he a leading figure in the Sabini Gang, and in prison he showed signs of mental illness.

The imprisonment of Joe Sabini was a blow both to Darby Sabini personally and to the Sabini Gang, changing its dynamics. Though Darby had always been the outright leader, his younger brother had been a trusted, dependable and loyal lieutenant. A major figure in the rise of the gang and in its victories, he would not rejoin it after his release, as will be discussed. If Darby Sabini had also lost Alf White, then the Sabini Gang's swift ascent to gangland power might equally swiftly have been challenged by new enemies.

However, White's successful appeal was a major boost to Darby Sabini and White would go on to play an increasingly important role in the Sabini Gang, which will be made clear. And, most importantly, Sage and Gilbert had lost. At the end of a spring and summer of slashings, shootings and beatings, they had not become the 'top dogs'. The Sabinis had kept their grip on the southern racecourses, bolstered as they were by their legitimacy as stewards for the Bookmakers' Association. As for their enemies, the Elephant Boys would resume hostilities in 1925, and whilst the Titanics faded away, some of its members would carry on fighting the Sabinis. So too would former members of the Camden Town Gang, although as an entity it disappeared along with its co-leader, Fred Gilbert. For a man whose life had been so public, it now became highly private, and the last documentary reference for him was 1925, when he was still living in a flat in Moreland Street.[384]

Unlike him, Sage continued to be involved in racing, and there is some slight evidence that he may have remained in control of the rackets on the open part of Epsom – perhaps as part of an understanding with the Sabinis.[385] What is certain is that his propensity for violence was unabated. In December 1925, when he was fifty-one, he was arrested for a brawl with a twenty-seven-year-old man over a betting dispute outside Tattersall's in Knightsbridge. This was the premier venue for auctioning race horses and its weekly events were also a rendezvous for racing men. Describing himself as a clerk, probably for a bookmaker, Sage pleaded guilty and was bound over.[386] By 1939, he, his wife and their three children were no longer living in their grand home in Mornington Crescent and were at Pemberton Terrace, Junction Road, Islington. Indicative of his changed circumstances, it was a three-storey house with basement accommodation and was shared with two other families, whilst Sage gave his occupation as builder's labourer. Following the death of his first wife, he was able to finally marry Ellen Brookes in 1942. George 'Brummy' Sage died five years later.[387] He had been one of England's first nationally notorious gangland leaders but his name was quickly obscured by that of Darby Sabini – the country's first 'personality' gangster and first acclaimed guv'nor of London's gangland.

Chapter 5

THE SABINI GANG SUPREME

DARBY SABINI: THE CHIEF

At the start of August 1922 and in the midst of the Racing Feud between the Sabini Gang and the Camden Town Gang, the *Empire News* trumpeted that there had been no more amazing feature in English crime over the last hundred years than the supremacy in the underworld of the 'S– Gang'. A detailed piece revealed that the rank and file of the gang consisted mostly of Whitechapel Jews, who carried out the operations ordered by their leaders. These 'banditti' were three London-born Italian brothers, very well known to the police, who 'speak our language and know our ways as well as any Englishman'. Those who worked under them rarely dared to retain any of their ill-gotten gains for fear that their portion would be immediate punishment in the form of a huge slash down the face with a razor. Indeed, the depredations of the 'S– Gang' were enough 'to make people wonder whether or not we are living in a civilised country with a large, highly paid police force'.[388] Though well informed about the Sabini Gang's activities and feuds, the

137

language used in the *Empire News* article reflected deep-rooted prejudices against Italians, Jews and un-Englishness. These bigotries were to the fore in an anonymous letter sent to the Metropolitan Police in August 1922, during the trials of the Racecourse Feud.

Ungrammatical and with misspellings, the complainant asked whether the authorities were aware that 'these Italian mobs are walking about, cutting people face with razor, and shooting them, are all well known boxer, and that they never done a Day work since they been in this country'. Darby Sabini was personally accused of shooting Billy Kimber and having his friend [Solomon] put up for it, whilst the Italians were allowed to do things an Englishman could not. Supposedly they kept gambling houses, which were never raided by the police, and they were allowed to travel to race meetings and 'demand money from all the Bookmakers there, and nothing is said to them, why because they are Italians'. The letter ended with the plea, 'We Englishmen only want Fair Play, and justice done, that is not much to ask for. God know who face will be cut next.'[389]

A few days later, a similarly ill-formed letter in a different hand was sent to the Home Secretary, Edward Shortt. Its envelope was postmarked Leicester and it was signed with the pseudonym 'Tommy Atkins', the popular generic term given to British soldiers. As an ex-serviceman and Englishman, and ostensibly uninterested party, he wanted to give a few 'facts' regarding the Racing Feud and the 'Sabina Gang' [*sic*]:

> The Financier and Brains of this gang of Cuthroats on the Race Courses of England are Foriengers [*sic*] named Edward Emanual and Gurchan Harris, these two men

finance all the large clubs and Gambling Houses in the
West End of London, and they pay large sums of money
to other foriengers, 'The Sabini Gang' also the 'Flying
Squad' of Scotland Yard to safeguard their interests.

'Tommy Atkins' specifically pointed out that 'none of the
'Sabina Gang' was in the 'Service' during the War and I think it
is disgrace to the country to let such 'Terrors' to go about and
attacking Englishmen that have done their 'Bit' to uphold the
Tradition of the British Empire'.[390]

Of the two men picked upon, Gershon Harris had come
to the East End from Poland as a young man in the 1870s.
Originally a tailor, by 1900 he was the 'owner of a great deal
of house property in the Jewish Quarter of Spitalfields'.[391] A
wealthy man who was living in Shepherds Bush by 1919, he
was also a boxing referee and a leading fundraiser for the West
London Hospital.[392] There is no evidence connecting him
with the Sabini Gang. However, the same cannot be said for
Edward Emanuel. He had close connections with Darby Sabini
and had brought in the Sabini Gang to protect the Jewish
bookies from the blackmailing of the Birmingham Gang.
But he was not a foreigner. Emanuel's Jewish family was long
established in England, and behind him was the Englishman
Walter Beresford, the prominent bookmaker and president
of the Bookmakers' Association.[393] Nevertheless, in a period
when foreigners were too often looked down upon as aliens,
the ancestry of Emanuel and the Sabinis provoked fear, outrage
and ignorance. This 'alienism', as Heather Shore has insightfully
shown, 'fundamentally allowed the press and the Home
Secretary to characterize the metropolitan confrontations as
something essentially 'unEnglish' and potentially dangerous'.[394]

The 'unEnglishness' of the Sabinis and their Jewish allies was accentuated by the 'alien' nature of their neighbourhoods. Although Alfie Solomon was from Covent Garden in North London, the Jewish gangsters were mostly associated with Whitechapel in the East End. Frederick Wensley, Chief Constable of the CID at Scotland Yard, began his policing career there in the 1890s when 'it was full of the criminal classes. They lived there and largely worked there'. The lodging houses were full of ne'er do wells, the 'slum' areas were nests of crime, and the streets were infested by infamous women. Although he was at pains to emphasise that the East End was not an unrelieved haunt of vice and crime, and that he had met people of the finest character among Jews and Gentiles, the negative image of Whitechapel was the dominant one in the press.[395] So too was that of the 'Italian Colony' in Clerkenwell.

An article on 'Alien Criminals' in the *Pall Mall Gazette* in 1901 reported that it had been 'discovered' that no less than 25 per cent of the cases at the Clerkenwell court were concerned with foreigners. This 'influx of criminal aliens' was denounced and the whole district, including as it did 'the East End Jewry and the Italian colony', was besmirched as 'more alien-ridden than any in London, or, for that matter, in England'.[396] No account was taken of the proportion of the population that was Jewish and Italian and of how that related to the proportion of criminals. Impressions and images were what mattered, and these fuelled prejudice. As observed by Lucio Sponza in his groundbreaking work on Italian immigrants in nineteenth-century Britain, they were the subject of continuous adverse comments and judgement on what was perceived as their violent character. In particular, according to evidence given to the Royal Commission on

Alien Immigration, it was believed that they all carried knives and were quick to use them in a fight.[397]

There was a further connotation between the Italians of Clerkenwell and violence: the Sicilian Mafia. In a piece from 1907 entitled 'Byways of Babylon. Naples in London', the celebrated journalist and commentator, George R. Sims, depicted the 'Italian Colony' as a 'colourful' district at the centre of which was 'a slumbering volcano' – the Mafia:

> That dread society that deals terrible punishments to those who are denounced and condemned in secret council, has its agents among the 'colonists', and the 'order' of vengeance is sometimes carried out in the heart of London without the slightest suspicions being entertained by the matter-of-fact citizens that the order of a world infamous secret society has been executed in their midst'.[398]

Yet there is nothing to suggest any Sicilian Mafia involvement in London's Little Italy. The great majority of its people originated not from Sicily but from Lombardy and Emilia Romagna in the north of Italy, or else from Tuscany in central Italy and Campania in the south, between Naples and Rome.[399]

And nor were the Sabinis Sicilian. James Morton has written a riveting account of the life of Bert 'Battles' Rossi, a major post-Second World War gangster. His parents were immigrants and his father 'came from Piacenza in northern Italy, the same region as the Sabini family'.[400] A Sabini was first recorded as living in Clerkenwell in 1851, and he was from Parma, near to Piacenza – and both are in the same region as Emilia Romagna. The Sabinis' father left there as a child and went on to marry an Englishwoman, Elizabeth Handley, yet the *Empire News* maintained that their sons resembled 'the Mafia gangs of Italy and America with this difference: that the London band does not ordinarily bother with the average citizen'.[401]

Another journalist even asserted that 'the Sicilian activities of the Sabini gang seem less deplorable on the little hills of Clerkenwell than on British racecourses'. The similarities between Little Italy and Naples meant that '*la vendetta* is appropriate here, and if the gang were artists they would apply their art in the right surroundings'.[402] The Englishness of the Sabinis was continually ignored, and because many of their gang were Jewish, it was looked down upon as practically all of foreign extraction. The *Empire News* deplored the fact that for a long time, these 'aliens' had sought 'to establish their exclusive right to rob and plunder all regular frequenters of racecourses in the South of England'. They had terrorised most of their opponents into submission and had defied the efforts of Scotland Yard's Flying Squad to restrain them.[403]

Darby Sabini himself was not an ostentatious gangster and did not seem to court such publicity. He drove a small car and dressed modestly in a shirt with no collar, dark suit and waistcoat and a light-checked flat cap.[404] And unlike Kimber, Sage and Gilbert, he had been named rarely in newspaper coverage of the racecourse wars. In 1921, he was mentioned only in the Greenford attack, when his surname was misspelled as Sabni and his forename was incorrectly given as Charles. In fact, as he wrote in 1940, 'my real name is Octavious Sabini not Frederick Sabini or Fred Handley. I used the name of Fred Handley has [*sic*] my boxing name Darby is my nickname. My friends call me Fred but I am not the same has Frederick Sabini my brother.'[405] Even in the Racecourse Feud of 1922 and its numerous court proceedings, Darby Sabini was alluded to but briefly when it was suggested that he was the leader of one of the racing gangs. The Jewish bookie Margulas denied this, stating, 'I know Sabini well, and he is not the leader of a racing gang.'[406]

This contention was contradicted just a fortnight later when, in another gangland article, the *Empire News* announced that Sabini was indeed the 'Chief of the "Sabini Gang"'. On 3 September, it was revealed that he was telling his story of the 'notorious brothers' and their activities. His motives for doing so are not known, as he had previously shied away from the press. However, given the negative publicity about his gang, it may be that he wanted to project a more positive image as an Englishman and defender of the weak. Nevertheless, the *Empire News* persisted in associating him with 'foreignness', introducing him as a 'dapper, sturdy-looking little man, with the quick, flashing eyes of his race', even though Sabini himself quickly affirmed his family's patriotism: 'My brothers and I were born and reared in the Italian colony in Saffron Hill. My father was an Italian and my mother was an Englishwoman. They have lived in the quarter for years and are widely known.'[407]

Sabini was one of six brothers, none of whom ever went to Italy and all of whom were educated at elementary schools in London. Not having attended Italian classes, they were unable to speak or understand Italian, whilst the family had no relations in Italy. Sabini later emphasised that 'all our people are English' and even though he had been brought up in Clerkenwell, 'I never mixed with Italians. It was always English boys'.[408] That was mostly true, as those with Italian surnames with whom he did mix had been born in England and were regarded by the

Italian-born as English. Importantly, Sabini's wife, Ann Potter, was a local Englishwoman and they married in 1913 – not in the Catholic church of St Peter, which was deeply associated with the Italians of Little Italy, but in the Anglican church of St Philip, Clerkenwell. Their eldest daughter would also be christened in the Church of England.[409]

Significantly, Sabini's two eldest brothers, Frederick and Charles, were named after their English maternal uncles. In 1899, both were imprisoned for larceny and receiving but thereafter they seem to have stayed clear of crime. It was Fred who went into racing first as a proper commission agent, putting on bets for owners of racehorses and receiving a payment in return. According to Darby, his brother had considerable success, and so Joe and Harry joined him.[410] Like all of the brothers, Fred married an Englishwoman, and from 1928 became a bookie under the name of Joe Wilson at Haringey and White City dog tracks. He had no involvement with the violent activities of his brothers. Nor did Charles, although he benefitted from them. From the late 1920s, he supplied racings lists, stools, betting forecast tissues, sponges and other 'services' to bookmakers at West Ham dog track in a business the police believed could 'aptly be described as a racket'. He did so for Joseph Levy, a regular associate of Darby and Harry Sabini. Another brother, George, carried out the same services at Haringey and White City.[411]

In his self-glorifying piece in the *Empire News*, Sabini emphasised that when the First World War broke out, all the brothers volunteered for military service, only two being rejected on the grounds of being medically unfit. Serving abroad with the East Cheshires, Joe Sabini was badly wounded having been shot through the right ankle. Now a cripple for life, he was in receipt of an Army pension. Another brother, George, joined the Middlesex Regiment for about eighteen months, but on account of his health was not sent on foreign service; and Darby himself was in the Surreys and served in a home battalion for a couple of years. Actually, he had been in the East Surrey Militia for five years from 1907 and, when war was declared, he tried to rejoin but failed to pass the medical examination owing to ear trouble and deafness.

Sabini went on to explain that as a youngster, he had become very interested in boxing and joined a little club set up by the local Catholic priests. It was open to:

> . . . all the youths in our colony, and here we used to have some very exciting contests. All my brothers learned to box and we became passionately fond of the game. The knowledge which we gained in our little amateur tussles became valuable later, especially in the West End where betting clubs began to spring up like mushrooms. At that time bookmakers were being persecuted and subject to a good deal of intimidation. I was offered an appointment as a doorkeeper at one of the clubs and naturally I soon began to get an insight into the racing fraternity.[412]

This daring story of the young amateur boxer coming to the rescue of persecuted bookmakers deliberately left out a significant portion of Sabini's background. After his father died in 1901, his mother carried on their small business in which he worked as a carman, driving a horse-drawn cart and delivering goods. He then joined the Militia, where he learned to box properly. After his service, he fought professionally as

Fred Handley (Clerkenwell), taking his English mother's family name. Although not regarded as skilful, Sabini was marked out by 'the strength of his arm', especially his right-hand punch, whilst he did not shy away from hitting below the belt and mixing it in a rough and tumble.[413] As a tough man, he did become a doorman, a euphemism for a minder, and in 1918, he was employed at a gaming club in the East End earning £3 a week.[414] Two years later, in May 1920, he was prosecuted after having been found at a gaming house and with having been 'concerned with another in keeping, managing and conducting said premises'.[415] The most likely 'another' was Emanuel.

Playing on his role as the 'saviour' of the bookmakers, Sabini went on to tell the readers of the *Empire News* that he saw that bookmaking was not the most pleasant of occupations. In 1918, a coterie of roughs habitually threatened and demanded money from those in London, and they were compelled to suffer this systematic terrorism because they dared not take proceedings. Sabini soon came to their aid.

It was at Greenford Park trotting races that I got into the wars. I went alone to the races. A quarrel arose between a Jew and two well-known racing figures. The Jew was seriously assaulted, being struck on the head with a cup. It seems as if there was an organised attack on the bookmakers that day, of whom the Jew was one.

I intervened and demanded to know why the bookmakers were being bullied and blackmailed, and instantly I was set upon. A gang of about 30 men attacked me. I was thrown to the ground, kicked like a football, till finally the police rescued me, and no doubt saved my life.

In this heroic-type account, Sabini failed to mention that he had drawn a revolver to protect himself and that he had members of his gang with him.

Then, he continued, the bookmakers formed their Association and because he knew the ringleaders of the blackmailers, he was taken on as honorary steward. So too were his brothers, Joe and Harry, together with a number of other men who were considered 'suitable' for such posts. Sabini emphasised that it was not easy dealing with some of the people who preyed upon bookies, but the Association and its stewards were successful in keeping undesirables away from meetings – so much so that even the Jockey Club and famous racing people had commented favourably on the satisfactory state of the racecourses since the Sabinis had become involved. Bookmakers, backers and the general public were able to attend without molestation and everything had passed off 'fairly well until the recent disturbances, which are really an echo of old feuds'. Keen to reinforce his selflessness, Sabini stressed that:

> We are not an organised gang and never have been. So far from encouraging feuds and outbursts I have endeavoured in every way to keep the warring factions far apart so that there should be no violent conflicts of any description.
>
> I have spoken to men whom I knew were likely to be troublesome, and I have warned them not to go out of their way to make mischief, as it wasn't worthwhile.
>
> It is amusing to hear the Sabini 'gang' blamed whenever there is any disturbance on the racecourse or in the streets.
>
> The truth is that some of those who know the good

work we have tried to do for the B.P.A. (the Bookmakers' Association), have no friendly feelings towards us, and when any little episode occurs the cry goes up 'The Sabini Gang again'.[416]

Much as he strove to dismiss suggestions that there was an organised Sabini Gang, it was the firm leadership of Darby Sabini, surrounded by a close group of lieutenants, which distinguished his gang. That cohesion had been a key factor both in forcing the Birmingham Gang into ceding control of the rackets on the southern racecourses and in defeating the Camden Town Gang alliance. And much as Sabini pushed himself forward as an honourable and generous man, his motivations were not altruistic. They were driven by self-interest. He was a violent man leading a violent gang and had become a racing man because he wanted to make a lot of money easily through blackmailing bookmakers and other rackets. The Birmingham Gang's racist attacks on Alfie Solomon and other Jewish bookies gave him the pretext to bring in his gang as saviours when in effect they were nothing of the kind. Backed up by force and the fear of beatings, extortion carried on unrestrained after the Sabini Gang takeover, and it became as much a parasite on the bookies as had been the Birmingham Gang.

SABINI'S RIGHT HANDS

Darby Sabini contrasted sharply with Gilbert and Sage, the leaders of the Camden Town Gang. A thinker and a planner, he had more nous than his enemies, who were roughhouse fighters always in the thick of it. It was something that he was proud of, explaining in 1922 that he did a little bit of work as a commission agent, sometimes for himself and sometimes for someone else, but, as he professed, 'I'm always honest, the last day's work I did was three years ago. I live by my brains.'[417] Yet, as bookmaker Prince put it, Sabini may have been 'the gentleman of the mob but he feared nobody' and clearly did not shy away from violence.[418]

Divall vouched for that through personal experience, recalling the occasion when a group of North Country hooligans had come to the Hawthorn Hill races near Windsor, well within the Sabini Gang's territory. They were obviously welchers and put up an apparently respectable man and clerk to make a book for them. As the racecourse official, Divall challenged the pair, and when they couldn't provide satisfactory references, he stopped them working. Infuriated, they and their friends made several quiet threats against him throughout the afternoon and, after the racing, they suddenly surrounded him. One of them swore with a terrible oath 'that he would kill me; he made for me and was just about to carry out his intention, but Darby Sabini rushed up to my aid and knocked the chap down with a heavy blow in the mouth. The others, seeing the "red light", got hold of the wounded warrior and hurried him away.'[419]

Sabini could clearly handle himself with his fists, but he would also use a weapon. Dave Langham was the bookmaker son of Sabini's lifelong friend George Langham, and he disclosed that, 'Darby was a razor man, although he was a good fighter but he was a bit vicious. Darby would come up and put his arm round you and then . . . [Langham made a slashing motion with his hand].'[420] Fighting man as he was, Sabini generally left the physical side of the gang to his closest associates, but he was still clearly 'the boss, the head of the whole gang', as recognised by his hated foe Gilbert.[421] By comparison, the Camden Town

Gang combination had no unifying force. Having several leaders, it was an unwieldy, shifting grouping without the structure or discipline of the Sabinis. It also lacked a tight core of loyal 'lieutenants'. Darby Sabini may have lost his brother Joe through imprisonment, but he still had Harry Sabini, Georgie Langham, Alf White, Alfie Solomon and Jim Ford. Some of these men were bonded together by ties of family and upbringing; others like Solomon by necessity, having needed to find support against the Birmingham Gang.

In Raphael Samuels' 1981 book, *East End Underworld*, Arthur Harding claimed that 'there wasn't an Englishman' among the Sabini Gang.[422] Yet there was. Sabini himself was an Englishman, as were his brothers Joe and Harry, the two who also joined the Sabini Gang. Born in 1890, Joe Sabini was two years younger than Darby. Just under 5 foot 7 inches, he had a dark complexion, black hair and hazel eyes as well as several scars on his head, neck and arms. Before the First World War, he also worked for his mother in her small family business of carting. He then joined the Royal Welsh Fusiliers in the spring of 1916, later transferring to the 13th Battalion the Cheshire Regiment. Just after midday on 21 October 1916, it captured the forbidding Regina Trench but the cost was high. Three officers and seventy-four men had been killed, with another 120 wounded. Joe Sabini was one of them. Invalided out of the Army in March 1917, his character was given as good. His service entitled him to the Victory Medal and British War Medal and a pension. It contrasted starkly with the many deserters in both the Birmingham Gang and Sabini Gang.

The police later stated that Joe Sabini was not the gang's originator. Nor was Harry. The youngest brother, and often called 'Harryboy', he was eighteen months old when his father died in 1901. Unlike his older brothers, who went to the non-denominational Laystall Street Council School, he attended St Peter's Catholic School in Clerkenwell until 1914, when he found work with an optician. Seeking to better himself, he moved on to a job in a munitions factory and, with the coming of peace, worked on commission for a bookie and boxing promoter. It is more likely that Harry Sabini was a minder, as he became for Walter Beresford, whom he joined in 1921 during the Racecourse War with the Birmingham Gang. Like his older brother, Harry put a positive spin on the rise of the Sabini Gang, later contending that it became involved to support bookmakers because 'there were some Birmingham chaps that used to try and get the pitches. There used to be fights over the pitches, and people used to say "the Sabini gang", and we got that name.'[423]

Of course, the Sabini Gang was made up of more than just the Sabinis themselves. Another Anglo-Italian who featured importantly was George Langham, the English name of Angelo Gianicoli, whose parents also came from around Parma. He and Sabini were staunch pals and he was viewed as 'Darby Sabini's right hand'. [424] Bookie Dell recalled Langham as 'a nice man. Very quiet. But he was one of the minders [...] a very good bantamweight'.[425] This last detail is clear to see in historical records, along with his success at boxing flyweight as well. A 'rugged customer' yet skilful fighter, he boxed professionally and was good enough to take on Charles Ledeux, the French bantamweight champion, in Monte Carlo, although he was knocked out in the fourth round.[426]

Langham was born in 1889 in Little Italy and was the second eldest of six children to Italian parents. His father worked in a kitchen and his mother took in washing and the whole family lodged in overcrowded conditions with another large Italian family. Unlike his parents, Langham had violent tendencies and when he was fourteen, he was discharged from malicious wounding. After his release he became a mosaic floor layer, but in 1913 he served six months in Wandsworth Prison for unlawful wounding. That year, he also pleaded guilty to breaking and entering a shop with 'a gang of desperate criminals'. As he was not the 'brains' of the gang but a boxer of some repute who had been introduced to it through a girl, he got away without imprisonment.[427]

These offences were committed under the name of Angelo Gianicoli and his family believed that during the First World War, he went on the run. It is likely that his desertion led to his change of name to Langham, under which it seems he was again enlisted, as official records show that he served with the London Regiment and was wounded at the end of July 1918.[428] With the coming of peace, he started boxing again but it was obvious that he was associating with a rough crowd. In November 1920, Langham was the firm favourite in a three-round contest against a boxer from Swansea at a bout in London. Drawn against a comparatively unknown man, he thought that he could take liberties, as it was reported, but his opponent out-boxed him and his supporters became 'disturbed', all the more so as many of them had bet on the local favourite's victory.[429] The referee was Moss Deyong, and at the end of the fight he knew the Welshman had won because Langham 'had been boiled down to make the weight limit and had no fire or punch in him'. Notwithstanding this, the three judges could not agree on a decision, leaving Deyong with the unwanted role of determining the winner. He was approached by the worried promoter of the event and told,

'Use your brains, Moss. All Clerkenwell is here to see Langham win.' With the situation ugly, and notorious characters in the audience, Deyong announced that there would be a fourth round, believing that the Welshman was so far ahead that he couldn't lose even if Langham took the round. Yet once again the judges failed to agree, and despite his consternation at their indecision, Deyong awarded the fight to the Welshman.

> Two seconds after I had given it a man jumped into the ring and kicked me in the face, while at the same time another roughneck was approaching me from the rear. I dealt with the kicker first, and turned just in time to grab the man behind, and we fell to the canvass together.
>
> I took good care that I was on top when we fell, and to be truthful I made no effort to fall lightly. We were in the process of tearing each other to pieces when two detectives jumped into the ring and pulled us a part.[430]

Another inner-circle member of the Sabini Gang was Jim Ford, a good pal of Langham's, who was also said to have boxed. The eldest of eight children, in 1911 Ford was living in Holborn, on the borders of Clerkenwell, and was an errand boy, a low-paid casual occupation. Having hazel eyes, brown eyes and two tattoos, he could readily turn to violence, and, when he was just seventeen, he pleaded guilty to actual bodily harm. Strangely for his later associations, his victim was an Italian. Ford then joined the Royal Regiment of Artillery and served in France in 1915 before he was posted to Salonika in Greece. Two years later, because of deafness, he was transferred to a Reserve battalion, from which he deserted. Although he was absent without leave several times, the military deemed him to be intelligent but unreliable and not amenable to discipline. Pertinently for his later life as a racecourse rogue and gangster, he had shown no aptitude for a particular employment in civilian life.

Like Ford, Alf White was another of Darby Sabini's henchmen who was of English descent. Branded by the police as a violent character and racecourse ruffian, White was viewed as clearly 'one of the leading lights of the Sabini Gang'.[431] Raised by the Angel, Islington and apparently an only child, his father had various occupations including as a clerk and a carpenter but eventually as a bookmaker. As for Alf White himself, Jim McDonald of the Elephant Boys reckoned he was actually an early leader of the Titanics.[432] There is no firm evidence to support this belief, although interestingly White had started out as a pickpocket and was connected to the Titanics through his marriage. In 1913, when he was twenty-six, he was one of four London men convicted for stealing a purse of money from a Scottish farmer at Carlisle railway station.[433] Another man imprisoned with him was Charles Wooder, White's brother-in-law, who was a pickpocket, racecourse thief and definitely a Titanic.[434] If White was also in that pickpocketing gang, then it's surprising that he switched allegiance, given its antagonism with the Sabini Gang and his family links. It may be that he did so because he had settled in Clerkenwell – the Sabinis' stronghold – where he had a business as a florist. As Brian McDonald astutely observed, White 'sat uncomfortably astride a fence with the Sabinis on one side and East Enders on the other'. Perhaps a more compelling reason for joining the Sabini Gang was that White was an enemy of the Birmingham Gang and its London allies. He had formed the King's Cross Gang, which was one of the first to terrorise bookmakers on southern racecourses after the First World War, but it was forced out in 1920 by Kimber's takeover.[435] Soon after, White joined the Sabini Gang, quickly becoming one of its top men.

The main Jewish personality amongst the Sabinis was Alfie Solomon. He was unusual amongst his peers, as historical records suggest he had a comfortable upbringing. Born in 1892, both his parents were English and his father was a fruit merchant, employing several people and, nine years later, the family was living with a servant in Covent Garden. By 1911, two of Solomon's five brothers were clerks to racecourse bookmakers, but although he was nineteen, he was recorded as 'at home' and of no occupation. In January 1915, however, he gave himself as a horse driver when he volunteered to join the Royal Field Artillery. His physical development was good. Fresh complexioned, his eyes were blue and hair brown. Solomon went on to serve for over three years in France, receiving the 1914–15 Star, the British War Medal and the Victory Medal.

Unlike Kimber, Solomon was not a pickpocket and had served his country loyally. It is obvious, though, that he was interested in gambling. In August 1907, he was fined for frequenting premises used for betting on horse racing; and in April 1916, whilst in the Army, he was given seven days' detention for gambling with dice.[436] His only other misdemeanour was a charge for insubordination to a non-commissioned officer. After he left the Army in January 1919, Solomon was bound over for betting and he became a bookmaker. Two years later, he was ordered to pay £10 damages relating to eleven cases of welching. Importantly, however, there is no evidence to suggest that he was a gangster until after he was so brutally assaulted by Thomas Armstrong of the Birmingham Gang. Subsequently, though, he became one of the most violent men in the Sabinis, responsible for the cutting of Gilbert, the shooting of Kimber and other vicious assaults.

Around the core of the Sabini Gang were numerous violent men who did their bidding, with claims they totalled 250–300 men.[437] However, such a figure needs to be treated gingerly. A former pickpocket in a race gang reckoned there were between thirty and sixty in each mob.[438] This was a more realistic assessment. The Titanics numbered around twenty to twenty-five, but could call upon other 'roughs', whilst the Birmingham Gang was made up of small groups each of between four to eight rogues. Several of these bands may have operated on the same racecourse at the same time and occasionally they came together in much larger numbers, as at the Epsom Road Battle. Seventeen men were imprisoned for that melee, several more were fortunate not to be convicted, and others escaped from the scene. Given that and the reports of the other Birmingham Gang members at the actual Epsom races, there may have been around a hundred or more who showed up that day. This was exceptional, as was the turnout at Bath, when again there could have been a hundred or more, but this figure would have included roughs who were not regular associates of the Birmingham Gang and were there for the row.

When the Sabinis went to Hurst Park in revenge after Bath, they took two coachloads of men, totalling fifty to sixty in number. It is likely that this would have been the gang's maximum strength without hangers-on, but they were brought together in a much tighter and ordered force than the unruly bunchings of the Birmingham Gang, each with its own top man, and over which leaders like Kimber and Towey had much less control than did Darby Sabini. With the firm support of his inner circle and the wider gang, with the Birmingham Gang staying in its manor, and with the Camden Town Gang grouping defeated, Sabini was now almost at the height of his power. But the power of a gangster chief is precarious and he quickly faced new challenges. The first was the loss of legitimacy derived from his role as a steward with the Bookmakers' Association; and the second was opposition from within Little Italy from his former supporters, the Cortesi brothers.

THE FEUDING SABINIS & CORTESIS

As shown by the majority of the key men in these gangs, those from poorer backgrounds were more susceptible to becoming drawn in to gang culture. Bert 'Battles' Rossi articulated why some such men became gangsters. Born in 1922, he grew up in Saffron Hill in a house shared with three other families, and, as he tellingly pointed out, 'when you come from the slums if you didn't get out and grab it you suffered. [We] struggled to pay the rent, struggled to put food on the table, thieving's better than jumping on a bus every morning, struggling to pay for a holiday once a year. Do what your brains tell you.'[439] Edward Emanuel was also of that ilk. Formerly a 'terror' of the East End with convictions for assault, pickpocketing, operating spielers, and illegal street bookmaking, now he was well on his way to legitimacy. Through his close association with Beresford and his position as vice president of the Bookmakers' Association, he was able to set up the Portsea Press printing company to provide bookmakers with the lists of runners for each race as well as other printed material.[440] Within four years, the business was so successful that Emanuel was advertising it as 'The Largest and Most Efficient Sporting Printers in the Kingdom', but it was the racing lists that provided the impetus for this rapid growth.[441]

At first, they were sold on behalf of the Association by their stewards, led by Darby Sabini, but on 15 May 1922, an allegation was received that they were demanding a royalty of 1 shilling on every set.[442] This amounted to large sums of money. Sabini himself admitted that each set was sold for 5 shillings, and that between £100 and £200 a day could be earned.[443] A month later, further complaints were dealt with; and on 4 September, the day after Sabini went public in the *Empire News*, the Association's general committee agreed unanimously to dispense with the services of the stewards.[444] No doubt their decision was also affected by the unwelcome publicity arising from the Racecourse Feud. In his trial, Alf White had highlighted his role as chief steward of the Association; and in Langham and Ford's case, the prosecuting counsel had accused the Sabini Gang of carrying on 'an illicit profession on racecourses, parading themselves under the quasi official of the Bookmakers Protection Association', an organisation formed ostensibly to report roughs who tried to blackmail bookmakers.[445]

At the height of the Racecourse Feud, Albert Emmanuel, the secretary of the Association, tried to deflect such criticism. In all probability this statement was more likely to have come from Edward Emanuel, as records show that the secretary was actually named Albert Marks.[446] The day after Gilbert was threatened with a gun by Harry Sabini at Paddington Station, this Emmanuel issued an official statement, dismissing the fracas as 'a bit of a shindy' (quarrel). In fact, he assured the press that it was now a pleasure to go racing as there was no 'molestation of bookmakers whatever and there are no more attempts at blackmail'. His denial provoked a swift reaction. On 26 August 1922, the *Daily Herald* alerted its readers to 'Terrorism on the Racecourse' and revealed that its representative had interviewed prominent bookmakers to ascertain their feelings about Emmanuel's 'prosaic voice of the commonplace'. They did so under condition of anonymity and one of them gave a representative response:

Mr. Emmanuel's optimistic statement is very interesting, because Mr. Emmanuel ought to know, if anybody did. I can quite believe his assertion that it is a pleasure to go racing nowadays, but that is a purely personal statement, of course. Most of us, however, fail to see the pleasant side. What are the facts? Well, it is as much as any bookmaker's life is worth to refuse money to members of the gang when they ask for it. The least that will happen, if you're on the course, is that they'll shout 'Welsher!' knock your satchel up and pocket the doings. If they don't do worse than that you can consider yourself lucky.

As for the backers. They're easy. They're either gone over on the train down, or robbed on the course, or relieved of their winnings, if any, on the return journey. The likely 'mug' is marked from the start, and you've got grin and bear it, take it from me!

I know one man, a member of your profession, who had his money-pocket slit and emptied on Newmarket Heath, and *knew* it at the time. He also knew that the 'operator' was being covered by the rest of the mob – every racing man knows 'em by sight – so he said nothing. If he had shouted the odds, he'd have been for the cottage hospital or the mortuary, and the gang would have been well away.

The bookmaker finished by acknowledging that it was difficult for the police to get witnesses to speak out – and he himself would not risk it without police protection. But this was the sort of job they were paid for, and whilst he did not go in for politics, it struck him as a bit funny that although the police wasted no time in dealing with unemployed processions of thousands, 'they don't seem over anxious to tackle half a hundred racecourse thugs'.[447] They were interesting observations. Just a few months later, Inspector Grosse, the head of the Flying Squad, confidently told a court that whilst allegations had been made that bookmakers were blackmailed by their own stewards, he had never heard this from the bookmakers themselves. Indeed, since the stewards had been organised, the police had received no complaints of blackmailing, and 'there was no doubt that the Bookmakers' Protection Association had done a considerable amount to prevent the blackmailing that had gone on'. Before this 'happy state of affairs', he had done practically nothing for eighteen months but look after the gangs.[448] Such an interpretation flew in the face of the evidence and suggested that because of the Sabinis' truce with the Birmingham Gang, Grosse was relieved that he no longer had to focus on the racecourse gangs.

Emmanuel gave his statement at Bath races, now in the territory controlled by the Sabinis. Yet it was obvious that under the cloak of their legitimacy as stewards they were operating the same rackets as had the Birmingham Gang. They carried on doing so after they were stripped of their role. Prior to this, two of the stewards had left the Sabini Gang. They were

Enrico and Gus Cortesi, and with their brother, George, they had formed a gang to compete with the Sabinis. Enrico, the eldest, was often known as Henry or Harry. Born in 1884 in Paris, hence his nickname of 'Frenchie', he was eleven when his father, an Italian and a widower, had settled in Clerkenwell. By 1911 Harry had married an Englishwoman and was a hat block maker. Later he would move to Ellington Street, Islington. In a rare photograph from Islington Library, showing the early Sabini Gang soon after the First World War, Harry Cortesi is in a prominent front-row position and is the only one sitting. Yet no convictions were recorded against him until 1923 and the feud with the Sabinis.

Contrastingly, his younger brother, George, became embroiled in criminality and fighting early on. As a teenager, he was active in the gang fights between Italians and English roughs, including those from Hoxton, and in 1907 he and a friend were arrested for wounding during these disturbances. He was fortunate to be discharged as the other youth was sentenced to six months' imprisonment. [449] His good fortune held out, as he was discharged again in 1909, when he was involved in a row between his friend, Vincent Sabini, and an Italian who was stabbed. It is indicative of how the English-born children of immigrants were perceived that the victim had shouted at Sabini, 'I will give you English bastard something.'[450]

That year, the second-eldest brother, Augustus 'Gus' Cortesi, a hat maker, pleaded guilty to common assault after knocking his victim down and breaking his left arm.[451] Viewed by the police as 'a very violent man, especially when in drink', in 1912 he and George were found guilty of jointly attacking an Italian in a case dubbed 'Foreigners at Strife'. The sentences were weak: one of them had to provide bail for good behaviour and the other was fined 20 shillings.[452] After war broke out, George Cortesi served with the Oxfordshire and Buckinghamshire Light Infantry and was awarded the Victory Medal and British War Medal. His brother, Gus, was an interpreter and was praised as a 'very clean & hardworking man. He speaks French & Italian fluently'.[453] Standing a little under 5 foot 5 inches, he had hazel eyes, and dark-brown hair, which was thinning on top. He was also scarred by fighting, having marks on the right side of his forehead and chin.

By the summer of 1922, the Cortesis were making their presence felt, and it was reported that as well as the Sabini Gang, the Birmingham Gang and the Gilbert Gang, there was now an Italian Gang.[454] The core of this latter group was the Cortesi brothers. It might have been expected that George or Gus, who were obviously fighting men, would have led it, but the chief was actually Harry Cortesi. Ted McLean had been a 'broadsman', a pickpocketing member of a turf gang, and in his 'confessions', he indicated its make-up.

> Each gang has its own polished men-about town; women decoys; pugilists who use knuckle-dusters, a sandbag, or a knife, as well as their fists; and the 'gunmen'. There are the 'broadsmen', who, like myself played their by no means small part as pickpockets; and, most important of all, there are the men who scheme and organise – they are the 'brains' of the 'mobs'.

Enrico Cortesi was praised by McLean as the 'brains' of his mob, and his approach differed greatly to that of the Sabinis. Never a lover of the knife or the revolver, he was quiet and unassuming but had a wonderful brain for scheming and organisation. He seldom took part in the actual work of his gang because he was 'content to be the "man behind" who schemed the coups which the gang pulled off'. Consequently, blackmailed bookmakers feared him more than any other race-gang leader.[455]

The Cortesi breakaway was resisted forcefully by the Sabini Gang.[456] Living close to each other in and around Clerkenwell, the Sabini and Cortesi gangs were 'savagely jealous of each other's exploits', causing endless fights between them both on the racecourses and in Little Italy.[457] There was also some crossover between the two gangs, such as the case of Alexander Tomaso. Usually called by his English name of Sandy Rice, he left the Sabinis for the Cortesis, a move that further heightened tensions. There is no official record of these disturbances other than that in September 1922, when George Cortesi was assaulted in the Fratellanza Club in Clerkenwell by Harry Sabini, an Italian called 'Jumbo Exposito' and other Italians.[458] After Harry Sabini was prosecuted for the attack on George Cortesi, he threatened to 'mix it up' for Rice if he did not get Cortesi to withdraw the charge.[459] This threat failed and Sabini was fined merely £3.

Probably fearful of the next move against them, the Cortesi brothers acted first, leading the usually peaceful Harry Cortesi to resort to violence. In December 1920, he had been granted a gun licence because he had 'amounts of money' on him in the course of his business and required a revolver for protection.[460] He had that gun with him just before midnight on 19 November 1922 when he went to the Fratellanza Club, in the heart of Little Italy, where the Sabini brothers and close gang members met. It stood on the corner of Warner Street and Great Bath Street, where Gus and George Cortesi lived with their youngest brother, Paul. Three men were chatting outside the club that

night when they saw Harry, Gus and Sandy Rice coming down
the street. Gus had no jacket on and ordered them to, 'Piss off,
there's going to be some trouble'. At that, they walked away and
then heard the sound of shots coming from within the club. [461]

Louise Doralli was the daughter of the club's secretary and
was serving behind the bar in the big room. As the club had to
close at midnight, 'time' had just been called when Gus Cortesi
came in and ordered a coffee. His brother, George, was behind
him and then followed Harry and Sandy Rice. Doralli evoked
the scene in her evidence.

As soon as he asked for a coffee Gus looked at Darby
Sabini who was standing about the centre of the room.
Gus put his hand in his right trouser pocket and said
'Come on you bastard this is the time to fight'. As he put
his hand to the pocket I saw a revolver there and rushed
at him. I got hold of his hand and struggled and he
dropped the revolver back into his pocket and pushed
me aside. He then rushed at Darby Sabini . . . Sandy
Rice also rushed at Darby and hit him across the side
of the head with a lemonade bottle. At the same time
Gus took his revolver and fired at Darby but missed
him, the bullet going through the window near the
bagatelle table. As Gus fired I saw Harry Cortesi pull
out something and Harry Sabini just in front of him.
I rushed between them thinking Harry Cortesi would
not shoot but Harry Sabini just pushed me aside and
Harry Cortesi fired. Harry Sabini fell to the floor and I
knelt beside him and found he was bleeding from the
right side. Then I looked up and the Cortesis and Sandy
Rice had gone. It all happened in a very short time. [462]

Harry Sabini was shot through his right side, with the bullet lodging in the skin at the back of the abdomen wall. Although hospitalised, his injury was not life threatening and he recovered. It was surprising that the wound was not more serious. In fact, all the shootings during the racecourse wars resulted in non-life threatening injuries or missed their target.

Alerted by a witness about the shooting, a police officer quickly arrived outside the club, where someone said that Harry Sabini had been shot by 'Frenchie'. An attempt was made to arrest Harry Cortesi, but it was obvious he had plenty of supporters, as about twenty men from the French café opposite charged across the road, obstructed the policeman and rushed Cortesi away. His brother, Gus, was with the angry crowd and went for the witness who had called the police, punching him and kicking him before fleeing.[463] More police arrived, and he was arrested soon after, as were George and Paul Cortesi and Rice. Dramatically, the *Daily Mail* told its readers that armed officers of the Flying Squad were searching for 'Harry Cortesa [*sic*], alias Harry French'. They published the police description of him, which was loaded with negative stereotypes: he was sallow skinned, had sharp features, broad shoulders and a prominent nose, and was flat-footed and knock-kneed with 'a general Jewish appearance'.[464]

Harry Cortesi surrendered himself two days later at Bow Street Police Station saying to Detective Inspector Grosse:

I've heard you are making enquiries about me for shooting or something, so I've come to see you. You know Mr Grosse I don't get mixed up in these things, it's not my game, but on Sunday night I was at my mother's house about midnight, which is a few doors from the club. I heard there was a row and I went into the club. Everybody was struggling, some were on the floor. I hadn't a gun, I heard a shot fired and I walked out. I did not go home but went to some Turkish baths. I often go there.[465]

Despite his protestations, Harry Cortesi, his three brothers and Rice were charged with the attempted murder of the two Sabinis, riotous assembly and the unlawful possession of firearms. They pleaded not guilty. During the ensuing court case, Harry Sabini represented himself as a peaceful, law-abiding citizen who never attacked people.[466] So too did Darby Sabini. He stated that when he went to help his brother he was hit with bottles by George and Paul Cortesi, leaving him with a black eye, two or three cuts to the head, and broken false teeth. When someone shouted, 'Harry's shot', the attackers ran out. Cross-examined in court, Sabini insisted that he never carried a revolver and only had one when he was attacked by the Birmingham Gang at Greenford because a bookmaker had given it to him.[467]

By contrast, the Cortesis' defence strove to present the Sabinis as the aggressors, suggesting that it was Harry Sabini who had pulled a revolver from his pocket and in the struggle it was that gun with which he had been shot.[468] Recent cases had shown that the Sabinis had threatened rivals, and their attitude was: 'Do not prosecute one of us or you will be put away'. Additionally, it was a curious and convenient fact that each of the brothers had been convicted of the possession of a revolver.[469] Gus Cortesi himself stated that whilst he was struggling on the ground with Darby Sabini and two other men, he heard two shots. He saw Harry Sabini lying flat and a revolver beside him. It was picked up by an Italian known as 'Dead-Eye Dick', whom Cortesi chased out of the club and then hit.[470]

This story grabbed the attention of some newspapers, as did the bravery of Louise Doralli and the idiosyncratic contributions of the judge, Justice Darling. Darling withdrew the charge of riot and restricted Paul and George Cortesi and Rice to unlawful wounding. They were acquitted but Enrico and Gus Cortesi were found guilty of attempted murder and each was sentenced to three years' penal servitude. Darling pronounced that it was evident they had intended violence and the sentences would have been heavier if 'they had made an unprovoked attack upon people of good character'. He had also received undisclosed information from the police that had affected his sentencing, but perhaps the most important influence on his leniency was his attitude towards Italians. In addressing the Cortesi brothers, he informed them that:

I look upon this as really part of a faction fight which has raged between you and other Italians in consequence of some difference which the police do not entirely understand. There is nothing new about that. Anybody who has read Italian history – and I happen to have read a good deal of it – knows perfectly well that to determine the cause of the differences between the factions which existed in Italy in the Middle Ages baffled the skill of most people who tried to investigate the matter. This is a small affair. You are not historical parties, but your methods are the same. You appear to be two lawless bands – the Sabini and the Cortesi. Sometimes you are employed together against the Birmingham people and sometimes you are employed against each other. On this occasion you were carrying out a feud between you and the Sabini. I do not think there is much to choose between you, but the Sabini are within the King's peace while in England, and people must not be allowed to shoot them or at them.

Darling had received a strong request from the jury recommending the deportation of any aliens found guilty. He had the power to do so but would not, as he could see no reason to suppose that the French-born Cortesi brothers were worse than others who had been convicted in the racing feuds and who had not been recommended for deportation. Still, he alerted the whole 'Italian colony' that 'if this kind of lawless conduct goes on, the judges and the Ministers of the Crown who administer this particular law will take care that those who get convicted in future will be turned out of this country with their wives and children. Let it be a warning to you all to lay aside these lawless practices and settle down to observe the law peaceably.'[471]

In common with other newspapers, the *Westminster Gazette* disapproved of the sentences as too mild and was appalled at the disclosures from the trial, which 'serve to warn us that twentieth-century England IS not altogether either English or modern'. Referencing the feuding families in Shakespeare's *Romeo and Juliet*, it hoped that 'this is the last we shall hear of these Montagues and Capulets of the ghetto. Even medieval Venice found such feuds so tiresome, and so dangerous to the uninterested citizen that it was constrained to visit the severest penalties on the contending parties.'[472]

The Sabinis and Cortesis were nothing like feuding medieval Italians. Their rivalry was a very English affair and, like the

English Camden Town Gang, the Cortesi Gang vanished with the imprisonment of its leaders. Afterwards, George Cortesi married, and in 1939 was working as a hat block moulder and living in Fisher House, Islington. When he died in 1968, he left £1,368.[473] His brother, Gus and his wife opened up a café in Soho. He died in 1949.[474] The eldest sibling, Harry, was also a hat block moulder, although he was arrested as a suspected pickpocket in 1925 but was discharged.[475] He and his wife carried on living in Ellington Street, Islington and in 1939 their eldest son was a bookmaker's manager. Harry Cortesi died in 1954.[476]

BRIBERY AND POLICE CORRUPTION

The publicity around the racecourse wars of 1922 was bad for racing, as the stewards of the Jockey Club belatedly realised. They were also receiving complaints about the increased ruffianism at meetings. At first they regarded them as rumours and attached little importance to them, but when strong evidence was produced they felt it their duty to do everything in their power to overcome 'the evil'. Accordingly, in January 1923, a conference was held involving the Jockey Club, the Assistant Commissioner of the Metropolitan Police, and chief constables from across England. Charles Haughton Rafter, the chief constable of Birmingham, could not be there but was amazed at the statements that were made blaming the Birmingham Gang for all the troubles. After making extensive enquiries, he found that whilst Birmingham's detectives had attended about two hundred meetings during the year at thirty different places, they had not been asked to do so at any covered by the Metropolitan Police, and it was on these racecourses around London that problems occurred. Where a detective from Birmingham did attend a meeting, it was with a view to watching 'our local ruffians', but such an officer had no legal position if there were no agreement with the relevant police force.[477]

It was rumoured that the Metropolitan Police would take over all responsibilities at all racecourses, but no action was taken and policing outside the London area remained the responsibility of the local constabulary. As in the past, usually too few officers were taken on and those that did attend either didn't know the gangsters or else were bribed. In these circumstances, and with no opposition from other gangs, the Sabinis carried on their racketeering unchecked. It must have seemed to its top men that they were all but untouchable – Alf White certainly thought so. He had escaped a long term of imprisonment for the Shooting Affray and he wanted to do something for his pal, Joe Sabini, who had not been so lucky. White's actions, though, were foolhardy and from early 1923, reports emerged of 'the sequel to the Sabini case'. These followed the arrest of White and a George Drake for conspiring with others to solicit warders to convey documents to and from Joe Sabini whilst he was in Maidstone Gaol.[478]

On 15 February, a warder named Matthew Fright was on his way to work when he heard his name called from across the road. He saw Drake, whom he remembered meeting in the First World War, with three men. Drake approached Fright and, after asking a few questions about people with whom they had served, he explained that he was there to 'do a bit of good' for Joe Sabini, adding that it would be worth £2 a week for someone to look after him and get a note in and out. At this, Drake beckoned to one of the other men to come across. It was

Alf White, who proudly explained that he was the one who had got off an appeal and had been 'damn lucky' to do so. White also asked if anything could be done for Sabini, to which Fright replied, 'Yes, go straight back to London & leave him alone; if the authorities get to know that you are trying to get word into him they will transfer him away at once.'[479]

Undeterred, later that day Drake called at the home of another warder and offered £2 a week to get something in to Joe Sabini. Again the offer was refused. White and two other men then managed to visit Sabini by falsely representing themselves as three of his brothers.

Prison officials were anxious for White and Drake to be convicted as 'it would be a salutary lesson to others who are inclined to approach prison officers' to try and corrupt them.[480] The vengeful Cortesis must have been as anxious. In mid-March, and after reading about what the press termed the 'Sabini Sequel', an Ernie Thomas contacted the authorities at Maidstone Prison with relevant information. A professional boxer, he was friends with the Cortesi brothers, and he alleged that when attending their trial, he had overheard Alf White and Darby Sabini arranging to get George Drake's help in corrupting a warder at the prison on behalf of Joe Sabini. A few days afterwards, at Kempton Park races, Morris heard Darby Sabini and Edward Emanuel making further arrangements for Joe Sabini.[481] Thomas was not called to give evidence and was not needed, as in July 1923, Drake and White were found guilty and sentenced to two years' and eighteen months' hard labour respectively. They sought leave to appeal but were refused.[482]

Although the Camden Town Gang and Cortesis had disintegrated, the Sabinis still had enemies, and whilst White was on bail for the bribery trial, one of them struck. It was Ike

Kimberley of the Birmingham Gang, who was now living in London. On 17 May 1923, a friend of his, William Homer, was fined for street betting. Kimberley believed that the police had been set on Homer by Steve Griffin, a friend of Alfie Solomon. The next evening, Kimberley viciously attacked Griffin in a pub, striking him with a broken glass, severing the tendons of one wrist, cutting his head, and severely injuring the other wrist. Kimberley was charged with wounding. In court, although Griffin admitted that the two of them had been abusing each other, he could not swear as to the identity of his assailant. The magistrate responded firmly.

> Listen to me. We are here to protect you. You have your duty to the State as well as we. You are not doing it. If further danger comes to you, you will thoroughly deserve it. You are on your oath now, and you are not trying to speak the truth. Whether it is fear of further violence or not I do not know, but your best chance of avoiding further danger is to tell the truth.

Obstinately, Griffin refused to identify Kimberley, even though he had previously done so, and it was obvious that he was in absolute terror.[483] In spite of this, Kimberley was found guilty and sentenced to twelve months' hard labour. According to the inspector in charge of the case, he was a racecourse pest earning his living by blackmailing bookmakers, and his violent character and that of his associates had made it difficult to get witnesses.[484] Kimberley's brother, Mo, had taken a leading role in the Epsom Road Battle, and the two of them would later be involved in slashing in a feud within the Birmingham Gang.

The Sabinis' reprisal for the cutting of Griffin was swift and brutal. Solomon admitted that it had grieved him to see the hands of his old pal nearly cut off by Kimberley. In revenge, he teamed up with Alf White, who was on bail, James Harper, Matthew McCausland and two unknown men to punish Kimberley's friend, Homer. On 20 May, they assaulted him at his home. His wife, Kitty, was cooking dinner when McCausland came to the door. She saw him hit her husband with a hammer. Homer tried to close the door, but McCausland, Solomon and the two other men followed him into the house, knocked him down and kicked him. Kitty Homer recalled:

> I ran out with my baby to call the police and outside I saw White and another man standing by a taxi. I said to White, 'Do come and stop it; they are killing him; he has done nothing.' He said, 'All right. Hug your baby and go in. I'll stop it.' He went up the steps and called them, and the four men came out. I went in and found my husband lying on the floor, with his face swollen and his head bleeding. I got him up and ran for the police.

White, Solomon and Harper were originally charged with causing grievous bodily harm, whilst McCausland was also accused of trying to obtain £20 by threats. Once again, the police had difficulty in getting statements from witnesses, whilst even Homer himself put the attackers in a more positive light. Giving evidence, he said that when McCausland had arrived he had spoken of coming to terms as if he wanted peace, whilst it was Homer who had first pushed McCausland on the lip. Harper was discharged before the case went to the Old Bailey, where White and Solomon were found not guilty. McCausland was convicted of common assault. Surprisingly, the police inspector who gave evidence informed the court that the feuds between the race gangs had been more or less wiped out, and all concerned had become friends again.[485] They had not become friends and the Sabini Gang had certainly not been wiped out; in fact, it was at the height of its power. Such a positive yet inaccurate pronouncement raises suspicions of 'close relations' between some officers and the Sabinis, all the more so as serious allegations of police corruption and the gang were soon to be made.

A fortnight after the beating of Homer, Darby and Harry Sabini and a man called George Dido were accused of wounding Maurice Fireman, alias Jack Levine. A former professional boxer, Fireman was a minder for a bookie and alleged that on 4 June, when he was putting up a pitch on Epsom Downs, another man warned him that the spot was his. The two of them went into a beer tent where Fireman was hit in the jaw with a knuckleduster by Darby Sabini, after which Dido did the same. He was also struck the on the back of the head by Harry Sabini, who took out a penknife saying, 'I have a good mind to knock your eye out,' and touched Fireman's eye with the weapon.[486]

A different version of events was given by the defence for the Sabinis. When the row over the pitch with the other man had begun, Fireman had walked over demanding to know, 'Who says my guv'nor ain't going to have a pitch? I will fight any man in the "booze" for my guvnor's pitch.' He and Dido then had a supposedly fair fight – at least according to former Sergeant-Major Michael O'Rourke. The Sergeant Major had served in the Egyptian and South African campaigns as well as the Great War and had won the Victoria Cross and the Distinguished Conduct Medal twice. As a war hero, his 'interesting' evidence was influential, all the more so as it was shown that Fireman had a bad record. O'Rourke was at the meeting with others from the Ministry of Pensions Hospital and 'being an Irishman', upon hearing a row in one of the booths, he walked in. He saw Fireman 'put up his dukes and have smack at Dido. It was a plain up-and-down fight', which Darby Sabini had tried to stop. As might be expected given this evidence, the charges were dismissed.[487]

This event prompted another anonymous letter to the Home Secretary. Received on 11 June 1923, it was in a different hand to that of Tommy Atkins and the other unnamed letter sent during the Racecourse War with the Birmingham Gang, and it was well written with no spelling mistakes. The writer demanded action against the Sabinis. Racecourse roughs, they were 'instigated by that rogue Edward Emanuel the man who is responsible for all the disturbances which occur at all race meetings'.

This man Edward Emanuel is also the owner of the gaming house in Edgware Road known as the Titchbourne Club.

This place is the haunt of criminals of every description and Faro is carried on day and night.

I am writing this letter because it is really remarkable the number of Police Officers and C.I.D. men who are continually in this man's company well knowing that he is an ex-convict, felon and rogue.

They also know that it is he who finances the Sabinis. He pays them well to walk about for the sole purpose of blackmail, and keeps them in immediate vicinity immediately he discovers a new victim.

He directed a fight at Epsom on Monday the 4th inst.

He was not there but his confederates were – the Sabinis.

I distinctly heard Darby Sabini say that Edward Emanuel told him to do it when he was asked why he attacked a man.

He employs them only to avenge himself on anyone who dares to defy him. Nine racing men out of every ten live in absolute terror of them and would willingly report them, but they would go in daily fear of their lives. And for that reason I am also afraid to disclose my name but you can believe me Sir that every word which I have written is perfectly true.[488]

The complaint that Emanuel was paying police officers was well established, and Arthur Harding was certain that he did so. He claimed that one his pals 'used to give the police their weekly cut' from Emanuel, who drank with top detectives from Scotland Yard in the 'Three Tuns' pub in Aldgate.[489] Pertinently, the *Empire News* had revealed that this was the haunt of Jewish criminals, whose leader was 'a clever, far-seeing man who is a regular king of the underworld in Whitechapel'.[490] There can be little doubting this 'king' was Emanuel, but for all the allegations of police bribery against him, nothing had been proven. In his letters, Tommy Atkins had also alleged that the Flying Squad was bribed by the Sabini Gang to protect its interests, giving twelve instances of attacks without police interference. Consequently, a detailed report was made into these accusations in December 1922. It showed that four cases were trivial and/or never were reported; in another three, those assaulted refused to identify the assailants or to assist the police in any way; and in five, arrests had been made but only two convictions resulted because two of the victims absolutely refused to prosecute whilst another became a hostile witness. Apart from these cases, the police had made seventeen arrests regarding race-gang affrays, of which twelve had been tried with eight convictions. The report concluded that the arrests and convictions had been distributed quite impartially over members of both the Sabinis and their enemies.[491]

In the same month as this internal report, the prestigious *New Statesman* had finished a series publicising serious charges against a minority in the Metropolitan Police for blackmailing lawbreakers such as illegal street bookmakers, street traders and prostitutes. This system was believed to penetrate to comparatively high quarters, allowing the operations of about half-a-dozen notorious gangs of racecourse roughs and welchers. The Sabini Gang was the most infamous of them, and the commentator questioned whether its members were all known to the police and why it existed. It was then alleged that the Sabini Gang paid corrupt police officers over £5,000 a year for its immunity. The *New Statesman* accepted that this sum may have been incorrect, but was certain that the actual figure must have been big or else none of the gang would have been allowed on the racecourses – and it had evidence ten times over to substantiate its charges.[492]

Such proof was not made public but Harry Daley, who was a policeman in the East End during this period, insisted in his memoirs that the rottenness in the Metropolitan Police went right to the top. There is some evidence that it may have done so. In February 1923, a constable accused of accepting bribes from an illegal bookmaker told the court that he had not informed a certain chief inspector that he had been offered the money because he did not trust him. Indeed there were higher people than that whom he did not trust.[493] As will be discussed, five years later, a widely publicised case of police corruption would hit the headlines regarding a nightclub owner who was in all likelihood also paying protection money to the Sabinis. In these circumstances, it would therefore be foolish to reject claims that some police officers were receiving payments from the Sabini Gang and Emanuel – or, at the least, were colluding with them. Certainly, it is remarkable that Darby and Harry Sabini managed to escape serious charges throughout the racecourse wars of 1921 and 1922, whilst Emanuel had long been considered as a corrupting influence on the police. And the statements made by senior police officers previously addressed, indicate they accepted the ascendancy of the Sabini Gang on southern racecourses because it had ended the gang wars and brought a certain 'peace'. Yet it would be as foolish to suggest that all of the police in London thought this way or that all were corrupt given the attempts made by some of them to break up the Sabini Gang, as evidenced by the imprisonment of Joe Sabini and Alf White.

NIGHTCLUBS AND THE SABINIS

Paramount on the racecourses the Sabinis also levied tolls over some of the nightclubs that, as one newspaper expressed it in late 1919, had 'sprung up like mushrooms' in the West End, between Piccadilly and Soho.[494] They were places where people could drink unlawfully outside licensing hours, gamble illegally at cards, and dance 'to their hearts' content till the small hours of the morning'. But their principal patrons were damned as men and women from the scum of the underworld at home and abroad: crooks, cracksmen, thieves, card sharpers, impostors, degenerates, drug fiends, and blackmailers who found their prey in other habitués of nightclubs such as distinguished fighting men, politicians, actors and writers. One club of this type was a quiet-looking residential mansion with the blinds drawn and all lights obscured. Entry was by a little card bearing a number and thence down a narrow winding staircase to a basement. Then came another passage, dimly lit by a flickering gas jet, leading to a spacious room, where couples danced to the strains of the latest jazz music. On either side of the floor were little tables, at which sat men and women, some in evening dress, some without.[495]

By 1922, there were at least twenty 'questionable' nightclubs in and around Soho, although others were genuine meeting places for 'late workers' who wanted some leisure time and to enjoy a dance – activities which they would not otherwise be able to do. And then there were 'the latest and swellest' nightclubs, like one guarded by a uniformed commissionaire at the door and with a more exclusive clientele. Here, couples 'tripped the light fantastic' on a beautifully polished floor to a jazz band of black musicians on a palm-decorated stage. Other customers were seated against walls tastefully decorated in frieze. But even here, young women in expensive evening dresses of Parisian creation were 'doing a bit of doping' with cocaine, whilst others drank brandy of 'the most poisonous stuff' for exorbitant prices.[496]

Clubs like this were magnetic to the race gangs, and Harry and Gus Cortesi found them especially alluring, spending their ill-gotten gains freely – so much so that when they were imprisoned at the end of 1922 it was regretted that the clubs had been robbed of two of their most familiar and characteristic figures.[497] Other gangsters, especially the Sabinis, focused on the clubs not so much for enjoyment but for the opportunity to blackmail the owners, the most celebrated of whom was Kate Meyrick. Dubbed 'the Night Club Queen', she opened her first club, Dalton's, in 1919 when she was forty-three. An Irishwoman, she was separated from her husband and was the mother of eight children on a paltry income. She soon discovered she could earn huge sums selling drinks without a licence in a sparsely furnished setting with a jazz band. And as soon as one of her clubs was closed down by the authorities she opened another; little wonder, as it was widely assumed that she could earn up to £1,000 a week.[498]

As Meyrick made plain in her reminiscences, for the first five or six years after the First World War, Soho suffered a reign of terror. A party of 'gentlemen' entering a club might transpire to be one of the numerous gangs of bullies or racecourse terrorists who held sway at that time. Of course, she admitted, mentioning 'West End gangs the name Sabini comes almost automatically to mind'. That gang crossed her path almost immediately after she entered the West End and 'they were responsible for some of my most exciting experiences'. It was the fashion to ascribe to the Sabinis most of the responsibility for the terrorism that then gripped London, and whilst it was absurd to paint them as angels, Meyrick wanted to show they often suffered for the misdeeds of others, for it was an easy way out to blame them. In fact, she bore no ill will towards the leaders of the Sabini Gang, as they had come to her rescue twice when her premises were in danger of attack by other members of the gang.

At Dalton's, she first noticed trouble with the race gangs when waiters complained to her one night that a party of 'gentlemen' would not pay for their drinks. This became a regular occurrence, and when Meyrick went over to them, invariably they were various gang members whose express purpose was to drink at the club's expense. Thinking that she would stop the problem, on one occasion she asked for payment and was laughed at. She then sent a waiter to find a policeman. He returned saying he had been unable to do so. Sent out again, he disappeared, apparently scared witless as to what would happen to him if he brought the police upon the gang. Meyrick became resigned to the situation, realising that if she did not want her club to be wrecked, the best thing to do was to suffer intimidation.

Unhappily, free drinks were not the end of the matter, and one night, events took a dangerous turn. Some gangsters believed to be Sabinis came in, and when asked to pay for their drinks, they offered to fight anybody who said that they should. An ordinary guest shouted 'Cad' at them, and the next thing a gangster produced a revolver. He fired two shots across the club, smashing a pair of mirrors.

In an instant there was pandemonium – women shrieked and clung to their male companions, men swore and the staff stood petrified. By the merest chance nobody was injured by those two shots, although one of them whistled by the head of a man not far from me, and the other ricocheted from the broken mirror into the pianoforte. The band scuttled to safety.

I glanced about me wildly. The gangster with the revolver was obviously intoxicated and it was as likely as not that he would shoot again and that murder would be done. The male guests seemed to be as panic-stricken as the women and everybody appeared too frightened to move.

Suddenly a young and slightly-built fellow, who, I

subsequently discovered, was a member of the Sabini gang, and a brother of the man with the revolver, crept up behind the gunman and seizing the hand that held the gun, broke his brother's grip on the weapon and it went flying across the floor. Two other gangsters then seized the gunman and held him in a vice-like grip.

Meyrick ran out for a policeman but, when she returned with one, the gangsters had disappeared. Though giants, her doorkeepers were as terrorised as everybody else by these thugs, and once inside, they swept everyone out of their path. The rest was plain sailing. Not surprisingly, these visits affected takings as respectable people stayed clear. In response, Meyrick decided to stand at the club's entrance, vowing that no gangster should be allowed in. On one of the first nights, she told a group of Sabinis and others that under no consideration were they entering. A beetle-browed fellow 'with an unshaven chin that spoiled the effect of his evening dress' ordered her to let them pass. After Meyrick again refused, he made to shove her aside. She resisted with all her might and pushed him back to the pavement. The gangster 'saw red', rushing straight at Meyrick with a shout and striking her a severe blow on the side of her head, knocking her to the ground. She screamed as she fell and he hit her again. Shrieking loudly for help, 'the brute' kicked Meyrick. She must have fainted for the next thing she knew, she was lying on a sofa in the club and somebody was holding a glass of brandy to her lips. The gangsters had bolted, chased up the street by about half of the male club members. Meyrick pondered whether to report the attack to the police. Before she had made up her mind, the next evening a gang member came to tell her that all the 'Boys' were extremely sorry for what had happened and that the man who had assaulted her was an outsider and only a casual friend of the gangsters. He wanted her to know that, 'Darby Sabini went home after him last night, and thrashed him within an inch of his life for daring to strike a woman'. Although there is no evidence that Sabini himself frequented nightcubs, this event and Meyrick's positive views of the Sabinis indicates a close relationship between her and them.

Meyrick next opened the 43 Club in Gerrard Street in 1921, and by then the gang menace had become so serious that she had to organise the male regulars as a sort of guard against unexpected raids. They stood in a bunch behind the door to prevent roughs from forcing it open, which was locked immediately when the gangsters were spotted approaching. But this strategy could only be adopted when there were enough regulars, and even then gangsters could still gain entry through subterfuge. This happened when fifteen or sixteen of them arrived in fancy dress. Alerted by the resulting sounds of disorder, Meyrick went to her office, which the gangsters were searching. Seeing her, they took hold of her handbag with about £50 in and fled.[499]

The belief that to stop the blackmailing and robberies of other gangs Meyrick paid the Sabini Gang protection money is boosted by their extortion of other club owners, for which the evidence though limited is telling. On the evening of 1 December 1923, two of the Sabinis' main henchmen, George West and Jim Ford, were embroiled in a disturbance at the New Avenue Club in Piccadilly. They claimed they had been attacked when they went there, but the prosecution argued they had started the trouble by throwing bottles about, one of which injured a man. Found guilty of various charges, the jury recommended mercy on account of the provocation the prisoners had received. West was sentenced to nine months' hard labour and Ford to six months.[500] The police and others must have wondered how the jury was convinced of provocation, as the wrecking of a club was either a punishment for the owner not paying protection or a warning as to what would happen if the premises were not 'protected'.

As for Meyrick, from about 1924 she was also bribing a police officer, Sergeant Goddard, to 'tip her off' about police raids. Four years later, and prompted by an anonymous letter, her club was raided by the Flying Squad without the knowledge of Goddard. In the high-profile court cases that followed, Meyrick was convicted on charges of corruption and conspiracy and sentenced to fifteen months' hard labour. Goddard was also found guilty and imprisoned for eighteen months' hard labour. During the trial it was revealed that although his police salary had been £6 a week, he had assets of around £18,000, £12,000 of which was in banknotes, some of which could be traced back to Meyrick.[501]

MANSLAUGHTER AT THE EDEN CLUB

Most of the nightclubs of London were the haunts not only of gangsters but also of the rakish, thrill-seekers, cocaine takers, exploitative older men, prostitutes and late-night drinkers. In January 1923, a reporter visited one that had recently sprung up in the shady streets of the West End. It was a fantastically decorated cellar with a bar and a jazz band playing. The bar closed at midnight but, in an upstairs room, bad whisky could be bought all night for two shillings a small glass. In the racist language of the time, the reporter saw that about 'a hundred people – negroes and yellow men among them – were jazzing on the dance floor'. Admission was by ticket, bought for ten shillings from a dingy room across the road. This particular jazz haunt opened at 11pm and closed at 6.30am, with breakfast served from a room above the cellar ballroom from 3am.[502] Such scenes were replicated in other nightclubs. With their polished floors, tables and chairs, and divans, they were places where men outnumbered women, who were always young.[503]

An even more lavish nightclub setting was the scene for a fight between the Shelby brothers and London gangsters in Series Two of *Peaky Blinders*. Called the Eden Club, it was owned by the fictionalised Darby Sabini and featured a huge, gold-painted low ceiling, a jazz band, fashionably dressed flappers, dancers shimmying energetically, cocaine sniffers, smart-suited men, and professionally attired waiters.[504] The real Eden Club was very different. It was not a nightclub and nor was it owned by Sabini. The proprietor was Isidore Hyams, and although it was registered as a social club, it was a spieler, an illegal gambling joint. Members played card games like faro and could also bet on horse racing via a telephone, whilst a ticker-tape machine provided the results. Based on two floors at 5 Eden Street, and above a motor garage, it was approached by a staircase from the street. On the first floor was a billiard room and kitchen, whilst the second floor was a card room and dining room with a bar. It was here that Alfie Solomon killed Barney Blitz, also known as Buck Emden.

Blitz worked for the owner of the club as a professional backer of horses. Arthur Harding knew him as 'a Jewish chap, a lovely fellow' and a bit of a fighter who got in with the Sabinis.[505] Blitz was a hard man, having convictions for wounding with a bottle and for striking a police officer on the neck with a bayonet. He was also a racing man and that led to enmity between him and Emanuel. Blitz had started to sell racing lists, a business that Emanuel monopolised. At Epsom in June 1923, Blitz was arrested as a suspected person, and he believed the police had been bribed to do so by Emanuel so as to stop him selling the lists. The grudge Blitz held led to his killing. He was in the dining room at the Eden Club late on the evening of 22 September 1924 when Emanuel, Solomon and two friends came in. They played cards and then Emanuel went to the bar. He was followed by Blitz, who wanted to know why Emanuel would not leave him alone. In response, Blitz was insulted as a 'boss-eyed ponce' (a squint-eyed man living off a prostitute). He retorted that Emanuel was a 'ponce' and a copper (police informant), vowing 'I will knock your f . . . . . . brains out'. Emanuel threw the contents of his glass at Blitz, who immediately hit Emanuel on the back of the head with his glass.

Going for each other, they fell to the ground struggling and were pulled apart by several members of the club. Though bleeding profusely and an older man, Emanuel offered to go outside and fight Blitz, who readily agreed. As they were rowing over who should go first, someone heard Emanuel say, 'Do it for him, Alf.'[506] A witness saw what happened next.

> Solomon suddenly picked up a carving knife from the table where the food was lying. I saw it in the air, in his hand, and I saw a flash of the knife. I did not see him strike Blitz, but immediately after I saw Blitz bleeding from the head or face. At that time Emanuel was nearest the door and Solomon came from behind Blitz when

he seized the knife. The whole of the members rushed towards the door, and at the same moment I missed Blitz and I saw Solomon, still with the knife in his hand, rushing after somebody towards the dining table.[507]

That somebody was Mick Abelson, the doorkeeper, who had punched Solomon on the chin after Blitz was stabbed. In the chase, Abelson fell on the settee, and though he tried to kick Solomon off him, he was stabbed. Covered in blood around his neck and on his shirt, Solomon uttered to one of his group, 'Look at the state I am in.' Everybody else had rushed out to the street, where they found Blitz lying on his face. He was turned onto his back by one of the members, who shouted for help and called Blitz by name. He simply groaned. Two police officers arrived and took him in a taxi to hospital, where he was pronounced dead.[508]

A 'wanted for crime' telegram was despatched by the police for two men. Edward Emanuel was described as well-dressed, dark complexioned and stoutly built. He walked with a limp. Alfie Solomon was of medium build, dressed in a dark suit and bowler hat and, like Emanuel, was of 'foreign appearance'.[509] Emanuel was arrested at his home in Golders Green but there was insufficient evidence to charge him. Blitz's relatives were so angered at this that his brother-in-law went to the Home Office, suggesting that Emanuel was the cause of all the trouble and that he had ordered Solomon to make the attack.

During the inquest into Blitz's death, the Coroner received two anonymous letters, one purportedly from a poor woman who had suffered from Emanuel's gambling dens. She claimed he was 'making his brags all over the East-End that his money will keep him out of this affair. I know him & know he paid Solomon to do this poor man some injury.' Emanuel professed 'to be a very good man by helping poor Jews and that is why they never say anything about him'.[510] Reporting on these accusations, Chief Inspector Brown said that there was considerable bad feeling between Solomon's partisans and those of Blitz, who had become obsessed with the idea that Emanuel should be charged with murder.[511]

Solomon was charged, and when he came to court in November 1924, it was reported that he was a young man of Jewish appearance, smartly dressed in a long blue overcoat, grey hat, and brown shoes.[512] Scars on his right wrist, left thumb, at the back of his neck and on his upper lip were evidence of attacks by Kimber and others. Solomon also had tattoos. His left arm featured a shell, a lion and a Japanese woman with a fan, and on his right arm he had another Japanese woman. Contrary to the evidence of witnesses, Solomon claimed self-defence. His counsel was the celebrated Sir Edward Marshall Hall, an acclaimed orator and barrister. He drew attention to Blitz's criminal record, previous violence and his 'murderous' attack on Emanuel. With his friend grievously injured, and thinking that he was about to be attacked again, Solomon 'picked up a deadly weapon lying to his hand, and seeing red, his sense of right and wrong weakened by drink, he plunged the knife into Blitz's neck and killed him'. But this was manslaughter and not murder, averred Marshall Hall. The jury agreed.

Before sentencing, the prosecuting counsel highlighted Solomon's membership of the Sabini Gang and his involvement with previous violent attacks, even though he had never been convicted of them. However, given his association with men like Alf White and Harry and Joe Sabini and his own reputation, it was unsurprising that other members of the club had hurried out when a knife was produced. Marshall Hall countered by producing Solomon's medals and Army discharge papers and by stating that four firms in Covent Garden had given him good references. Indeed, he himself had been instructed by 'members of the great Jewish community, who were providing the funds for the defence'. This showed that Solomon could not be the scoundrel that had been suggested. It was most likely that 'the great Jewish community' was actually one man, Emanuel, but with such glowing testimony, Solomon was sentenced to just three years' penal servitude.[513] It was believed by the police that he was exceedingly fortunate not to have been convicted of murder, for which he would have hanged.

In an article on the 'The Joy of the Sabini Gang', the *People* announced that there was great jubilation at 'Solly's' light sentence. Solomon had been prominent in many ugly scenes against their strongest rivals, the Brummagem Boys of Birmingham, but his only previous convictions were for the comparatively minor offence of welching. That was because, 'we always have our boys well defended', and as the gang members boasted, money was no object. If one of them was in trouble, he was well looked after and need not worry about his defence, as the best lawyer would be obtained, whilst witnesses would be intimidated. This meant that the police found it almost impossible to get one of the gang's victims to prosecute. For years the police, the Jockey Club and the bookmakers had been at war with the racecourse gangs, but as the newspaper stressed, nothing had been done to suppress them and they were still flourishing.[514]

Contradicting the report in the *People* about the ongoing strength of the Sabini Gang, a few months beforehand the breakup of the turf gangs had been acclaimed thanks to the efforts of Detective Inspector John Ferrier of the Metropolitan Police. Upon his retirement in August 1924, he was praised as 'a pitiless enemy of the racecourse brigands'. His courageous tactics had driven terror into the notorious Sabini Gang and the Birmingham Boys, pushing them out of their lairs and rounding them up in spite of the fact that they were armed with guns and knives. He did so by personal bravery and through introducing new tactics. In particular, he kept his men as close as brothers to the racecourse pests at all times and in all places. Scores of plain-clothes officers were detailed to visit their favourite clubs and to lay their hands on most of the minor members of the gangs. Then Inspector Ferrier went after the 'brains' of the tribe and, despite threats of personal violence, succeeded in putting their organisations out of joint.

But though they were quieter, the two main gangs had not been put out of joint. The Birmingham Hammers Gang, as it was now dubbed, remained in control of collecting 'tolls' from the bookmakers in the Midlands and the North up to the territory of the Newcastle Boys, whilst the Sabinis continued to be 'busy'.[515] That 'business' remained intimidation and violence but, with no opposition from other gangs, there was little reporting of their activities. An exception was an attack on 29 September 1924 at Wye races, and it attracted only brief notices. About twelve of the Sabini Gang had surrounded two London bookmakers who had crossed them. One was hit and the other managed to run away, only to be caught, knocked down and savagely assaulted. His head was held by one man, whilst another punched him in the face with full force. The victim was then kicked four or five times in the ribs before he was rescued by the police.[516] Four men were charged with assault, including Harry Sabini. Still saying that he was a fruit salesman, yet again he was discharged, probably because the three others gave evidence that he hadn't been involved. Each of them was sentenced to one month's hard labour. They included Thomas Mack, who had recently been released from prison for his part in the Shooting Affray with the Camden Town Gang. The other two were Pasqualino (Pasquale) Papa, better known as Bert Marsh, who will feature later, and Antonio Mancini.[517] A commission agent, Mancini would be hanged for murder in 1941 after he knifed a man in a West End club.[518]

By the end of 1924, the Sabini Gang was the most feared race gang in the country, as was maintained by the *People*. A law unto themselves, they had been prominent in many ugly scenes in their long-standing feud with their strongest rivals, the Brummagem Boys. The Sabinis flouted the law openly, living in a manner more daring, if less picturesque, than any highwayman or bushranger. While shooting was not their favourite means of fighting, 'they do not stop at that if they think it necessary'. But more often, many victims who had been afraid to prosecute had been 'maimed for life by appalling razor attacks, in which most of the gangsters are expert'. In itself, this was proof, if it were needed, of the Sabini Gang's foreign origin.[519] This focus on 'foreignness' ignored the realities of what was an English gang fighting its English rivals. The slashing an enemy with a razor was not a sign of 'foreignness'; it was mostly a British phenomenon. Razors were used by Scottish gangsters in Glasgow and by English gangs in London, as well as in Sheffield, which was soon to be thrust into the public eye as a city notorious for its race-gang war.[520]

Chapter 6

THE SHEFFIELD GANG WAR

TOSSING RINGS AND THE MOONEY GANG

Boxing Day 1924, and instead of being filled with goodwill, the *People* announced on its front page a 'New Phase in Feud of Race Gangs'. It centred on Sheffield, which, like London and Birmingham, was scarred by its race-gang pests. Terrifying citizens and taxi-drivers with free fights and 'rough stuff' tactics, they had necessitated a special watch in the city centre and all-round police vigilance. A feud between two gangs had been raging for several years, but recently the conflict had become more frequent and desperate: 'Revolvers, truncheons and razors are used by the gangs and the police know that many men have received dreadful injuries from razor-slashing attacks, but are powerless to prosecute because the victims are scared, and dare not give evidence against the assailants'. The rivalry had blown up over leadership of Sheffield's premier race gang, and so bitter was the feud that several original members had fled the country. Most worryingly, the Birmingham hammer gang, possibly the best-known gang of racecourse ruffians in the country, was thought to be 'taking a hand' in the Sheffield warfare.[521]

Despite its sensationalism, the article was correct. There was a vicious gang war in Sheffield between the Mooney Gang, led by George Mooney, and the Park Brigade headed by Sam Garvin. Both were racing men and previously they had been partners in crime, but after falling out their animosity knew no bounds. To make matters worse, the feared Thomas Armstrong of the Birmingham Gang had now arrived in Sheffield to support Mooney. But unlike other gang conflicts throughout the country during this era, this war was not fought over racecourse protection rackets; it was over control of a lucrative gambling site at Sky Edge, a high ridge of wasteland looming over Sheffield's city centre.

The gambling here concerned the tossing of coins. Centuries old and easy and simple to play, this game was deeply embedded in male working-class culture and was widespread across England, Scotland, Ireland and Wales, as well as Australia, where it was called two-up. Illegal as it was, it could be played between a group of a few men after they had left the pub or between large numbers in what was termed a school, usually found in remote locations, which provided more safety from the police. Often these bigger tossing schools were controlled by local hardmen, who took a cut from the winning gamblers, and they were highly profitable, sometimes leading to confrontations when takeovers were attempted. The gang war in Sheffield was the most bloody and infamous of all such conflicts and was one of the reasons why the Home Secretary would declare war against the race gangs in 1925, a move to be discussed in the next chapter.

Tossing involved men gathering in a ring around a largish

space into which stepped one of them who would be the banker. He gambled that he could toss two ha'pennies or pennies into the air to land heads upwards. If they came down tails he would lose, while if they showed one head and one tail there would be another toss. The banker himself might stake any sum, depending upon the size of the school. This could be covered by one person from the crowd or several, and side bets could also be staked amongst those watching. Before each toss, the coins were examined to make sure that they were not two-headed or weighted. Then they were placed tails up on the index finger and middle finger of one hand, although in some tossing schools, predominantly those in Ireland, they were rested on a piece of wood known as a feckin (throwing) stick. When tossed, the coins had to turn all the time at a reasonable height to ensure no cheating. This was because some men surreptitiously 'flammed' – put their thumb to the side of one coin to stop it spinning and ensure it stayed heads up.[522] If there was any doubt about the throw, anyone in the ring could shout out 'bar that toss' before the coins touched the ground, and there would have to be another throw. Bets were paid out at even money.

In Scotland, there were numerous big birling (spinning) schools along the Clyde, as well as in the woods and pit banks of Lanarkshire; whilst the gamblers of Swansea met on the beach or in the local quarries. In the Midlands and the North there were also large tossing schools in secluded spots near to urban centres. Coldwell on the moors in East Lancashire was notorious in the early 1920s. Just over three miles from Nelson, it had big and little rings depending upon the stakes gambled. Most days, about a hundred youths and men attended, some walking there in their clogs and weekday attire, others arriving by car or a special bus. Gamblers could even purchase pies, cakes, cigarettes and hot tea for refreshment.[523] Isolated rings elsewhere in England included Tudhoe Wood in County Durham. Here the hoying (spinning) of the coins was taken on by someone referred to as a 'bebber', a professional spinner who was paid by winners. To ensure fair play, he tossed his own supply of 'jubes' – Queen Victoria Diamond Jubilee ha'pennies.

Such larger schools were protected from police raids by 'crows' or 'pikes' (scouts), often paid 10 shillings a day, and were run by 'tollers' who levied a fee of around 2s 6d in the pound from winning punters.[524] These tough-nut 'masters' of the ring were like 'Two Ton Titley' of Cannock, strikingly portrayed by Arthur Hopcraft, a child of a respectable and chapel-going working-class family.

> He was holding money in large quantity. He was the pivot around which the other men conducted themselves. They brought him coins and notes, and sometimes he gave them some back. He kept up an encouraging, belching banter, his puce face prickly with pinheads of sweat nestling in its creases. 'C'mon lads, yer luck's in. Doa be frit. The wife woa know.' He had money in his hands, in his pockets and often between his teeth and tucked between his trousers-top and his swelling midriff . . . He was a picture of godlessness, rampant with beer and blatant in his love of money – of the feel of it, of its corrupting desirability. He was immodesty personified. He was wicked. Two Ton looked gigantic and unassailable in this setting. He was at work, selling sin with a grand flair.[525]

The prevalence of tossing during this period is clear from the sheer spread of the activity. It was also very popular in Ireland and large gatherings were commonplace in Dublin, unlike the big cities in England. Mick Doyle recalled several tossing schools in the lanes near to Townsend Street, down by the quays south of the River Liffey, prevalent even during the hard days of the 1930s when unemployment was rife. Big money was involved and they were very much organised, with each one having a ring man who controlled everything.

> He was a heavy and he looked after it. Oh he'd have a belt, swing his belt, take off his belt and swing his belt and that'd keep order. They'd give him so much depending on how much they'd win. Always ha'pennies and they wouldn't say heads or tails like you'd say [in England], they'd say heads or harps. Heads or harps. 'Harps, harps a hundred pound. Heads a hundred pound'. If you had your money to put down you could get in. So long as you got your bet down he'd cover your bet, right. That's on the ground . . . You put your money down say twenty pound and he covers it. The man who's throwing he covers it, right. The ring man, he's the boxman and he looked after everything.[526]

One of the best-known boxmen in Dublin was Sartini. He and his partner ran the school in the Greenhills, beyond Griffith Bridge. Máirín Johnston evoked him as if he were the ringmaster in a circus . . . 'he stormed about the centre of the toss-school circle wielding a short-handled dray driver's whip. The lash of the whip was about three feet long, and Sartini would use it mercilessly to enlarge the circle so as to enable the other boxman to get the bets down for the tosser, who would then throw up the two 'makes' (coins) off the 'feck' (stick).'[527]

Sartini's control was lucrative and, on one occasion, he had to fight off a challenge from the notorious Animal Gang from the Corporation Buildings and surrounding neighbourhood in inner city North Dublin.[528] Similar events happened in Yorkshire, where the Mexborough Boys of racecourse rogues tried to take over tossing schools near Huddersfield, an attempt that was successfully resisted.[529] But the worst violence arose between 1923 and 1925 over the control of Sky Edge, leading to Sheffield becoming dramatised as the 'little Chicago of Britain'.[530] This gang war was unusual both in its intensity and length, as most tollers gave up the control of their rings as younger and harder men came along, or else in a straight fight.

Sky Edge had both large and small rings and had been notorious for some time when it was raided in 1917 by the police and military looking for deserters.[531] The stakes gambled were high and many hundreds of pounds were won and lost, so extraordinary measures were taken to secure the school against surprise. Paid as much as £5 a week, 'crows' were stationed at all the important approaches. Aware of this, a large body of soldiers and police approached it from ten different directions and managed to collar over fifty men out of the two hundred gathered there. The ringleader made a desperate but unsuccessful attempt to escape by jumping about 40 feet over the cliff into an adjoining brickyard but sprained his ankle and was captured.[532] Most of the arrested were working men from Sheffield and fines of £3 each were handed out.[533] That makeup expanded in the gambling boom straight after the First World War, with Sky Edge drawing in businessmen and others from a wider area. It also pulled in the Mooney Gang, which had been involved in a smaller way in protection rackets at local tossing rings within the city.[534]

The gang's 'generalissimo', George Mooney, was of Irish descent and from West Bar, a district just to the north of the city centre that was associated with the Irish. In 1891, when he was a toddler, he was living in a lodging house with his mother and older brother but no father.[535] A decade later, the family was reunited, but Mooney was already set on a life of crime. Fined for theft when he was eleven, over the next twelve years he was convicted of stealing, shop breaking, conspiracy, assault and loitering. He had also been arrested seventeen times for drunkenness and swearing, and been discharged from unlawful wounding.[536] Married at sixteen to Sarah Wigley, they separated a year later. His wife had one child and was expecting another, but she was frightened to live with him because of his cruelty. He had thrown her out of the house more than once, saying 'Take your hook; I don't want you.' Once, she and the baby had even been turned out half-dressed in the middle of a rainy night. He also kept her short of money, sometimes giving her a penny or two for breakfast, or perhaps tuppence for supper.[537] Sarah later returned to Mooney but died in 1921.

By 1911, and ostensibly a barman, he was involved with the local Spring Street Gang, which terrorised publicans into giving them free drinks and sometimes money. Within two years it had become 'the notorious Mooney gang' when he and his henchman, Peter Winsey, were convicted of assault.[538] That year, 1913, Mooney was damned as 'a dangerous character' and was imprisoned for two months' hard labour for punching a woman and kicking her on the ground after he had attacked her husband.[539] He seemed to revel in his notoriety as a 'newspaper hooligan'. In another assault, when his various convictions were referred to, he quipped, 'You will have me put down as a modern Dick Turpin if you go on'.[540] What Mooney could be put down as was a dirty fighter. In 1914, in a stand-up scrap outside a pub, one of his gang kicked away the legs of his opponent. Mooney then bit off part of the man's ear and, going back into the pub, punched his friend with such force that he knocked out four teeth. Despite the familiar story of victims withdrawing charges and witnesses changing stories or being too fearful of giving evidence, Mooney was imprisoned for two months' hard labour.[541] Within weeks of his release, he was back inside for hitting a policeman so hard that he knocked him out.[542]

During the First World War, Mooney deserted from the York and Lancashire Regiment. Going on the run, in 1918 he was arrested for frequenting in Liverpool and pickpocketing in Leeds. Described as a commission agent, he was 5 foot 8 inches tall and was marked with tattoos of a dancing girl and a banjo on his right forearm.[543] The next year, he was back in Sheffield and in control of Sky Edge. He took over with the support of his older brother, John Thomas, Albert Foster and William Furniss, three hardmen with shocking records who lived in the Park district, which was overlooked by Sky Edge.[544] Three other key members of Mooney's gang were John James 'Spud' Murphy, Frank Kidnew and his childhood friend, Winsey. Another was Sam Garvin, although this relationship was soon to become something altogether uglier.

THE PARK BRIGADE ASCENDANT

Apart from controlling Sky Edge, Mooney also extorted protection money from legal off-course credit bookmakers and associated with the Mexborough Boys at local races such as Doncaster.[545] In September 1919, he was arrested there for loitering and imprisoned for three months. Through attending these meetings Mooney met Sam Garvin, another racing man, who in 1919 would be described as one of the Mooney Gang.[546] Born in 1885, he was a little older than Mooney and, as a child, lived nearby in Acorn Street with his maternal uncle and aunt and two younger brothers. By 1911, the three boys were with their mother but their father was again living elsewhere. Garvin was now a coal heaver working underground, but soon he became a career criminal. In 1909 when he was twenty-five and a 'burly-looking individual' of no fixed abode, he was convicted of assault.[547] Thereafter he would lead a life of violence, intimidation and thieving. Quickly he became a travelling rogue, and in 1910 was fined for frequenting at Doncaster and for gaming with dice at Gosforth Park races near Newcastle.[548] A year later, he was living in Brightside in Sheffield's East End with his wife in her parents' home when he was named as a bookmaker's clerk and the leading figure in a 'terrorist gang'. Like Mooney's mob, Garvin's also went to pubs to cause mayhem or be paid off. On this particular occasion, Garvin had severely beaten a man who had tried to help the landlord eject him. The victim did not appear in court, and although he was damned as a terror to the whole neighbourhood and a menace to society, Garvin was merely fined for refusing to leave the premises.[549] He was not so fortunate in 1912 when, without provocation, he knifed Billy Foulkes, Sheffield United's former goalkeeper, and was sentenced to two months' imprisonment to be served consecutively with a similar term for another assault. Disdainful of the law, some of Garvin's friends threatened one of the witnesses before he left the court and he had to be escorted home by the police.[550]

Strangely, three years later, and describing himself as a racing man, Foulkes appeared as a witness on behalf of Garvin when he was accused of burglary in Cardiff. But with the police reporting that he belonged to an expert team of housebreakers, he was found guilty and imprisoned for twelve months.[551] After his release, Garvin went back on the run to avoid military service, and in December 1917 a warrant for his arrest was issued in Liverpool. Standing 5 foot 7 inches, he was clean-shaven and of medium build, with light-brown hair and blue eyes. Very smart in appearance, he favoured a serge suit, Melton overcoat, black bowler hat and blue starched collar.[552] Returning to Sheffield after the war, Garvin teamed up with Mooney in running the Sky Edge tossing rings, but he was not the kind of man to share ownership of anything where large sums of money were to be made. And there was a lot of money to be made. The school attracted gamblers not only from Sheffield but also from Rotherham, Barnsley and elsewhere and there could be 200–300 in a ring. Mooney himself had once won £200 and he knew of a man who had picked up £1,000. After he lost control, the ten tollers at Sky Edge each made £2 a day, and that was after they had paid out two shillings a head to touts, lookouts, which were mostly unemployed men. Over a week, that gave a substantial total of £140, on top of which was the big cut taken by the chief of the gang.[553]

Although now living in Crookes, on the other side of the city to Sky Edge, Garvin plotted to oust Mooney. He rounded up fighting men in the Park district, riling them up against the outsider from West Bar who was running what should have been their tossing school.[554] Amongst those hardmen was William Furniss, who deserted Mooney's gang. With Furniss's backing and that of other street fighters, Garvin gathered a large force known as the Park Brigade. In April 1923, they congregated on Sky Edge, simply pushing out Mooney and his handful of gangsters. On this occasion there was no serious fighting but this would not last.

Determined to hit back, on 29 April, Mooney ordered an attack on his one-time ally, Furniss. His house was broken into in the middle of the night and whilst in bed, he was badly beaten with a poker by Spud Murphy and Frank Kidnew. Furniss declined to take proceedings, but revenge was swift, and on 27 May, Kidnew was found on waste ground in the Park district.[555] To an eyewitness he 'looked as if he had been in a slaughterhouse', with his face and hands one mass of blood and his hair clogged with blood. His coat was in ribbons and his right trouser leg was cut open. Through the slit was a wound six inches long: 'It was horrible; you could lay two fingers in it. The front of his skull was battered in, you could hardly see his nose for blood.' Despite his wounds, Kidnew was smoking a cigarette and casually observed, 'I reckon they've spoiled my suit.' Seriously injured, he was hospitalised.[556] He told the police that he had been walking with John Thomas Mooney and Spud Murphy, and on turning a corner he was struck on the head with a blunt instrument and knocked to the ground. He named Garvin, his brother, Bob, and Furniss amongst the men whom he saw but declined to prosecute any of them.

On the evening after Kidnew's beating, Mooney's second wife, Margaret, rang the police asking for special attention to be paid to their house, as she was scared of an attack. Mooney sent similar messages. The police complied but 'nothing extraordinary happened' until about 1am on 16 June, when Furniss and others of the Park Brigade tried to storm Mooney's house in West Bar.[557] With trouble expected, it had been barricaded and, inside with Mooney, his wife and brother were Winsey and Foster. Cries of, 'Come out and fight, you Irish –' were heard, along with threats of setting fire to the house with petrol. Shots were fired from both sides and one of the attackers was injured. He was George 'Ganner' Wheywell, an extremely dangerous man regarded by the police as a ringleader of the new gang. The windows of Mooney's house were broken and its doors smashed and grates wrenched. Despite the violence and shooting, both sets of gangsters were merely bound over to keep the peace by the courts on 26 June.[558]

That afternoon there were 'exciting scenes' when 'women relatives of members of the two parties took a hand in the game'. About six of them went to the Park district to confront the wives of their husband's enemies. They were armed 'with such things as pieces of furniture and domestic implements and a battle took place between them, lasting nearly an hour'. Receiving an urgent message, the police sent a strong force, including three mounted officers. The Park Brigade women were the aggressors, as the only woman injured was a Mrs Smith, the mother-in-law of John Thomas Mooney. Her head was cut open by a blow from a potato masher, although the wound was not serious.[559] This brawl between the wives of gangsters was a rarity. There is no evidence whatsoever of the wives of Kimber, Sabini or any other of the race-gang leaders taking an active part in their criminality, let alone their fights. Brian McDonald's intriguing study, *Alice Diamond and the Forty Elephants*, has brought to the fore an all-female gang of pickpockets in London, but the clash in Sheffield is more reminiscent of how some young women associated with the street gangs of the peaky blinders in Birmingham and the scuttlers of Manchester and Salford.[560]

A day after the 'bust-up' between the wives, a report was

received on 27 June that Mooney had shot at members of the Park Brigade near his house. This could not be corroborated but it led to a police search of his home. They found a small rifle, sporting gun, revolver and rounds of ammunition. Mooney was arrested along with the other men in the house. They were Murphy, Winsey, Foster and Thomas Rippon, who, as soon as he was released on bail, was assaulted by Ganner Wheywell. Wheywell was arrested but Rippon withdrew the charge. Badly outnumbered by the Park Brigade, which was strong enough to attack him in his own neighbourhood, Mooney had decided on a radical move – to give his story to the *Sheffield Mail*. It was published on the same day as the arrests, 27 June. Mooney revealed that there were only five in his gang, the same number as those running the Park Brigade, but because its leaders were afraid they went about with a crowd.

> They think that if they can get us to slash with razors, or kill, whatever is going to done – and they are trying hard to provoke trouble – we shall be out the way and that the Park gambling ring will be left to them and their claims will not be tampered with. But we do not want to clash, and we do not want to interfere with them. There is no need for trouble to put us out. For four years we have been trying to live down the title of the Mooney Gang.

The *Sheffield Independent* wryly noticed that 'the spectacle of Satan rebuking sin is always entertaining'. Mooney had painted an appealing picture of outcasts trying to live down their past and having been prevented from doing so by the unwelcome attentions of their former, and temporarily victorious, associates. But the correspondent asked if this laudable desire would have been so evident if Mooney and his friends had not been precariously placed and forced to retire to their castle.

To rid the city of the gangs, the newspaper called upon the local authorities to follow the example of Birmingham, which had always treated such lawlessness with a stern hand. Twenty years previously, peaky blinders had 'inspired terror by their operations and outbursts of open warfare but though their ramifications were peculiar and extensive and for a time they were a law unto themselves the police eventually cleared the city of them'. [561] Sheffield's chief constable, Lieutenant Colonel John Hall-Dalwood, was indeed alert to the local gang problem, having previously expressed his concerns that there were too few police in the city whilst the sentences passed by the magistrates were too lenient.[562] The same issues had been raised in Birmingham during the 1890s, when the ruffianism of the peaky blinders had seemed unstoppable. As it was, the Sheffield police believed that they had taken every possible action and 'in fact have gone beyond their strictly legal powers in endeavouring to deal with the circumstances as they have arisen'.[563]

On 28 June, a day after Mooney's interview, Albert Foster, another one of his gang, was attacked. His assailant was sentenced to two months' hard labour. After the case was finished, Foster went into a pub where he was beaten by Wheywell, Furniss and two other men of the Park Brigade. One of them struck Foster with a billiard cue, causing a severe wound and much bleeding. All four attackers were committed to two months' hard labour. In gangster terminology, 'it was on top' for Mooney's Gang and now his closest pals turned on him for 'coming the cop on us in the paper' – naming them. The same day as Foster was first attacked, on 28 June, Mooney and his long-time pal Spud Murphy fought in the street. Murphy got the worst of it. He and Winsey were then accused of throwing bricks at Mooney's house, one of which struck his wife. Found guilty of assault, Murphy, calling himself a bookmaker, was imprisoned for six months' hard labour. After the sentence was passed there was a disturbance when some women tried to get at Margaret Mooney and her witnesses.[564] This was another rare example of women connected to gangsters becoming embroiled in gangland rivalries.

Abandoned by his mates, over the next few months Mooney mostly remained in his fortified house, but even that was breached on Christmas Eve 1923. He was lying ill in bed when, at about 5.45pm, the back window and locked-and-bolted door were smashed in by several men. Inside the kitchen was Mooney's fifteen-year-old daughter, Mary, his sixteen-month old son, his ten-day-old baby, asleep in a pram near the fire, and a Mrs Flynn, who was helping his wife. The toddler had been playing on the floor, but fortunately when the shattered glass and framework of the window crashed into the kitchen, he was shielded from the flying splinters. One of the intruders mockingly told Mary, 'I have come to wish your father merry Christmas.' She and the older woman 'pluckily tried to prevent the intruders getting upstairs' but were pushed back. Mary fell to the ground but shouted to alert her father. One of the men called out, 'Give him some razor,' but as they had to climb two awkward flights of stairs, Mooney had time to switch off the electric light and hide in a wardrobe. Thwarted at not finding him, the intruders smashed several sacred images, which had belonged to Mooney's mother. Hearing that the police were coming, they ran off. The four men were quickly arrested.

They included Sam Garvin and one of his top fighters, Charles 'Sandy' McKay Bowler from the Park district. Another was Frank Kidnew, who had been badly slashed by the Park Brigade but who had since switched sides. All four were charged with wilful damage. Garvin was acquitted whilst Kidnew and Bowler were each sentenced to three months' hard labour. For the assaults on Mary Mooney and Mrs Flynn, each was fined a paltry 50 shillings.[565] Such sentences justified police complaints about the leniency of the magistrates.

Throughout the Racecourse War between the Birmingham Gang and Sabini Gang, the Racecourse Feud between the Camden Town Gang/Titanics and the Sabini Gang, and the feud between the Cortesis and Sabinis, no attacks had been made on any of the homes of any of the gang leaders. The forced entry of Mooney's house was another unusual feature in the Sheffield Gang War and it was more reminiscent of the Garrison Lane Vendetta in Birmingham, fought as it was by people who lived close to each other. It also underscored the bitterness between Mooney and Garvin and the maliciousness of Garvin's 'win at all costs' mentality that made him oblivious to harming women and children. None of the 1920s gangsters were to be admired but Garvin was a particularly odious man.

By the start of 1924, Mooney's gang had broken up. Two of his main fighters had turned coat, he had fallen out with his best friends, his brother had emigrated to America, and Foster had fled to Birmingham. Now Mooney left Sheffield for Glasgow.[566] Unopposed and in the ascendancy, Garvin must have felt as untouchable as had Alf White – and he acted as if he were. In September 1924, he beat up a man who then refused to prosecute, and he and his gang stole £100 from an employer as he was leaving the bank with the money to pay his workers. Found in a pub sharing out their 'loot', Garvin and his accomplices were arrested, but the victim failed to identify them and they were discharged. He and his men even had a charge of obstructing the police dismissed in October.[567] Their absolute contempt for the law was displayed on 8 December when they assembled in Fitzalan Square in the city centre and marched three quarters of a mile to attack the home of Thomas Rippon in West Bar, where former associates of Mooney had gathered.

Craftily, Garvin and his brother stayed back, letting others take the initiative. A shot was fired, a brick was thrown through the window and the front door was forced off. As the Park Brigade charged inside, a general melee ensued. Most of the Mooney Gang managed to get upstairs to safety. Henry Dale did not and he was beaten severely with the leg of a stool. His wife was with him and appealed, 'Don't kill my husband. I have five children and am expecting another.' Ordered to get out of the way, she was told, 'We shan't hurt you.' Subsequently, Sandy Bowler, ostensibly a miner, and three others of the Park Brigade were arrested and charged with causing grievous bodily harm. The police found a revolver and bullet and other weapons including an iron bar, razor and hammer. According to one officer, the attack was 'old broth being warmed up'.[568]

This did not end the violence. In fact it was the catalyst for its escalation. Ganner Wheywell, a friend of Garvin and a top man in his gang, had refused to take part in the 'tanning' of their West Bar enemies at Rippon's house, saying he had three children to look after and was going home. Enraged, Garvin had threatened that, 'Alright, you are on one. We will cut you up a bit. We will tear you to pieces when we have done with that mob.'[569] The next evening, 9 December, the gang tried to carry out the threat. Wheywell was pounced on in a pub by six men. Whisky was thrown into his eyes and he was punched on the chin. He caught hold of one of his attackers, John 'Jack' Towler, and struggling they got outside and fell on the floor. Towler was on top, choking Wheywell, who was kicked by other men. He managed to get up and run off and, soon after, the police found him bleeding from a wound to his upper lip. His coat was off and his trousers were badly torn. A fearsome fighter, though outnumbered, Wheywell had inflicted serious wounds on Towler, some of them allegedly with a knife.[570] Charged with wounding, Wheywell was found not guilty, the jury finding that he was not the aggressor. It was a verdict with which the judge agreed.[571]

Wheywell was now the one to change sides, quickly palling up with Mooney's former men. On the afternoon of Christmas Day, he was with Dale when they were spotted and chased by Garvin, his brother and about a dozen others. They were caught and assaulted. In defence, Wheywell pulled out a revolver. The police were quickly on the scene to break up the fight. At a later date, Wheywell was discharged from having a firearm without a certificate and Robert Garvin and another man were each sentenced to one month's hard labour with assault. Then, on the evening of Christmas Day, a bookmaker called Newbould was accosted by the Garvins and three others. He was ordered to hand over £10 to obtain a solicitor for some of the gang who were in trouble. The bookie refused and he and a friend were beaten. Newbould brought a prosecution but also fetched in a bruiser from Birmingham to take reprisals on the Garvin Gang. He was the dreaded Thomas Armstrong of the Birmingham Gang and he quickly went to work, threatening Sandy Bowler.

Given this upsurge in violence, it came as a surprise to the public when, on 1 January 1925, the *Sheffield Daily Telegraph* announced that the previous evening, the Sheffield gangs had met and ended their feud. It reported that all the responsible leaders had been involved directly or through representatives. After 'as much palaver as at the conclusion of peace between Germany and the Allies', an Armistice had been agreed, whereupon each side was to appoint six men as 'delegates' and both gangs would share the profits of the tossing rings at Sky Edge.[572] This was a seemingly strange development. There was no need for a truce, as Garvin and the Park Brigade had clearly won, as the police realised. Having made inquiries as to whether the arrangement was genuine, the Chief Constable was emphatic that 'no reliance whatever could be placed upon the word or promise of these men'.[573] As J. P. Bean discerned in his work on the Sheffield gangs, the truce was a ruse. Four of the top men in the Park Brigade were due in court for the attack on Dale, and so too were Garvin and others for assaulting Newbould. All of them faced imprisonment if found guilty. Consequently, as part of the agreement between the gangs, Newbould dropped his charges.[574] In the other case, Dale, who was the chief prosecution witness and a friend of Newbould, went missing. Despite his absence, the four Park Brigade men were found guilty. Bowler was sentenced to nine months, two others for six months, and a fourth for twelve months. Yet even with their loss, Garvin's gang remained stronger, and of course he soon reneged on the deal to share Sky Edge.[575] It was with justification that a judge called him the *deus ex machina* pulling the strings for the puppets to dance.[576]

Albert Foster of the Mooney Gang had now returned to Sheffield, and on 22 January, he and Armstrong went with two others to Sky Edge to meet the 'head ring man' to fix a meeting for a share out as had been previously agreed. They didn't know that Garvin had gone back on his word but quickly found out as they were emphatically told that he had changed his mind and was going to run the ring himself. Mooney's men were angered and challenged the Park men: if terms couldn't be agreed then they would settle matters in 'a stand-up fight to take place at a pre-arranged place in the country'. The Mooneys were then stoned and bricked by about fifty youths attached to the Park Brigade. Armstrong, Foster and the other pair fought back but the numbers against them were overwhelming and they bolted into a nearby house, 'somewhat astounding the occupant', as it was put by a local newspaper. Inside, they barricaded the top of the stairs, 'collected a few ornaments, and prepared for the worst'. The stairway was very narrow, so that only one of the attackers could go up at a time. It was not something that any of them fancied, given the frightening reputation of Armstrong. Gathering outside the house, the Park Brigade was dispersed when a posse of mounted and foot police arrived.

Soon afterwards, Mooney's eldest son boasted that his father was back in town and was going to clear off all the Garvin Gang.[577] It was true: Mooney was back and it wasn't long before he was embroiled in an altercation that sparked a series of violent conflicts between the two gangs. In early February 1925, Mooney was with Albert Foster and Ganner Wheywell and his brother when they came across Frank Kidnew of the Park Brigade. Breaking down an advertisement board, they threatened him with obscene language. Days later and in retaliation, another former gang member was beaten up by Garvin amongst others – but again he walked free from a charge of assault. As he left court, the Park Brigade lined one side of the street. Opposite them, they were faced off by the revived Mooney Gang.[578] The conflict intensified. On 1 March, the bookmaker Newbould answered the door to his house in West Bar to three members of the Park Brigade. One of them was Jack Towler, the man who had fought with Wheywell. They asked if Armstrong was in and, when told otherwise, Newbould was hit on the head with a beer bottle by Towler before they left the scene. Towler was soon arrested and his defence argued that Newbould employed Wheywell and was financing the Mooney Gang and paying Armstrong to assist them. Having been found guilty, Towler was sentenced to four months' imprisonment. A day after the assault on Newbould, one of Garvin's chief supporters was hit on the head so severely with a heavy instrument that his life was endangered. He pulled through, but in July 1925, his assailant, Albert Foster, was sentenced to eighteen months in prison after he had been arrested in Birmingham, indicative of the connection between the Mooney Gang and the Birmingham Gang.[579]

The police described the men involved in the Sheffield gang war in disparaging terms. It was a description that would have also held good for the members of the Birmingham Gang, Sabini Gang and Camden Town Gang.

They frequent race Meetings for various purposes, engage in tossing, promote boxing contests, and generally prey upon bookmakers, publicans and similar persons who are in some instances too easily terrorised by them. Some of them engage in breaking into shops, warehouses etc. and others provided means for the disposal of stolen property, Samuel Garvin being suspected of being particularly active in this direction. On every occasion they appear before the magistrates they are most ably defended; the evidence adduced in their interest almost invariably coming from members of their own party is often tainted, if not altogether perjured. They appear to have acquired quite a contempt for Police Court proceedings ... these men have committed many acts of violence; on nearly every occasion the persons they have attacked have been members of the opposite party.[580]

Whilst the violence between the gangs was despicable and destroyed the peace in the city they called home, events took a devastating turn when a man not at all involved in the gang wars was attacked.

THE GARVIN GANG AND MURDER OF A HERO

William Plommer was the antithesis of the gangsters and a positive example of a tough, hard-working family man. A Glaswegian aged thirty-three, he was well built and muscular and, until 1912, had served in the Army, where he had a good boxing record. Two years later, he was called up and served throughout the war, becoming a sergeant. After he was discharged, he was always in regular employment and he and his wife, Elizabeth, settled in Princess Street in the Norfolk Bridge neighbourhood of Sheffield's East End. On Sunday night 26 April 1925, their friend Harold Liversedge came to their house covered in blood. He had been drinking in the Windsor along the street, and at closing time had been hit without provocation by Wilfred 'Spinks' Fowler. One of Garvin's Gang, Fowler had been in the group that had besieged Armstrong and Foster after they had been chased away from the tossing ring at Sky Edge. Returning to the pub with the

Plommers, Liversedge challenged Fowler to a fist fight, and Plommer was heard to say, 'Let them have a fair fight.' Fowler was knocked down and, as he was helped up by the sporting Plommer, he was hit on the head from behind by an unknown person. Fowler blamed Plommer and cursed him as, 'You Scotch bastard. You're in for a tanning tomorrow.'

Early the next evening, Sam Garvin and three others went into the Windsor. He talked about Plommer and another man, then swore, 'We'll kill the bastards.' By now, some of his gang were parading up and down Princess Street and Wilfred Fowler was overheard saying, 'He's done our kid (younger brother). He's done our kid and we'll do him in.' Knowing that mischief was brewing for him outside, Plommer left his house unarmed and on his own to bravely front the men looking for him. Obviously worried, his wife watched him and recounted what happened.[581]

I saw my husband standing at the junction of Princess Street and Attercliffe Road. I saw 7 or 8 men go up the street to him and attack him. I was at my door, about 50 yards away. It was light. I saw a man with a bandaged head strike my husband who seemed to break away from the lot of them. I can't say what the man struck with or where he hit my husband. I commenced running up the street and as I got there I saw Lawrence Fowler strike my husband with a poker hitting him on the back of the head ... He was wearing a tweed lightish overcoat and had no cap or hat on ... My husband then tried to get on a passing motor-car and was pulled off. My husband then walked round the corner by the Rawson's Arms and passed close to me. I heard him then shout to the men 'Come one at a time'. Wilfred and Lawrence Fowler were stood against me and Lawrence Fowler said, 'Let's do him in whilst we've got him'. My husband then began to run down the street. The two Fowlers ran after him. Wilfred Fowler picked up a scooter and threw it at my husband. But it did not hit him. I saw my husband go into our house. In 2 or 3 minutes I joined my husband in our house . . . When Wilfred Fowler said 'Let's finish him', he had a razor in his hand.

Only ten years old, Thomas Plommer witnessed the cowardly attack on his father. Going outside 'to see what some men who were walking up the street would do to him', he must have been traumatised to see his father hit with a poker, then with a leather cosh by Wilfred Fowler, whose head was bandaged. In fact all the attackers had weapons, including heavy chains and thick rubber tubes with lead in one end, whilst one of them had a bayonet. Even so, and outnumbered as he was, one neighbour declared that Plommer 'stood like a hero and fought them all'. He knocked down Wilfred Fowler and then, slipping on the tramlines, fell to the ground, where he was beaten by the others and seemingly struck on his left side by Lawrence 'Lol' Fowler with something in his hand. The police arrived soon after Plommer managed to get into his house and was rushed to hospital where, tragically, he died. His waistcoat, scarf, shirt and vest were all bloodstained and there were cuts to his clothes. He had suffered three wounds to his scalp, a cut to his hand and two cuts to his stomach. It was these abdominal wounds that had killed him and they had been caused by a bayonet or something similar.[582]

William Plommer was buried on Saturday 2 May 1925. His coffin was draped with the Union Jack and it was estimated that 20,000 people turned out on the streets and at the cemetery to pay their respects.[583] Ten men were tried for his murder. During the trial, witnesses were threatened and afterwards Elizabeth Plommer received an anonymous letter telling her that she would be 'done in'. Courageously, she defied the warning, stating that 'I shall follow my husband's example. He did not run away, and nor shall I. I intend to carry on as best I can with my mother, who is seventy, and my four children, whose ages range from four months to eleven years. The police have been very good to me, and I have every faith in their protection.'[584]

Three of the accused were discharged for a lack of evidence. They included Bob Garvin and Frank Kidnew. Sam Garvin and another man were acquitted. On 31 July, three others were found guilty of manslaughter: two were given ten years' penal servitude and the third, seven years. Although they had protested that William Plommer had been the aggressor and that they had not delivered the fatal wounds, the two Fowler brothers were found guilty of murder and sentenced to death. Both were from Brightside, a working-class neighbourhood in the East End adjoining the Norfolk Bridge area. William Fowler, the younger brother, had a very bad record, with convictions for theft and assault from when he was ten. Aged fifteen, he was sent to reformatory school. Reoffending after his release, he was ordered to Borstal for three years. He was discharged early in 1922 as someone reliable who ought to be a success. Still, there were concerns about him returning to his parents' locality and attempts were made to settle him elsewhere. They failed, and after returning to live with his wife and young daughter at her parents' home, he could not find work. As feared, he drifted back into crime and, according to the police, he was not known to do any honest work and was continually seen in the company of thieves. The company he was drawn to was that of the notorious Sam Garvin.

Lawrence Fowler was two years older than his brother and was believed to have led him astray. A bookmaker's clerk, he had convictions for theft, assault, malicious wounding and street betting, and he was suspected to be a receiver of stolen property. When sentenced he shouted, 'I am absolutely innocent. This is an impossible thing.'[585] Both brothers appealed unsuccessfully against their sentences. Wilf Fowler then petitioned the Home Secretary. He emphasised that he had never had an opportunity to prove himself a good citizen, as he had not had the influence of good training like most youths. After his release from Borstal, he had found work, contradicting official reports, but the police informed his employer that he was a Borstal boy and he was immediately discharged. He concluded that, 'I can assure you I have not had a single chance. I humbly beg of you Sir on behalf of my wife and two little children, to give me one chance to live the life of an honest and respectable citizen'.[586] His youngest child was a few days old. The petition failed.

In letters to his wife and friends, Lawrence Fowler had focused his hopes on people in the know coming forward to divulge the name of the man who had actually stabbed William Plommer. It seems that they finally did so and his solicitor sent this information and relevant documents to the Home Secretary. In his final letters, Fowler also wrote that his innocence could be proved by his brother, who was going to tell all. Just before he was executed, Wilfred Fowler did reveal the name of the murderer to his solicitor. He was one of the men who had been convicted of manslaughter. Calling him the kindest husband possible, Fowler's wife said that he had not disclosed this information in court because it would have meant giving a pal away and he had not thought the case would take so serious a turn for him. His statement was also sent to the Home Secretary, who later denied knowledge of it.[587] Wilfred Fowler was hanged on 3 September and Lawrence Fowler the next day.

The three men convicted of manslaughter were George Wills, Stanley Harker, and Amos Stewart. All three were in their early twenties and, like the Fowlers, they lived in Sheffield's East End in the lower valley of the River Don.[588] A wide industrial area including Brightside, Attercliffe, Norfolk Bridge, Darnall and Tinsley, it was crammed with polluting factories and badly built, insanitary back-to-back houses. As such, it had much in common with the older, central parts of Birmingham, from which the members of the Birmingham Gang were drawn. But like those districts, Sheffield's East End was not an abyss filled only with a frightening, criminal people. As one former East Ender recollected, it 'may have had its darker side, but I don't remember it as unpleasant or dangerous', whilst another stressed that despite the terrible poverty in the 1920s, 'the people in the area had remarkable spirit and independence'.[589] Born in 1904, Frank Harris also came from the East End and was associated with the Alfred Road Gang, noticeable for its members wearing a white silk scarf knotted at the front, as opposed to the red silk of the Park Brigade.

He had knocked about with the Fowlers and recalled that Lol Fowler had been involved in running a local tossing ring during the First World War. Afterwards, he and his brother Wilf took bets illegally on the streets for a bookmaker and also went racing. Always well dressed, they were not really tough, and on the afternoon when Plommer was killed, Wilf Fowler had been to Uttoxeter races. Harris remembered that when Fowler returned home, Amos Stewart told him, 'Go up to Norfolk Bridge. Your kid's in trouble.' The two of them joined others to back up Lawrence Fowler against Plommer, who was on his own. A hard man and 'straight battler'. Harris was certain that 'he would have duffed 'em both up' without the gang.[590] In court, Wilfred Fowler had stated that he had been to Uttoxeter races and that he had gone to Norfolk Bridge with Amos Stewart, who was identified by Thomas Plommer as one of the men who had attacked his father. When sentenced for manslaughter, Stewart had bowed with mock politeness, thanked the judge and left the dock laughingly – obviously pleased with a ten-year term and not one of death.[591] He belonged to a violent family and, in 1934, not long after he had been released from Dartmoor Prison on licence, he was convicted of assault and sent down for another twenty-two months.[592]

Whoever actually killed William Plommer, many people in Sheffield believed that Garvin was behind the murder. Harris was one of them, emphasising that Garvin had got to know that Plommer was running a local tossing school under Norfolk Bridge. Garvin 'wanted to run all the lot or get summat out on it', but Plommer 'wouldn't cough up', and the Fowlers and their mates were sent to sort him out. Garvin and his brother, Rob, may have jumped on a tram before the attack but 'they were the instigators and the Fowlers were only underdogs. They shouldn't have been hanged. The Garvins were useless on their own, tha' knows it. If they was with the gang they was like lions. They ruled by force, fear. Man to man Plommer would beat them.' Unlike him, the Garvins would use razors and other weapons, a despicable thing because 'if tha' can't fight with fists what use are thee'.[593]

Above: The Elephant and Castle pub, 18-19 Green's End at Beresford Square in 1957. This pub gave its name to the Elephant Boys gang of South London

Below: The corner of East Road and Nile Street by Allerton Street, Hoxton, in 1936. Nile Street was the site of the Battle of the Nile in 1921 between Hoxton's Titanics and the Sabini Gang.

Above: A street scene in Hoxton in about 1902. A large group of local residents are lined up for the occasion. The location may be Boot Street, adjacent to Hoxton Market.

© *Mary Evans Picture Library*

Below: Mornington Crescent, on the corner with Hampstead Road, Camden, where George 'Brummy' Sage lived in comfort in the early 1920s thanks to his criminality.

© *Mary Evans Picture Library*

Above: The Sabini Gang in 1920. Second from the left is Joe Sabini and seated is Harry Cortesi. To his left and without a hat is Angelo Gianicoli and to Cortesi's right is Darby Sabini in a flat cap and collarless shirt. Next to him is Gus Cortesi and peering behind him on the right is Harry 'Boy' Sabini.

Below: A group of Italian men sit in the sun or lounge in doorways in a Saffron Hill street, the focal point of Clerkenwell's Little Italy.

Left: Alfie Solomon at Hurst Park racecourse in the 1920s.

© *Brian McDonald*

Right: A betting ticket for Sydney Lewis, whose real name was Simeon Solomon. Simeon was the younger brother of the real Alfie Solomon.

© *Carl Chinn Bookmaking Archive*

George Langham, real name Angelo Gianicoli, a lifelong friend of Darby Sabini and one of the Sabini Gang's inner circle in the racecourse wars.

Above: A small group of young men gambling on the tossing of coins. The banker is in the middle and has just flicked the coins into the air with his right hand, and the other lads are looking upwards at the spinning coins.   © *Alamy*

Below: Taken in about 1925, this photo shows George 'Ganner' Wheywell on the left wearing the braces. Originally in the Park Brigade and Garvin's Gang, he later switched sides to the Mooney Gang. Standing on the right and wearing the trilby hat is Harry Rippon, also of the Mooney Gang.

Above: The junction of Attercliffe Road and Princess Street by the Rawson's Arms and close to where William Plommer was attacked and received his fatal wounds on 27 April 1925. *The National Archives PCOM8/58*

Below: Wilfred Fowler, one of the two brothers hung for the murder of William Plommer. *The National Archives PCOM8/59*

Above: A photo of Darby Sabini later in life, in his garden at his home in Hove.

Right: Billy Kimber on one of the cruises he enjoyed with his second family in the 1930s. His first family was not so fortunate, living in poverty in Birmingham after he abandoned them in 1910, with his wife, Maude, dying in 1926. Her great granddaughter, Juliet Banyard, recalls that her own mother, Sheila Jones, once tried to find Maude's grave but as she had a pauper's funeral, there wasn't one: 'She's still mad about this, knowing Billy had money.' This photo was sent to Sheila's mother, Annie, Kimber's second daughter of his Birmingham family.

The prosecuting counsel in the murder trial had also maintained the importance of 'King' Garvin, as he dubbed him, in the murder. However, in his summing up, the judge informed the jury that as Garvin had not been alleged to have been at the affray itself, if he were to be found guilty they had to be satisfied that he had been 'privy to the instigation or the directing mind of the actual assault'.[594] Although he was acquitted on this legal basis, there can be no doubt that he was the ringmaster not only of the Sky Edge tossing school but also of other criminal activities across Sheffield. Since the start of the gang war, he had expanded his activities and was reputed to be a receiver of stolen goods. The Park Brigade had been essential in gaining control of Sky Edge and it was also unchallenged in the city centre. But it was now one element in what had become Garvin's Gang. He lived distant from the gang wars, though, in a three-bedroomed terraced house in Walkley, over three miles from the city centre, where there was a much better standard of living than in the East End and Park district. Yet far as he was from these poorer working-class neighbourhoods, it was from them that he pulled in gullible and criminally prone young men. Garvin gave the orders, but when it suited him he would pull away from them – as he did with the Fowlers, for in court he said that he had only ever spoken to them a few times.

Garvin was cunning and it was well known that, whilst he hadn't been convicted of assaults by his gang, he had sometimes been in the vicinity.[595] But the day after his acquittal for murder, he was finally prosecuted for violence. Leaving Princess Street shortly before the killing of William Plommer, Garvin had been seen with a razor in his pocket and was heard saying that he was going to do Spud Murphy of the Mooney Gang. He and his brother Rob then left and, a short time later, joined up with other gang members. Coming upon Harry Rippon, another of Mooney's men, Garvin whipped out his razor and tried to slash Rippon's face. He warded off the blow with his hand, which was cut, but was then struck violently on the head with a life-preserver by Bob Garvin. Dazed, Rippon was taken to hospital with severe scalp wounds. The Garvins were charged with malicious wounding. As usual, Sam Garvin denied any involvement and defence witnesses testified that he had been in a different place at the time of the attack. But their evidence was inconsistent and, without retiring, the jury found the Garvin brothers guilty on 1 August 1925. Sam Garvin, one of the cleverest criminals in Sheffield and the mastermind of the gang, was sentenced to twenty-one months' hard labour. His brother Bob was given nine months because his 'character had been very good until recently and his downfall was due to the bad influence of his brother'.[596]

Though hating each other, the lives of Garvin and Mooney were inextricably linked. They had come to blows at Lincoln races in March 1925 and now Mooney was imprisoned soon after his enemy.[597] On 1 August, the day of Garvin's trial, Mooney fought on a train with a Sheffield bookmaker called William Cowen. Mooney protested that he had been attacked first but the jury preferred the evidence of witnesses and Cowen, who had not wanted to press charges and had been forced to attend court by a subpoena. He had been punched, knocked to the ground, kicked several times and had three of his ribs broken and part of his left ear gnawed off. Mooney was sentenced to nine months' hard labour.[598]

The murder of William Plommer and the ongoing problems caused by the gang war led to radical police action. In May 1925, Chief Constable Hall-Dalwood formed a Sheffield Flying

Squad with the sole purpose of suppressing the gangs. Led by Sergeant William Robinson, it was made up of twelve tough and strong policemen.[599] Complaints about their rough tactics were soon made when prisoners appeared in court with black eyes, noses bandaged and other injuries, and in January 1926, one solicitor asserted that the squad had been formed to give 'pests' 'a tanning'.[600] It had, and a few months later it was given free rein by the new chief constable, Percy Sillitoe, who vowed to fight force with force. The Flying Squad were taught ju-jitsu and other methods of attack and defence, but as Sillitoe stressed, 'It was surprising how little teaching they needed.'

Divided into small teams for patrol work, one of the most famous pairings was Loxley and Lunn. Walter Loxley was 6 foot 3 inches tall and weighed eighteen stone. In Sillitoe's words, there was 'not an ounce of soft flesh on him. He was granite hard, and to hit him, even with boxing gloves, was like striking a brick wall.'[601] Herbert 'Jerry' Lunn was a military hero. A sergeant with the Royal Garrison Artillery, he had been gassed and awarded the Military Medal in 1917 for keeping communications intact and rescuing wounded men under heavy shellfire.[602] Not quite as tall as Loxley, he 'was a beautifully balanced man who could hit like the kick of a mule'. As the two of them walked down the streets, 'they looked like a battleship with an attendant destroyer'.[603]Another celebrated team was that of Sergeant Robinson and Patrick Geraghty, 'a giant of a man' who was 'the dread of wrong doers'.[604]As Frank Harris remembered, 'Geraghty, Lunn'd come round in taxis and'd break 'em all up. They'd set about them. If the gangs were in a pub the landlord'd ring up. Two'd come in and order 'em out and two would be outside and give 'em some hammer. That broke the gangs up. People appreciated it. The coppers were all big 'uns. Six foot, fourteen, fifteen stone. They wouldn't let them rest.'[605] Nor did they, and the police relished the chance to fight the gangsters.

From all his memories of those troubled years, Sergeant Robinson remembered best of all the night the Flying Squad as good as challenged one of the mobs, probably Mooney's.

> We heard that they were going to get us because we had turned them out of a pub the night before. I decided not to wait for them to come to us and I took Loxley and Lunn to a pub in West Bar. Sure enough they were there, about a dozen of them. I knew we would be in trouble, so I told them I was going to search them. We found razors and coshes on them, but they knew we were out to settle it once and for all. Then the fun started. It was quite a set-to, and I shall never forget it. It was the only way to settle them, and we three showed the twelve of them what for. That's how we stopped it. We kept after them all the time. I told them that three or more was a crowd and I wouldn't let them get together in the bars. If I found them together my boys split them up. We harried them until we wore them down.[606]

Accounts like these are vital in illustrating how the police dealt with the gangs. However, not all are as well informed as Robinson's. In his self-glorying life story, Sillitoe claimed that the Mooney and Garvin gangs each had hundreds of members.[607] Like the supposed numbers in the racecourse gangs, these were exaggerated. Robinson's assessment of about a dozen main men in each gang is more realistic, although hangers-on could increase this total by twenty to thirty.

The fighting fire with fire tactics of the Flying Squad seemed to work, but with Garvin's release from prison the gang war looked set to erupt again in 1927. Mooney was already out of prison and he and his old friend, Spud Murphy, had made up their differences and, in March, they and Ganner Wheywell went into a pub where the Garvin brothers were drinking. Insults and threats were thrown about and Wheywell shouted at the brothers, 'You have got two young ones hung and we will get you yet.' The police were called and they left, but later that evening Mooney and Murphy were arrested for assaulting Sergeant Robinson. Each of them was sentenced to two months' imprisonment. It is more likely that they were the ones assaulted, with their solicitor asserting that 'at one time Sheffield was noted for its gangs, but now it is more notorious because of its organised gangs of police, who chase these men from one licensed house to another, and will not let them behave themselves when they want to'.[608]

Yet the Flying Squad's rough tactics did prevent the gang war reigniting upon Garvin's release, but towards the end of the next year, there were renewed fears. On 18 November 1928, Mooney, Spud Murphy and a third man forced themselves into the house of Sandy Blower, a key figure in the Garvin Gang. He was out but his wife was warned by Murphy, 'We are going to have him. We are going to murder him.' Panic-stricken, she fled into the street crying, 'Murder'. Her fifteen-year-old son ran after her to protect her and was said to have been hit by Murphy and Mooney, who was carrying a piece of lead.[609]

On 12 December, Chief Constable Sillitoe called Mooney and Garvin in to meet him and cautioned them that he would not tolerate a gang war. That very afternoon, the Mooney and Garvin gangs clashed but it would be for the last time. Mooney and Murphy were with Gilbert Marsh and George Sawdon, both of whom had been in the Park Brigade but had switched sides. They came across Garvin and Bowler with 'a Jew from London', alleged to have been 'imported' to get Mooney into trouble. When he saw Mooney, he went up to him saying, 'You took advantage of me yesterday, and I will have you today.' He struck Mooney, who hit back, but was kicked at by Garvin, who was then chased off by Mooney. The Jewish man pulled a knife, which was knocked out of his hand by Sandon with his umbrella. Mooney and his men and Garvin and Bowler were each bound over keep the peace.[610] Thus ended the Sheffield Gang War and the Flying Squad was disbanded at the end of 1928.[611]

A year later, Mooney was involved in an affray with the police when his friend, Spud Murphy, was badly beaten up by officers; and in 1930, he was sentenced to three months' imprisonment with hard labour in Dublin for loitering at an international rugby match.[612] Thereafter, he appears to have become law abiding. In 1939, he was living with his wife and their youngest children in a terraced house in Rose Street (now Roselle Street) in Hillsborough. Formerly giving himself as a bookmaker's clerk he was now a file cutter's labourer. He died in 1961.[613] Sillitoe had seen some decency in Mooney but no such spark in Sam Garvin. It seems there was none and he did not change.[614] He carried on travelling the country, sometimes bookmaking and often pickpocketing, for which he was sentenced to six months' hard labour at Nottingham in 1930.[615] And he continued to be vindictive and vengeful. He fell out with William Furniss from his gang and attacked him and his friend in October 1931. As usual, Garvin did not act alone, having with him his son-in-law and Bowler. Nor did he fight fairly. He hit Furniss with a beer glass and then kicked him on the ground, whilst Bowler used a razor. Garvin and Bowler were each sentenced to six months' hard labour. Aged forty-seven, Garvin was now living in the Park district in a terraced house like that of Mooney. Incorrigible as he was, in April 1937, Garvin was sentenced to eighteen months' hard labour at Lincoln for theft.[616] Two years later, he said he was a bookmaker's clerk and he and his wife had managed to move to a council house in Cemetery Road, probably under the first phase of the clearance of bad housing in the Park district. He died in 1952.[617]

Neither Garvin nor Mooney had made enough money from their criminality to become prosperous and move their families permanently into a middle-class lifestyle. In that respect they had much in common with the leaders of the small groups of thugs making up the Birmingham Gang. In sharp contrast was Billy Kimber, who would buy respectability for his children with his criminal proceeds. So too would Harry and Darby Sabini. In 1925, at the height of the Sheffield Gang War, Darby Sabini had begun to edge away from his gang and towards semi-legitimacy. That move would soon be followed by a relocation away from London to Brighton and Hove on the south coast. This slow but marked change in Sabini's circumstances opened up opportunities for his enemies. An alliance of the Elephant Boys and Bethnal Green Mob quickly took advantage of his loosened grip on the capital's gangland, leading to a new race-gang war, which quickly drew the spotlight of the newspapers.

Chapter 7

WAR ON THE RACE GANGS

ELEPHANT BOYS & THE BETHNAL GREEN MOB

Apart from the Joe Sabini corruption case and the killing of Barney Blitz, there had been a lull in publicity on the activities of the race gangs in 1923 and 1924. With the truce between the Sabini Gang and Birmingham Gang and the London enemies of the Sabinis defeated, there were no major gangland clashes and there was little that was newsworthy. The Sabini Gang, in particular, was in a commanding position. Bookmakers who paid them protection were cowed, the Jockey Club apparently lacked the will to rid the racecourses of 'undesirables', and the police seemed unable to break up the Sabinis. Their criminality was unfettered and their stranglehold on the racecourse rackets in the South seemed unassailable. Yet within two years, the power of both the Sabinis and the Birmingham Gang had begun to wane and, by the end of the 1920s, both were spent forces on the racecourses of England.

This rapid turnaround in circumstances was unexpected but was propelled by a reaction to the domination of the two main gangs. Wearying of their reign of ruffianism, the bookmakers' associations came up with the ploy of giving leading gang members 'jobs' to provide the 'services' that had been extorted. Stirred to action at last by the weight of evidence about roguery, the Jockey Club organised a strong body to rid racecourses of pickpockets, welchers and blackmailers. Furthermore, embarrassed by a frenzy of headlines about the race gangs that erupted in the spring and summer of 1925 because of the Sheffield Gang War and renewed gang rivalry in London, the Home Secretary declared war against the race gangs, sending in the Metropolitan Police Flying Squad to make the racecourses safe around the capital. Their efforts were bolstered by those of the Birmingham Police against the Birmingham Gang. Crucially, this combination of factors was reinforced by the desire of some senior gang leaders to move away from gangsterism and towards legitimacy so that they might buy respectability for their children. The most notable of them was the most unlikely of them: Darby Sabini.

The waning of the race gangs, however, did not look possible let alone likely in the spring of 1925, when reports surfaced that the agreement between the Sabinis and the Birmingham Gang had been scrapped. They were invading each other's preserves, whilst 'peril and confusion' had been exacerbated by the emergence of new and independent gangs. Their terrorism on the racecourse was exaggerated by some as 'a modern replica of Fenianism, or of the Italian Camorra or Mafia'.[618] Other articles emphasised that the 'boys', 'as the get something-at-any-cost brigade are called, have increased a hundred per cent, in numbers'. The cheap rings were full of ex-convicts and cut-throats. Pickpocketing was rife, and at one small jumps meeting 'several charabancs were held up half a mile or so from the course, and the passengers were relieved of their cash in as complete a way as the train robbers do in a film story'. In the past, detectives had stopped such things by standing at the train barriers and preventing suspects from travelling but now motor traffic had developed so much that it was 'impossible to restrict the roguery at the fountain-head so to speak'.[619]

The *Daily Express* was in the forefront of the reawakened interest in the gangs. It announced a 'Racing Gang Outrage' on 16 February 1925, reporting on a wild melee the previous afternoon when rival gangs believed to hail from London and Birmingham had clashed in Aldgate East. In a lively running fight involving about a dozen men, one had cried out, 'They are murdering me!' before he suffered a severe razor slash stretching from the temple to the mouth. His assailant fled, but in full view of the crowds thronging the pavements the victim was thrown to the ground and kicked in the body and head by five other men before they bolted down a side street. So feared were the racing gangs in the East End that scores of men, women and girls who had witnessed what had happened would only reply to police enquiries by saying, 'I saw nothing'.[620] But this was not actually a clash between rival gangs, as the injured man was a bookie on his own. He had been in an argument at Lewes races and, according to Greeno, one of the policemen at the scene, six or seven of the Bethnal Green Mob sought him out. After the slashing, his face was 'criss-crossed like a lace curtain' and he was left scarred for life.[621] The bookmaker was Moses 'Moey' Levy, who had been 'the terror of Aldgate', with numerous convictions for assault and carrying a revolver but whose power was wilting. A friend of Alfie Solomon, his brother, Bobby, was associated with the Sabini Gang and this slashing was the first indication of a new challenge to the Sabinis.[622] Five men were arrested, including Jack 'Dodger' Mullins, leader of the Bethnal Green Mob, and Thomas 'Monkey' Benneworth of the Elephant Boys. When charged with malicious wounding, Mullins disparagingly called Levy 'the King of the Jews'. Each man was granted bail of £500, or 'a monkey' in bookmaking parlance, and all of them were later discharged.[623] As Brian McDonald observed, that Benneworth was able to pay this hefty sum gave him his nickname.[624]

Though only 5 foot 6 inches, Dodger Mullins was an intimidating presence. With scars above his eyes and left arm and a broken nose, he was covered in tattoos, including 'in memory of my mother', a dagger, a boxer, clasped hands and Britannia. Arthur Harding, a villain himself, detested Mullins as someone 'ignorant as bloody hell and brutal with it'. A terror, he lived by tapping money from people who were frightened of him, and Harding had once watched Mullins kick a little white dog to death because it had bit him. [625] Former detective Greeno had a differing opinion of Mullins. One of the toughest gang leaders, he 'was the original, crazy mixed-up kid; a genial little rogue – only 5ft. 8in. and slightly built – who had the DCM (Distinguished Conduct Medal) from the Kaiser's war and could turn into a fighting tearaway at the drop of a hat.'[626]

Harding believed that Mullins was the son of an Irish father and Jewish mother, but he was baptised Church of England by his parents.[627] His father was a violent man, convicted in 1898 of maliciously wounding a woman, and his mother died five years later.[628] Mullins and his brother and sister appear to have been abandoned by their father, and in 1911 they were living with their widowed grandmother in Bethnal Green. She was sixty-nine and still having to work at home as a finishing tailoress. A sweated trade, she would have worked long and hard for little pay. Mullins was ostensibly a paste maker for a confectioner, before becoming a labourer and full-time criminal. Whether or not he was awarded the DCM in the First World War, afterwards he and his henchman Timothy Hayes, another terror, were reckoned by the police to be the leaders and pioneers of the gang warfare on the racecourses.[629] By then, Mullins was living with Minnie Cooper and their children. They had a tempestuous relationship, and one May evening in 1920, after coming home, she refused to make his tea, telling him to 'sling his hook'. In response, he struck her in the neck with something sharp and she ran away. Mullins was charged with malicious wounding but he wrote to Cooper apologising. She told the court that she didn't want to proceed with the prosecution as she had a temper and knew how to get Mullins into one quicker than anyone. Besides he was very fond of their children and 'that was a good fault about him'.[630] Her change of heart was ignored and Mullins was imprisoned for six months' hard labour. Described as a very dangerous man whose gang was the terror of the neighbourhood, his imprisonment also ended his involvement in the racecourse rackets in the South, facilitating the takeover by Kimber and the Birmingham Gang. [631]

Following his release, Mullins became involved with Henry Bargery, one of the leaders of Hoxton's Titanics, and then teamed up with Thomas 'Monkey' Benneworth of the Elephant Boys.[632] Born in 1894 and hailing from Bermondsey, Benneworth was a printer's labourer like his father and older brother, another criminal. In 1922, when Benneworth was sentenced to eight months in Wormwood Scrubs for receiving stolen goods, he was described as a little over 5 foot 5 inches with a scar above his right eye. Two years later, in June 1924, he pleaded guilty to loitering at Epsom races. He appealed to the magistrates that he had been trying to go straight, and 'if he were now sentenced, he would lose his trade union card as a printer, and it would be practically impossible for him to find work again in his trade. He had a wife and four children, the youngest of whom was only a few days old.' Benneworth's plea fell upon deaf ears and he was imprisoned for three months.[633] Given his record, it is doubtful whether he would have forsaken criminality anyway.

The leader of the Elephant Boys was now Wal McDonald, and because of continuing trouble with the Sabinis, his nephew, Brian McDonald, believed that the fighting arm of the gang had to be resurrected.[634] Benneworth was recruited to lead it. Quickly, he pulled up with Mullins, but their alliance was first indicated not in London but in Leeds, and it suggested support for Mooney in the Sheffield Gang War. Late one evening in January 1925, Mullins, Benneworth and four other Londoners fought on the streets of Leeds with Sam Garvin and members of his gang. Each of them was fined.[635] Then, in late spring, numerous newspapers reported that on the evening of 20 May, ten armed men in a large blue taxi had made several mysterious visits to London's West End. The driver had picked up two foreign-looking and well-dressed men in East London who had instructed him to drive to Epping Forest and afterwards to Walworth, where he picked up more men by the Elephant and Castle. Then he was ordered on to Aldgate, where others were crammed in.[636]

Given the pick-up locations, it was apparent that they were Elephant Boys and some of the Bethnal Green Mob. They were, and included Benneworth and Mullins as well as John Jackson. He had been with them in the slashing of Levy and, as one of the Camden Town Gang, his brother Joe Jackson had been imprisoned for his part in the Shooting Affray.[637] The police believed that the ten men in the taxi had been looking for one of the Sabinis. They found him in a small betting club above a shop in Paddington. It was Alf White and he was pummelled badly. So too was a Jewish gambler, who having been asked if he were Italian, foolishly replied that he was. The men then went on to a club on the Tottenham Court Road.[638] In his memoirs, Greeno wrote that in one these clubs a Sabini Gang member was stabbed to death and another was thrown onto a fire.[639]

There is no evidence of the stabbing, although Brian McDonald revealed that at the betting club, Alf White's friend was held against the open fire until he told Benneworth and Mullins the address of Harry Solomon, the brother of Alfie, who was still in prison.[640] The next destination was Maiden Lane, Covent Garden where eight of the men went to the entrance of a sporting club. Its doorman stopped them and the alarm must have been given because thirty to forty members 'made a precipitate retreat to the back of the house and down the fire escape'. The men then kicked in the door at another building in the street where it was believed a rival gang leader was hiding, with the battering waking the tenant of the flat above. Putting his head out of the window, he shouted down, 'What do you want?' One of them called out, 'We are Nobby's friends', and they left.[641]

Following this rampage, Benneworth and another Elephant Boy were quickly arrested. On 25 May, they were charged with breaking and entering a house. Bail was refused and they were remanded in custody for a week.[642] This ensured that they could not go to the Epsom Derby meeting, where it was feared that the gathering storm of a new racecourse war would burst.[643]

As the other gang leaders were in hiding, Scotland Yard was watching and searching their favourite haunts and was ready to make 'a clean sweep of all undesirables'.[644] On the day of the Derby itself, on 28 May, the police left nothing to chance. Every carriage of trains leaving London was scrutinised by detectives; motor patrols paraded the roads leading to Epsom 'to get on the track of these desperate stick-at-nothing men'; and on the course itself, there were over four hundred mounted police, 'as well as an extraordinary number of constables, detectives, and Metropolitan police reserve men'.[645] With such precautions, there was no trouble. Mullins and two other Elephant Boys were also later charged. As was the norm, witnesses were not forthcoming and, with no evidence of breaking and entering, all that the magistrates could do was bind the men over to keep the peace.[646]

THE BIRMINGHAM GANG FEUD

But peace was not forthcoming and, within a few weeks, violence broke out in Birmingham. In his dramatised version of Darby Sabini's life, Edward Hart wrote that a reprisal was ordered on the Birmingham Gang on their own manor following the violation of a young Italian woman kidnapped at the Epsom meeting. Led by Harry Bates, the enforcement wing of the Birmingham Boys were playing snooker in the upstairs room of the George on Radley Street when the Sabinis came in with shotguns. They ordered their enemies to line the wall, but the Sabinis' leader cheerfully said that the guns were just for insurance. The intention was slashing – 'the honed razor was already in his hand, and that hand was as steady as a rock'.[647]

But in reality there was no Radley Street, no Harry Bates, and no attack by the Sabinis. Instead there was fighting *within* the Birmingham Gang. On 16 June, newspapers carried reports of a sensational affair that had occurred in a pub in Birmingham city centre the previous evening. Thomas MacDonald, aged forty-nine, had been hospitalised after his face had been slashed. The wound on his left check stretched from the ear to the top lip and he had also received two hard blows on the head. A mysterious feature of the affair was that the victim refused to make any incriminating statement.[648]

Originally a caster from Hockley, MacDonald was a serious racing rough. Born in 1877, he was known as both Thomas McDonough and George White. At just over 5 foot 6 inches tall, he had thinning brown hair and hazel eyes. His left forefinger was missing and he had scars from fighting on his head and legs. Like so many of the Birmingham Gang, he had been a peaky blinder and, from the age of thirteen, he was convicted for numerous offences, including assault, wilful damage and gaming.[649] He committed a more serious offence in 1895 when he was imprisoned for eighteen months for wounding with intent to do grievous bodily harm. This resulted from a disturbance in a pub when he had struck a man, who was then stoned returning home. Falling down, he was hit on the head with a stone by either McDonald or his companion. The victim had a fractured skull and his life was endangered. He pulled through but was left permanently injured with memory loss and partial loss of speech.[650] By 1904, McDonald had also served time for stealing in Sheffield, and that year he was sentenced to six years for housebreaking in Birmingham. Released on licence, he continued to reoffend, and in 1912 he was again found guilty of grievous bodily harm, this time in London. It might be speculated that he had joined Billy Kimber but there is no firm evidence to prove this. After a three-year sentence, MacDonald returned to Birmingham, found work in a munitions factory and joined the Devonshire Regiment, but in 1917, and whilst in uniform, he was arrested in Derby for uttering counterfeit coins. A persistent housebreaker and base coiner, he was imprisoned for five years. [651]

Violence and criminality coursed through MacDonald's being, and in 1922, not long after his release, he was again charged with grievous bodily harm but was fortunate that the case was withdrawn.[652] Two years later, he and James Cope were summonsed for unlawfully demanding money with menaces from a part-time bookmaker at the pony races in Tamworth. When he had refused to pay up, he was punched on the side of the head by MacDonald. Obviously scared, the victim made it plain that he had no vindictive feeling and did not want any unduly harsh course to be taken against MacDonald, who was merely bound over to keep the peace. The charges against Cope were also withdrawn.[653] Another top man in the Birmingham Gang, he had been pickpocketing with Billy Kimber in Dublin in 1917.[654] Now, in May 1925, Cope was named as the leader of seven men who had terrorised and blackmailed bookmakers at Chester races. They were rounded up after 'an exciting conflict' in which a hammer was used and bottles were thrown. Cope was sentenced to twelve months' hard labour for robbing a London bookmaker who had fled in terror.[655]

The Birmingham Gang had always been an unstable gathering of small groups of racecourse rogues like Cope's. Kimber had managed to bring them together into a fierce body in the racecourse war of 1921, but after a decade living in London and following the truce with the Sabini Gang, his authority must have waned. The Birmingham Gang fell apart, once again becoming the Birmingham Boys, a disparate collection of small bands. MacDonald belonged to one of them and his assailants to another. Described as a very dangerous race gang, it was led by Ike Kimberley and included his brothers, Mo, William and Charles, and two other Birmingham men. Ike Kimberley had actually travelled from London to fight with a friend of MacDonald's, 'Cunny' Cunnington, with whom Mo Kimberley had been seen at the Epsom Road Battle. Since then they had become enemies and Cunny's mob had cut Kimberley with a smashed pint glass in a London club. When Ike Kimberley arrived in Birmingham for the set-to with Cunnington, he teamed up with his brothers and went to a pub close to the Bull Ring markets that was popular with the city's racing men. MacDonald was already there on his own, and he fronted Ike Kimberley. They started to fight and the rest of Kimberley's mob joined in. One had 'a vicious instrument', a loaded stick with a strap, two of them had iron weapons, and another had a cut-throat razor. After the one-sided fight, MacDonald was found outside in Smallbrook Street dazed and bloodied.

Five of the Kimberley Gang were arrested and charged with unlawful wounding. In court, the bandaged MacDonald was named as one of the most notorious fighters and bullies amongst the Midland racing gangs. Admitting to being in a rival gang to the Kimberleys, he declined to give evidence. The case for unlawful wounding was discontinued and the defendants were bound over to keep the peace. MacDonald was then charged with 'being a disturber of the peace and likely to persevere in such conduct'. He promised not to attempt anything in Birmingham but vowed, 'I have made up my mind, I don't care who knows it, to get my own back. They are a lot of cowards.' MacDonald was also bound over. [656]

The Birmingham Boys were said to be becoming more dangerous and reckless.[657] They were, especially men such as Thomas Armstrong. Aggression simmered in him, always ready to boil over, as it did on 29 July 1925, when he and two others cruelly attacked four men. No longer needed as a minder in Sheffield, Armstrong was now in Brighton with pickpocket Sidney Payne and violent thief William Glynn. Payne had been to the Embassy nightclub and, returning to their hotel, he complained of having been insulted by Isaiah Elboz, a Jewish professional backer of horses originally from Whitechapel. Unhesitatingly, the three Birmingham gangsters sought vengeance at the club.[658] Elboz was leaving and, seeing the trio arrive, asked Payne, 'What's the game? Why have you brought these two with you?' Immediately, Payne raised his hand and struck Elboz, who collapsed in a pool of blood exclaiming, 'They have got me. I am done.' He had been slashed across the face from one ear to his lip with a wound five inches long. Trying to ward off the blow, his right forearm took a three-inch-long cut. An employee sought to stop the assault, but was kicked by Armstrong and knocked down. Striving to rise, he was hit unconscious. Two other men attempted to help but one was slashed across the wrist and the other above his left ear.

The three attackers were arrested at their hotel and brought to court the next day. Its entrance was closely guarded by the police and no member of the public was admitted. The prosecutor declared that he had never heard of 'a more cold-blooded attempt to maim and disfigure other men for sheer spite'. Terrified witnesses almost had to be dragged there and Elboz, especially, was scared to testify.[659] When the case came to a higher court, he maintained that he couldn't remember anyone else having been with Payne. The judge had no doubt that Elboz had been induced to pretend that he didn't recollect all that had happened. In spite of this, Armstrong, Payne and Glynn were found guilty and each was sentenced to eighteen months' hard labour.[660] Armstrong was fifty. He died six years later in 1931 in Birmingham.[661] His passing would have not been mourned by the many whom he had injured and terrified.

WAR DECLARED ON THE RACE GANGS

'Fifty Men Fight with Razors. Race Gang Battle in Aldgate', so cried out the headline in the *Daily Express* on Friday 21 August 1925. The story reported that the previous evening at Aldgate East, many men had been injured in one of the greatest race-gang fights in recent years. According to the article, it began in a pub over a dispute about Lewes races and 'suddenly, without warning, about fifty men split up in two rival sections, razors were drawn, and the two gangs began fighting'. Supposedly a scene of astonishing confusion followed, as 'a mass of struggling and excited men surged out of the tavern into the street, where they were joined by about one hundred more people'. The fighters were circled by a large crowd watching the battle, stopping the traffic. Police reinforcements from every nearby station were hurried to the scene. But the article reported that when they arrived 'the fight had assumed such a serious aspect that the crowd that had gathered had fled for safety and the two gangs were left in undisputed possession of the field'. However, with the arrival of scores of police, the gangs broke up and vanished into the side streets; as they ran, many of them could be seen trying to bind their wounds.[662]

Yet this story was a fabrication. No battle had taken place in Aldgate East. The City of London Police investigated the allegations and reported that they had found an unconscious man near a pub and that he had been taken to hospital. The usual crowd had collected to watch but there was no disorder. When the man came round, he explained that he had been drinking and, having fallen down in the street, injured himself. This incident could not 'by any stretch of imagination account for the sensational reports in the papers'. In fact, it was unthinkable that any such scene could have taken place without the police knowing, as there were many of them in the vicinity for traffic and other purposes. The police also interviewed the manager of the pub, who told them that nothing of the kind as described in the press had occurred.[663]

The non-existent Aldgate battle was one of ten race-gang outrages listed by the *Daily Express* for 1925. Like the slashings of Levy and MacDonald, some of them had occurred, but others were 'hyped up'. They included a fight between twenty men on Hampstead Heath on 3 August, which the police said was an ordinary Bank Holiday row with no evidence relating it to race gangs. This was followed on 16 August when another twenty men were reported to have battled with razors in Shaftesbury Avenue, injuring four of them. Nothing was reported to the police and, as far as they knew, it was pure invention. But with pressure from the press mounting, on 24 August, days after the non-existent Battle of Aldgate, Sir William Joynson-Hicks, the Home Secretary, declared war on the race gangs.

> I intend to break them up. The fight between rival race gangs in Aldgate East on Thursday night shows the existence of a state of affairs which cannot be tolerated in a civilised community. In Sheffield the race gangs have been effectively dealt with. There are

two men now under sentence of death, and three or four others have been sentenced to long terms of penal servitude. If it were brought to my notice that the police in race-gang-infested districts are influenced by threats of vengeance, I should at once take steps to increase the police strength there. It may be difficult to get rid of these gangs all at once. But give me time. The responsibility is mine. I mean to discharge it.[664]

Embarrassingly, the day after his widely publicised declaration to stamp out the gangs, the *Daily Mail* headlined '40 Men in Race Gang Fight'. The previous evening, it was said, a pitched battle had been fought between North and South London race gangs in Waterloo, in which razors, jemmies and iron bars had been wielded.[665] The police revealed a less melodramatic event. In a pub, Benneworth and two other men had rowed with a pickpocket, who had fled across the road to seek refuge in a hairdresser's. Benneworth had then broken the shop's window with the leg of a pub stool. As the police reported, even though he was in a dangerous race gang, there was no evidence that the attack was part of a race-gang feud or that a razor or any other murderous weapon had been used. Still, when arrested by two policemen, Benneworth had taken a fighting pose and warned, 'Nark it or I'll f......g well do you', and he later threatened to murder and chivvy (knife) them. Convicted only of wilful damage, he was fined.[666] Benneworth was another one who seems to have begun to believe in his invulnerability and, within a few weeks, he was again arrested. This time, he and two associates were accused of maliciously cutting and wounding two Italian brothers, the owners of a club in Soho, but with no apparent connection to the Sabinis.[667] As had become usual in such cases, the victims were unable to identify the attackers and other witnesses would not testify. The police offered no evidence and the charges were dropped.

By now, the Home Secretary's declaration of war against the race gangs had gained wide support. London's *Evening News* had been highlighting the problems caused by racecourse ruffians since before the First World War, and it welcomed his determination to put a stop, once and for all, to the organised warfare between the gangs. It conjectured that a three-pronged approach would be adopted: greater co-operation between the London police and other forces throughout England; joint action between the police and railway companies to stop rogues travelling to meetings; and the formation of a special body of plain-clothes detectives who would get to know the villains.[668] The *Daily Express* also reported that a law might be passed 'empowering magistrates to inflict heavy punishment on police evidence alone in the case of gang hooligans who are brought to book'.[669] But the Home Secretary himself did not clarify what he would do other than stating that he favoured sterner sentences and would apply more vigorously the existing organisation for dealing with the race-gang nuisance.[670] That existing organisation included police surveillance of the gangs, race trains and racecourse entrances; the detention of 'undesirables'; police patrols at meetings; and the exchange of information between London's police and those elsewhere.[671] But the Home Secretary's main response was to send in the Metropolitan Police Flying Squad.

None of the ten outrages listed by the *Daily Express* actually happened on racecourses, having taken place in London, Sheffield and Birmingham. But the Home Secretary was convinced that every mob was a race gang. Determined 'to smash gangdom', as Chief Inspector Fred 'Nutty' Sharpe expressed it, the Flying Squad was ordered to drive the gangs from racecourses in the London district. Sharpe himself was crucial to that strategy, becoming almost revered by bookmakers like Sam Dell.[672]

> There used to be one copper, the famous one was Nutty Sharpe and when he walked on the racecourse they ran for their lives, all the villains ran. And I can remember an incident once where Nutty Sharpe saw a mob of them get on a bus, you know, a push (group of pickpockets), what they call a push up on the bus and he commandeered the bus and drove it in to the nick (police station), pinched them all. Nutty Sharpe was a famous policeman and he used to talk to us all but any crooks came in sight of him, he was a man of great honesty. Honest man and he hated villains. And he was fearless.[673]

This commandeering of the bus with the driver taking it to the police station under Sharpe's orders happened in Shoreditch. Notable for jauntily wearing a bowler hat, he stood out, and on one occasion at Epsom, his approach was signalled by the bookmaker's tic-tacs, men employed to transmit betting information by hand signs. Thus warned, the pickpockets jumped over the rails to escape him. Sharpe's reputation was fearless; whenever he saw a mob of gangsters, it was said that he would stride forward on his own and order them to 'Clear Off'. Any who argued would be hit with a powerful punch.[674]

Cleaning up racecourses was neither an easy nor a swift process. It was gradual and not 'headline-grabbing', but by the late 1920s there was a distinct improvement for bookmakers and racegoers. It was a change for the better helped greatly by the Birmingham police. Virtually unnoticed, they had all but ended the Birmingham Gang's activities. In May 1931, one of the gang's leaders was interviewed by the *Daily Herald*, and despite the article's flippant tone it suggested an important point: police prevention. The race-gang leader explained that Birmingham was the best-behaved industrial city in the country because 'our lads are as goody-good as choirboys in their own town. It's the police you have to thank.' They had sent detachments to most of the racecourses and:

> . . . while you were on your way to the racecourse a nice chap you would recognise as a Birmingham copper came to you and said – 'Hello, Joe, there's a fine train home leaving in half-an-hour, dining-coach and everything. I'm sure you'd like to catch it.' What could you do but take the tip? You'd be spotted, and that's that. You found yourself leaning out of the carriage window to shake his hand while he shouted, 'Pleasant journey'. Sometimes you were persuaded before you left Birmingham. As sure as you were going for an honest day's racing they would come up and say, 'Hello, Bill, here for a little flutter, I hope' and then put you on your honour.

The gang leader finished off by announcing that 'race gangs are pretty well wiped out now'.[675] They were, and their disappearance owed much not only to police action but also to that of the Jockey Club, which played its part in ensuring that by the late 1920s 'gangs of roughs no longer vented their feuds violently in the vicinity of racecourses nor made their presence felt in any enclosure'. After decades of inaction, finally it did something constructive. Following a long period of discussions with the Home Secretary, the Commissioner of the Metropolitan Police and chief constables across England, it set up the Jockey Club and National Hunt Racecourse Personnel Department to supervise the rings. Headed by an ex-soldier, Major Wymer, it had three senior supervisors: one each for the North, the Midlands and the South. They engaged about sixty ring inspectors as Racecourse Detective Personnel, most of them retired senior CID officers from various police forces. Their duties were threefold: to watch the entrance gates and keep out 'undesirables'; to patrol the rings to spy out welchers and known bad characters; and to look out for suspicious cases of disputed bets. The supervisors and inspectors were instructed to work closely with the police, whilst the department's central office swiftly became 'a miniature Scotland Yard where records of bad characters who frequented racecourses were carefully compiled'.

Operations began at the start of the Flat racing season in 1925. In the most troublesome area, the South, the senior supervisor was another former military man, William Bebbington.[676] The situation he faced was grim.

> We were then witnessing pitched battles on our own racecourses between rival race gangs. In those dark days bookmakers were afraid to travel to meetings without surrounding themselves with bands of 'bodyguards'; and these bodyguards were often recruited from the gangs and were brought over in much the same way as the mercenary troops of mediæval times were enlisted. And there were hordes of pickpockets, card-sharpers and confidence men.

Quickly, Bebbington found that certain gatemen, ring officials and staff managers were making big money by selling pitches to bookmakers, admitting known thieves, and trafficking in complimentary tickets with 'undesirables' on a vast scale. The first move against 'gangsterdom' was to remove these corrupt officials one by one and replace them with men of integrity.[677] Like the police initiatives, this was a slow process, as was the clearing out of rogues, but it was a success. As a correspondent for the *Daily Mail* affirmed in 1931, 'the Sabini gang has gone, killed by the secret agents of the Jockey Club and the plain-clothes men of Scotland Yard'.[678] It had gone, but a key factor in its disappearance was overlooked: Darby Sabini's move away from gangsterism.

SABINI LEAVES LONDON

The Sheffield Gang War and the fracturing of the Birmingham Gang were important factors in the upsurge of race-gang activities in 1925. So too was the diminished position of Darby Sabini. For the previous two years, he had been the 'emperor of the racetrack' in southern England and nobody had dared to attack him personally on the Turf.[679] But now, at Ascot, he was beaten up by one of the Hoxton boys before eight of his own men could rush to the rescue. Carrying him to a downstairs washroom, they were followed by Detective Greeno. The gangsters were twisting Sabini's ears, 'a painful but effective way of bringing a man out of a fist-induced coma, and I grabbed him from them, pushed him up the stairs, down the covered way and on to the railway with his coterie of assorted thugs tagging on behind, muttering'. Tending to liken himself to a sheriff in the Wild West, Greeno ordered Sabini and his men to board the next train to London. They did so, like a flock of morose sheep, half-dragging their leader with them.[680]

After the imprisonment of the Cortesis, Darby Sabini's position had seemed invulnerable. Yet in 1925, the Elephant Boys and the Bethnal Green Mob sensed an opportunity to challenge his gang in London, if not on the racecourse. It was an opportunity of Sabini's own making because he was in legal trouble, although not with the police. Adept as he was at steering clear of arrest, he made a major error of judgement when, in the name of Charles Sabini, he sued the *Topical Times* for libel in connecting him with the Sabini Gang of racecourse pests. A weekly publication with a high sports content, it was owned by D. C. Thomson, one of the most important newspaper companies in Britain. In the spring of 1924, it serialised the 'Confessions of a Turf Crook', purportedly by a broadsman called Ted McLean. One article emphasised that the London Turf gangs included many Italian cut-throats, and that the Sabini Gang was the most powerful in the country. Purportedly with over a hundred members, it was big enough to stand on its own whilst others in London had to make alliances. More detail was included on 12 April:

No story of the Turf gangs could be complete without a reference to one or two of the men whose activities in this direction have made them notorious. I met most of them. The Sabini brothers, Harry and Charles ('Darby Sabini'), have earned themselves enough publicity.

The Sabinis are hot-headed fellows, and there are few of the men who followed them who did not know the dangerous game of gun-play from A to Z. It was the Sabini gang which started the idea of meeting bookmakers when they got off the train when they came back to town. 'Shell out!' snapped the Sabini 'broadsman', at the same time allowing the bookmaker to spot the butt of a revolver carried in the gangster's pocket. Invariably the bookmaker 'shelled out', for the Sabini Gang did not carry guns merely for ornaments.[681]

Two years before, Darby Sabini had revelled in the heroic image he had portrayed in the *Empire News*. The claims in the *Topical Times* destroyed that representation. Yet he could have ignored the articles, as he had previous reports that had linked him to the leadership of a notorious racecourse gang. He did not, and instead went to law, perhaps propelled by vanity, or perhaps, like Alf White, he had become convinced of the invincibility of the Sabini name. Whatever his motivations, he must have consulted lawyers in the spring and summer of 1925, because at the start of October, his libel suit was listed at the law courts. It was sufficiently interesting to be named with only one other prominent case in the *Westminster Gazette*.[682] Any idea, though, of a sensational racecourse trial was dispelled when it came to court on 15 December. D. C. Thomson had gathered 'voluminous particulars' in its defence that the articles had been true in substance and fact but Sabini failed to appear.

It was suggested that after he began the action, he may have thought that the publishers were not going to defend it and would insert an apology, giving the impression that the allegations were false. When he realised that D. C. Thomson was not going to back down, Sabini tried to discontinue proceedings, but they had gone too far. The case could only be disposed by a judgment of the Court, if for no other reason that the defendants could then recover their costs. Sabini must have realised that he was going to lose and went to ground, hence his non-appearance. Based on the weighty evidence presented, the Lord Chief Justice found in favour of the publisher and did award costs. He also directed that the alleged libel was justified and ordered that the papers from the case should be sent to the Director of Public Prosecutions.[683]

The action was a disaster for Sabini. He owed £737. Unsurprisingly, it was not paid and bankruptcy proceedings were begun. He did not attend a first meeting of his creditors on 10 June 1926, when it was revealed that his address was unknown as he had left Collier Street, King's Cross. Yet he was still seen at racecourses and it was said that he was making large sums selling racing lists. A resolution for bankruptcy was passed and the case was passed on to the Official Receiver.[684] Threatened with a warrant for his arrest, Sabini finally broke cover and appeared at the London Bankruptcy Court on 29 June. Described as a thick-set man, he was now living in apartments in Russell Street, Brighton with his wife and three children. He protested that the article in the *Topical Times* had done him a lot of harm and denied that he was the king of the Sabini Gang or that he had threatened bookmakers who refused to pay for particular pitches – the going rate for which was between £5 and £20 per day. Finally, he explained that he had not carried on his action, as he could not find the £75 to pay his solicitor, adding that he had no assets.[685]

It is most unlikely that he could not afford this sum and his decision not to continue legal proceedings coincided with a surprising move: in effect, he was leaving the Sabini Gang and London's gangland. Sabini had always been smarter than his rivals and he would have been fully aware of the pressures beginning to bear down on the race-gangs from 1925. Those pressures came at a time when he and his wife were making an important decision about their children's future. They didn't want them growing up in a gangster environment; they wanted them to have respectable lives. To do that they had to move away from London, hence the relocation to Brighton and Hove on the south coast. In 1940, Sabini's wife, Ann, wrote that their children had been 'educated in the best possible English traditions'. The daughters were brilliant elocutionists, one having gained 'the Gold medal for English and being the only girl to have passed this particular examination with honors and distinction'. The same year, Sabini emphasised his own pride in his children: one daughter was working in the Forestry Camp in Suffolk as part of the war effort; another, the elocutionist, hoped to_be an actress and was playing in little shows for the Spitfire Funds and YMCA, where his youngest daughter, a musician, also played. As for his son, he had attended Hove Grammar School and had ambitions to join the RAF.[686]

Sabini must have realised that if he carried on with his libel case, the publicity would have impacted negatively on his children at a time when he was relocating to Brighton and Hove. Most tellingly, his attempts to move away from gangsterism were made clear by his desire to change his name. Although he would continue to be known as Darby in racing circles, he later stressed that was a nickname.

> I said I did not want to be called that. I said, 'Do not call me Darby anymore; call me Fred' . . . They called me Fred because I used to use the name Fred Handley. I wanted to get rid of Darby, because I did not like that name, and when I went to Brighton, and mixed with different people, I did not want to use that name. I did

not want to go under the name of Sabini. That is why I used the name of Handley . . . Fred used to be my boxing name . . . [687]

This move away from gangsterism was gradual and was enabled by his new role within the Bookmakers' Association. Although he had been dismissed as chief steward at the end of 1922, it's apparent that close bonds remained as, a few months later, the solicitor for the Association had offered to pay the bail for White and Drake when they were first arrested in the bribery case relating to Joe Sabini's imprisonment. This ongoing relationship was soon made formal. At his bankruptcy hearing, Darby Sabini mentioned that since the end of 1924, he had been employed by the Association to sell the lists of the horses expected to run in each race.[688] Sold for five shillings each, he and another man made fivepence while the printer at Portsea Press made one shilling. Of course, that printer was Emanuel. Sabini denied that bookmakers were intimidated into buying these lists. They did so because they were members of the Association and, laughingly, he refuted the suggestion that he had made from £20,000 to £30,000 a year as head of the Sabini Gang. He only earned £8 a week from his commission for selling the lists. Out of this, he paid £1 and five shillings a day in travelling expenses, and a further five shillings a day for food and drink – and he went racing most days.[689] Such figures were unrealistic, as they would have meant that he brought in little or nothing. He obviously made more as he carried on selling the lists for the Association for the same commission until 1940, when he stated that he might sell a hundred a day at small meetings but 1,000 a week at big racing events like Ascot.

Sabini was not alone in drifting away from gangsterism. So too did Andrew Towey of the Birmingham Gang. Jim Cooper was a bookie in the Midlands and North from 1926, and he made clear the process.

There were gangsters when I started, just about . . . Now then the BPA (Bookmakers' Protection Association) was formed when I started to go to the racecourses. To get rid of the gangsters, do you know what they did with them? Give them bloody jobs. They created jobs for them. Now there were the Birmingham Gang under a feller named Andrew Towey . . . They gave them those jobs. They went in the three rings and they got half a crown, which was a lot of money in them days, from each bookmaker, which kept them going with money . . . Considering there could be at meetings like York all up to 60 bookmakers, it were a lot of money that . . . They brought the gangs up, to give them jobs. Towey was the top gang. When they gave them a job, well the other gangs couldn't get a living. When Towey was the head gangster . . . and they kept the other bloody gangs out.[690]

The formation of the Bookmakers' Association in the South had been swiftly imitated in the Midlands and the North, each having a Bookmakers' Protection Association by 1922. Leading bookmakers in these organisations obviously realised that to end the intimidation and violence by the two main gangs they had to offer Towey, Sabini and others something in return.[691] Quietly, almost secretly, they legitimised the 'services' formerly extorted by the Birmingham Gang and Sabinis in their respective regions, handing them over to the gang leaders and their closest associates. As George Langham's son explained, 'They did provide a service because they had to have the runners. If no-one knew the runners then the bookies couldn't write the runners up so they had to hire someone to do it'.[692] This 'legitimisation' was not recorded officially, but its existence was revealed in 1940 when the Northern BPA announced that it was entirely optional to pay for dots and dashes and number calling, and that after the death of Andrew Towey, both operations would cease in its region.[693] For Towey, Sabini and a few others, the new arrangement was beneficial, as they were now middle aged and no doubt were tiring of fighting other gangsters and avoiding the police. The handing out of jobs left out some in both the Sabinis and Birmingham Gang and all of the other mobs. This exclusion encouraged an unlikely North-South alliance: Benneworth and the Elephant Boys were joined by Yorkshire's Mexborough Boys in a vain attempt to take over rackets that were already melding into legitimate operations. It would result in the last battle on the racecourses between the 1920s race gangs.

THE LAST BATTLE

With the beginning of the Flat racing season in March 1926, hopes were raised that less would be heard of the gangs because of the strenuous measures that had been adopted by the Jockey Club and racecourse authorities.[694] Much less *was* heard. In 1925, there had been hundreds of newspaper reports about race gangs, even though many of them had nothing to do with such gangs and that other stories were concocted. But a year later, there was a substantial fall and the *People*, when writing about the gangs, even referred to the infestation of race gangs having been 'a few years ago'.[695] That was too optimistic, as in 1926, whilst the gang activity had seen a sharp decline, the conflicts were not quite over yet, as demonstrated by a major confrontation at Yarmouth races on 3 June. Yet the rarity of such an event now was made plain by the fact that it was covered only by the local newspaper. The clash was caused by the Elephant Boys, led by Benneworth and John Jackson, and the Mexborough Mob under John Tingle. A hard man, Tingle had a bad record with about forty convictions for larceny, gaming, assault on the police, affray, and stealing by trick.[696] Originally a miner, he belonged to a violent family. Aged seventeen, he and his brother were arrested for their part in a serious assault on two policemen. They were said to belong to the infamous 'Red Brotherhood' gang that was the terror of Mexborough and their father threatened one of the witnesses. On that occasion, Tingle was sentenced to six months' hard labour.[697] He later teamed up with others to form the notorious Mexborough Mob who mostly operated the three-card trick.[698] Now they had come south.

Bebbington had been forewarned about the probability of a fight at Yarmouth between the Elephant Boys, also known as the Walworth Road mob, and their Mexborough allies against the 'remnants of a gang of Italian and Jewish elements who were then employed in various capacities'. The ill feeling against the Italian-Jewish gangs, as he called the Sabini Gang, had arisen because they 'had been successful in securing many lucrative jobs on racecourses such as number-callers or salesmen of 'dots and dashes' cards to the bookmakers'. These observations reinforce the interpretation that not only Darby Sabini but also other members of his gang had become 'legitimised'. Alert to the danger, Bebbington had strengthened the usual quota of ring inspectors and CID officers in the cheaper enclosures, whilst the local chief constable was in attendance with a force of officers. The expected trouble began in earnest as the second race was about to start. There was a commotion at the bookmakers' joints with 'iron bars and spanners flying around and soon the Italian-Jews were in retreat'. In the attack on them, Tingle had shouted, 'The English fought the Germans. We are all Englishmen. Now it is the Jews. Leave us to fight it out.'

The Sabinis were escorted away from the fighting and the opposing gang broke up. Soon after, another row broke out between what was left of the two groups, and this time the Elephant Boys and Mexborough Boys received a very bad handling. It is suggestive that none of the Sabini men were arrested, another indication that their presence was now officially accepted on southern racecourses. By contrast, seven Elephant Boys and members of the Mexborough Mob appeared in court. Two of them had plastered hands and the legs of the others had been severely injured by kicks. Tingle, Benneworth and his henchman, John Jackson, were each sentenced to three months' imprisonment.[699] Their usual companion, Mullins, had not joined them at Yarmouth as he was already facing a serious charge of demanding money with menaces. On 9 July this 'captain' of the gang and 'nightmare of the East End', was sent down for four years. His right-hand man, Timothy Hayes, whom even Harding detested, was also found guilty of assault and imprisoned for nine years.[700] It is striking that whilst Mullins was clearly a vile man, he was admired by the most infamous gangsters of the 1960s, the Kray brothers. In their own story, they put him forward as someone who adhered to a code of criminal conduct, professing that he had 'played by the rules, which we admired. They never hurt women or kids or old people – they only ever did damage to their own kind'.[701] This rose-tinted image conflicted with the most unpleasant reality. Mullins and his ilk preyed upon their own and played only by their own nasty rules.

When he was sent down, Mullins protested that the case had been 'got up' by the Sabinis and 'some of the Yiddisher people in order to get Hayes and himself out of the way'.[702] Once imprisoned, out of the way they certainly were, and Benneworth and Jackson had lost two crucial allies in the war against the Sabinis. After their release from their two-month stretch, the two South Londoners returned to intimidation on their own manor. In March 1927, they were found guilty as incorrigible rogues. Terrorising tradesmen, publicans and stewards of working men's clubs, they ordered drinks and refused to pay for them, whilst they picked quarrels with innocent persons and demanded money. If their victims refused, they were attacked with broken glasses and razors. Whenever one or other of their gang were charged, the two men would go around with a subscription list for the defence, but the greater portion went into their own pockets. Jackson was sentenced to nine months' hard labour, but Benneworth was remanded on bail until 16 June to see how he behaved. He must have done so satisfactorily as there is no evidence that he was imprisoned.[703]

The 'Sharp Fight' at Yarmouth was the last major outbreak of violence in the 1920s racecourse wars. Benneworth was too weakened without Mullins, Hayes and Jackson to make any more attacks, whilst the Sabini Gang and Birmingham Gang were fading away on the racecourses. But excluded from the legitimisation of the bookmakers' services, smaller gangs of pickpockets, tricksters and bullies carried on. In 1928, Bebbington faced problems at Folkestone and Chelmsford and, a year later, on 4 September 1929, racegoers in Derby were urged to beware of nearly twenty-five pickpockets and card sharpers from Birmingham who had arrived for the races. Although they were dispersed, their movements were closely followed throughout the afternoon both off and on the course by plain-clothes men.[704] It is likely that apart from Towey and a few others, most of the Birmingham Gang were also excluded from the arrangement with the bookmakers. Amongst them was Philip Thomas, who had been arrested with Kimber for the attack on Alfie Solomon's clerk, Bild, in the 'Battle of Bath' and who was also linked to the Elephant Boys. On 16 July 1929, he and three others assaulted two bookmakers and tried rob them of between £600 and £700 after racing at Newmarket. Thomas and another man were arrested, but the judgements were mild: Thomas was discharged and his associate was bound over.[705]

However, there seems to have been more to this attack than robbery. One of the bookies, Benjamin Yeadon, was prominent in the Bookmakers' Association, which was taking an active role in prosecuting blackmailers and welchers and slowly clearing racecourses of rogues like Thomas, who were aggrieved.[706] By now the various bookmakers associations had also removed another money-making racket – the selling of pitches. Co-operating through an informal National Committee, they formed pitch committees to protect and safeguard racecourse bookmakers' rights and secured the co-operation of the Jockey Club in 1929. Henceforth bookmakers did not have to pay for their pitches, even to former gangsters, whilst they could not sell them. Instead they were allocated by the Racecourse Personnel liaising with the local Bookmakers' Protection Association. When applying for a pitch, a bookmaker had to have two established bookies willing to act as guarantors. The name was then added to a list and whoever was the most senior on it was entitled to a pitch when it became vacant.[707] With actions like this, the bookmakers' associations were as pivotal in the decline of the race gangs as were the Jockey Club's Racecourse Personnel and the Flying Squad. As recognised by knowledgeable commentators, by 1931, both the Birmingham Gang and the Sabini Gang were extinguished for all intents and purposes.[708] Whether this reality mirrors what has been told over the years as part of the myths and legends behind the gangs and their legacies, however, is another case entirely.

Chapter 8

GANGSTER REALITY & MYTHOLOGY

THE MYTHS DISPELLED

'I'm the Gangster Who Runs London's Underworld' splashed the *People* on its front page on 5 September 1954. The main story, it featured a photo of Billy Hill, England's first 'celebrity' gangster. Previously unknown to the public, crime reporter Duncan Webb exclaimed that Hill was 'in fact the Al Capone of this country – the most successful and desperate gangster in the history of British crime'. By wielding the knife and the cosh better than his rivals, he had smashed all the other gangs in London, welding them into one big fraternity with him at the top. The cleverest safe breaker ever known by Scotland Yard and the mastermind behind most of the big robberies in recent years, now he was sunning himself in Cannes on the French Riviera. Fingering a six-carat diamond ring, he announced that he was retiring from his position as 'Gangster No. 1' and was ready to tell his story.

His 'confessions' revealed a London underworld 'every bit as organised and determined as Dillinger and Capone ran'.

Serialised for four weeks in a newspaper that sold 4.5 million copies weekly, Hill told of how, in 1947, he grabbed power in 'One Night of Terror' from the Black Gang. This was actually the White Gang, led by one of the sons of Alf White. A key figure in Darby Sabini's inner circle, White had eventually become the leader of the gang after Sabini's move away from London and active involvement in its gangland. Hill ignored this reality, transforming Sabini into a legendary figure.

Don't think, though, that I invented the gangster set up in London. That was the creation of the notorious Darby Sabini. He started it in the late 1920s when he brought a gang of Italian cut-throats out of Saffron Hill and Clerkenwell and took over the West End. Sabini was the big shot of the underworld when I came out of Borstal in 1931, and he stayed on top for years. Soho was as tough as Chicago in those days. It was a lawless jungle of concentrated crime and vice in which you could drink and gamble round the clock if you knew the right spots.

Slot machines . . . gambling . . . booze and girls – that was the combination which made Al Capone rich. And Darby squatting like a fat spider the middle of the same gilded web in London couldn't go wrong either. With the income from his racecourse and dog-track rackets his personal cut was hundreds of pounds a week. That kind of dough spells trouble and there were terrible gang fights almost every night as ambitious rivals tried to muscle in on Darby's pitch.

But the Sabini's Boys always came out on top, and the tough and ruthless Darby ruled the roost right up until the outbreak of the Second World War. Then, almost overnight, his power was broken. Sabini and dozens of his mob were interned overnight . . . The Sabini Gang was bust, and at once its biggest rivals took overtook over . . . This mob was led by a man I'll call Bill Black.[709]

Striving to liken himself to a Mafia boss, Hill was keen to be seen as the successor to the 'Italian' Darby Sabini. But this intense portrayal of Sabini's power bore little connection to actuality. The Whites (Blacks in Hill's account) were not the Sabini Gang's rivals, having emerged from the gang. And the Sabinis had been at their most powerful in the early and not later 1920s. Sabini and his brother, Harry, were interned in the war on the ground of hostile origin – but were not joined by their brothers or dozens of their mob. And there is no evidence connecting Sabini with Soho following his move to Brighton and Hove in 1926. Officers of the local CID came to know him well, reporting that outside racing he did not appear to have any other interests and that no longer could he be described as a dangerous gangster and racketeer of the worst type. When in drink he was apt to turn violent, but such instances were very rare and a detective inspector observed that 'such conduct can be obviated by the use of tact and firmness'.[710]

Ignoring such realities, the 'Sabini myth' spread. In 1957, the *New York Times* included a 'highly coloured article' about how contemporary Brighton was 'a far cry from the days of the Sabini gang two decades ago'. These protection racketeers had 'terrorised the town with razor slashings and worse from the race track on the chalk downs above Black Rock to the sea front', but their violence had finally ended when they were driven out by the police.[711] Yet the Sabini Gang had not terrorised the town and Darby Sabini was not driven out, living there until he died in 1950. Eight years later, following a murder in Clerkenwell, blood was said have flowed again in Little Italy for the first time since 1925 when the Sabini Gang had been fighting to control the racecourses. One resident told the *Daily Mirror's* crime correspondent of remembering when the Birmingham Gang came down and fought the Sabinis, 'And the streets were covered in blood. They had razors, knives, and shooters.'[712] Even at their height, the Birmingham Gang had never confronted the Sabinis in Little Italy, where there had been no major gang violence other than the shooting by local rivals, the Cortesis.

A vital part of Billy Hill's inflation of Sabini's power was the comparison with Al Capone and Chicago, and even in death, Sabini's 'foreign origins' overwhelmed his Englishness. In 1963, crime writer Norman Lucas wrote that Sabini 'reputedly was a member of the notorious Mafia'.[713] He was not. Nor was he the 'leader of a Sicilian "razor" gang' who had imported over 300 henchmen from Sicily as enforcers, as some accounts have stated.[714] But the Mafia connection became accepted. In June 1971, Joe Colombo, 'America's most notorious Mafia chief', was shot at a rally and within yards of him was Englishman George Sewell. No ordinary bystander, as one newspaper recounted, he had been the lieutenant and bodyguard of Italian gang leader Darby Sabini in the 1920s and 30s, when the Sabini Gang ruled the British underworld. After the Second World War, many of the Sabinis had moved to New York and were adopted into the Mafia family of Joseph Profaci, but Sewell, 'forsaking his violent ways, had remained in London to become a reformed and highly respected citizen'. On this occasion, he had been on a brief holiday 'to meet old comrades-in-arms'.[715]

This, again, is untrue – none of the Sabini brothers or their inner circle went to New York and joined the Mafia. And George Sewell had not been a lieutenant in the Sabini Gang. As Brian McDonald expressed it, 'Sewell, who some called an enforcer, was more enforced upon than not.'[716] A boxer out of Hoxton, an enemy territory to the Sabinis, he joined the Bethnal Green Mob of Dodger Mullins, and Harding revealed that Sewell was knocked about by the Sabini Gang at Brighton races in 1920.[717] There is no mention of Sewell in the racecourse wars of 1921 and 1922, but in 1930 he and another man were attacked by a gang including Johnny and Toddy Phillips. Formerly of the Titanics and the Camden Town Gang, they had become allies of Mullins. Johnny Phillips went up to Sewell in a Soho pub and said, 'So you are with the Italians now? Why can't you be with Dodger?' Phillips then struck Sewell with a broken glass, resulting 'in serious injuries which would disfigure him for life'. In the ensuing court case, reference was made to the Sabini Gang and the judge remarked that he thought it had been broken up. The police informed him that there were still some rival gangs in London and that the old Sabini Gang was now known as the Italian Gang.[718] That name change itself emphasised that the Darby Sabini was no longer involved in what had been his gang. And in 1931, the year in which Billy Hill proclaimed that Darby Sabini was 'the big shot of the underworld' running Soho, the district was described as the home of 'the survivors of the old Sabini gang'.[719]

Despite his lack of involvement with the Sabinis in their heyday, Sewell was prominent in the biography of Darby Sabini by Edward T. Hart. A crime correspondent in Fleet Street in the 1950s and '60s, his information was gleaned from a variety of sources such as club-owners, doormen, boxers, jockeys, bookmakers, robbers and racketeers. There is no evidence of any of the interviews with these men, whilst Hart wrote in the style of a gangster novel. He included long conversations and musings from Sabini, who had been dead for many years before the book was published and whom Hart had never met, and he drew heavily on tropes of Italian immigrants rather than Sabini's Englishness. Hart stressed that his big breakthrough in researching Sabini's life came when he first met Sewell, 'Darby's lieutenant and right-hand man'. Known as 'the Cobblestone Fighter', he was the most feared of Sabini's warriors. Yet there is no evidence to suggest this was true, or that he was in Sabini's inner circle like Harry Sabini, Joe Sabini, Alf White, George Langham, Alfie Solomon and Jim Ford. Moreover, Sewell was not included as one of the British subjects associated with Italian gangsters compiled in 1940 by the Metropolitan Police.

The seeds of Hart's biography had been sown, though, not with Sewell but in a conversation with Jack Capstick, Scotland Yard's legendary commander known as 'Charlie Artful'. In the summer of 1956 he told Hart that 'compared to Darby Sabini, all the other British gang leaders down the years have been merely messenger boys'. He had it all: charisma, strength and intelligence. Though he could barely read or write, 'he possessed a tactical genius such as few army commanders will ever know'. Setting up to protect his people in Little Italy, he created a criminal empire 'the like of which Britain had never seen before . . . or will most likely see again'.[720] Capstick has rightfully been acclaimed as one of Scotland Yard's greatest detectives by writer Dick Kirby, a noted detective and an expert on the history of the Flying Squad. However, Capstick did not join the Metropolitan Police until 1925, becoming a detective three years later and joining the Flying Squad in the summer of

1929.[721] This was three years after Darby Sabini had left London for Brighton, meaning that Capstick's first-hand knowledge of Sabini must have been limited.

THE FINAL CHAPTER

Sabini's later life was nowhere near as startling as the Sabini Myth. After arriving in Brighton in 1926, he soon made his family home in Old Shoreham Road, Hove, a three-storey terraced house now divided into flats.[722] He did not remain for many years in a hovel in Little Italy with a holiday home in Brighton's Grand Hotel, as Hart claimed.[723] Although seeking to make his family respectable, Sabini's transition from gangster was unsure, and in 1928 he was discharged from assaulting three men in Brighton after two of them declined to say that he was the culprit.[724] A year later, after a dispute at Hove greyhound racing stadium, he was named as Darby Sabini when he twice assaulted a bookie, knocking him unconscious the second time. As usual there was a lack of witnesses, because, as the victim complained, 'It is impossible to try to get them. How can I get witnesses against a man like this, when everyone goes in fear of their life of him.' Sabini was fined only £5.[725] Then in 1931, and now in the name of Fred Handley, he and his old gang member, James Ford, were each sentenced to a month's hard labour for drunkenness. Returning from racing in a hired car, they had punched the driver and caused trouble in the police station after they were arrested. On appeal, the sentence was reduced to a 40-shilling fine.[726] This was Sabini's last conviction before the Second World War.

By the late 1930s, Sabini was bookmaking at Hove dog track

under the name of Dan Cope, working on commission with Emanuel's firm, the Portsea Press, and selling racings lists for the Bookmakers' Association – although he did not travel outside his patch in the South East. He also controlled services to the bookies. 'Mad' Frank Fraser became one of post-war Britain's legendary villains and, in his memoirs, he recalled that for three years from when he was about nine in 1932, he was a bucket boy for Darby, or 'Darbo' as called by his real friends. Fraser's task was to go round with a bucket of water and sponge so that bookies could wipe off the chalked-up odds of the horses after each race. They would pay Sabini and, depending on how things had gone, the youngster would receive 2s 6d or 7s 6d a day.

> 'Darbo' would tap me on the head and say, 'Take that home to your Mum', and I'd say, 'Thank you, Darbo'. He took a chuckle from it because he knew I was copying what I had heard; saucy little kid, but with the right style. 'Darbo' didn't have a menacing sort of style, just a nice man, but he didn't look a mug either. To me, even then, I could tell he was something special.[727]

Sabini had other sources of income. In the South East, he sold the pitches on the outside (unenclosed) parts of meetings like Epsom, which were not covered by the bookmakers' pitch committees and where the public gathered for free. He and his lifelong friend George Langham did the same at point-to-points – meetings where amateur riders raced hunting horses over the land of farmers. Unsupervised by the inspectors of the Jockey Club and National Hunt, they still gave opportunities for the blackmailing of bookies by small gangs of thugs. These were kept away by Sabini and Langham, who ensured that everything was 'all kept under control and that there was no fracas or trouble'.

Formerly a feared fair fighter and right-hand man to Sabini in their gang days, Langham had also moved into legitimacy. His son, Dave, became a respected bookmaker and he emphasised that by the time he and his siblings hit their teens in the 1930s, all the fighting had died out and, 'As far as I was concerned the Old Man was always a gentleman. He always dressed well. My Dad always had his own house. As a kid I always did very, very well. We were always looked after. I had plenty of food and he tried to see that we had a first-class education. We wasn't allowed to swear indoors at all.' Dave Langham revealed that his father also made money from controlling the runners who called the numbers of the horses on the racecourses around London. At these meetings and at White City and Haringey dog tracks, he shared the selling of the dots and dashes cards with Sabini. In the late 1930s, this led to problems with Harry Sabini.

> My Old Man never used a tool. He always used his fists, except for one time. The Old Man had a row with Harryboy. But it was over the dots and dashes. They wanted them from the Old Man and they wanted to get him out and he said no. They were shooting at each other with guns. They came with numbers so he had to [use a gun] because they were all fitted up. I think they expected it 'cus they knew it weren't going to be a give in. He was frightened of no-one, whichever way you wanted it he'd uses his fists except that one occasion. I know the Old Man got a cab and they shot at him. So it finished up, 'cus the Old Man at the time was getting

old, it finished up he was on a pension, so there was
wages every week. I can remember that 'cus I used to go
to their house [Harry Sabini's] every Sunday to get the
money. It was in an envelope.

This fall out with Harryboy did not spoil Langham's friendship
with Darby Sabini and 'the Old Man used to go religiously
every Sunday down to Brighton to visit him till he died. That's
how thick they were.'[728]

Sabini's more peaceful life in Brighton and Hove was a stark
contrast to his life in London, and in 1940 the local police
stressed that over the previous twelve years he had caused them
very little trouble. In fact, the well-informed CID confidently
stated that 'the Sabini gang could rightly be said to be non-
existent'.[729] Yet, in July that year, Darby Sabini was arrested and
interned at Ascot Prisoner of War Camp. MI5 had suggested that
if Italy were to join the Second World War then 'Italian consuls
and leaders of the Fascio will employ Italians of the gangsters
or racketeer type for certain acts of violence'. In response, the
CID in London compiled a list of such men, including British
subjects of Italian origin. Sabini was one of them. Reported
as having Italian sympathies and as a 'violent and dangerous
criminal of the gangster type', he was thought liable to lead
internal insurrections. His internment was strongly supported
by the London Police, though its officers had not had dealings
with him for several years. The Assistant Commissioner even
admitted that there had never been any intimation that Sabini
was politically minded. The only justification for his detention
was that he was a thorough rascal and an expert in racecourse
gang terrorism who had never done an honest day's work.
Nevertheless, it was asserted that if anybody wanted to employ

persons prepared to engineer acts of violence he could not make a better choice than Sabini – and the same went for his brother, Harry.

For all Sabini's previous criminality, this was preposterous. In appealing against his detention, he stressed that he was as fit as a fiddle and would 'protect my country and our home any time. I will have a go.' England was the only country for him and he had collected enormous sums of money for various hospitals. The Advisory Committee to the Home Office on Italian internees itself acknowledged that there had never been a very strong case against Sabini, other than that 'he was a low type person of Italian origin and an unscrupulous 'tough' who might do anything for money'. Consequently, he was released in 1941.[730] Afterwards, and perhaps because he had lost all his sources of income, he was tempted back into crime, and in June 1943 he and another man were sentenced to two years' hard labour for receiving stolen goods valued at £383.[731] It was not the kind of sum that might have been associated with a major gangster.

Soon after he was imprisoned, on 16 August, his only son, Flight Sergeant Harry Sabini, died of his wounds from a flying accident whilst serving with the RAF in Egypt. The loss of his son, of whom he was so proud, must have been a devastating blow. Later described as a dealer, Darby Sabini also continued bookmaking in and around Brighton. He died in 1950 after a debilitating illness, penniless according to some, whilst a story went around that his clerk was stopped leaving the country with £30,000.[732] There is no evidence of this though, and although Sabini left no will, he was not penniless. His wife survived him, living in the house in Hove that had been bought in her name until she died in 1978, leaving £16,730.[733]

Joe Sabini had moved away from gangsterism alongside his

older brother. After his release from prison in 1925, he carried on as a racing man, but as the police made clear, there was no indication that he rejoined the Sabini Gang even behind the scenes. He became a bookmaker at Haringey Greyhound Stadium, under the name of Harry Lake, and in 1939, was recorded a professional gambler. Like Darby, he married an Englishwoman, and by the outbreak of the Second World War, they were living in a large, three-bedroomed terraced house with a good-sized back garden in The Drive, Wood Green. They were still there when Joe Sabini died in 1969, leaving £6,000. His wife died five years later and left £14,500.[734] Joe Sabini's bookmaking and betting obviously paid, as these were large sums of money.

The youngest Sabini brother, Harry, made much more – both legally and illegally. By 1931, he and his English wife from Hoxton, the bastion of the Titanics, were living in Hamilton Park West.[735] Tinged with jealously, Inspector Greeno wrote that it was 'palatially decorated', and it was a most impressive detached Georgian house in Highbury, now worth between £2 and £3 million.[736] Nine years later, the house was paid for and Sabini owned other freehold property worth £12,000 and had savings of £1,500 in War Bonds. A further £3,600 was invested for his three children, and £3,000 was in his wife's name. He was a very wealthy man, much more so than his brother Darby who had no investments and a house mortgaged in his wife's name. There is some evidence to suggest that Harry Sabini made some of his money criminally, in particular from extorting protection money from nightclub owners. In 1935, four of his associates caused trouble in the Majestic Social Club. They smashed up windows and furnishings, and panic-stricken members 'flew for their lives'. As they did so, Thomas Mack, one of the original members of the Sabini Gang, shouted at the club owner, 'You ruined Harry Boy and we are going to ruin you. We warned you a few months ago. As you haven't carried out our warning we have come to enforce it.'[737] There were also suggestions that Harry Sabini was implicated in the theft of £21,000 of bullion from the Croydon airport strong room in 1935.[738]

Whatever his involvement or otherwise, he also earned substantial sums legally. From 1921 until 1932, he was employed by the bookmakers Beresford and Smith, afterwards becoming a professional backer of horses and a commission agent putting on bets for others. Walter Beresford died in 1931, and in all probability some of his customers were picked up by Sabini as he soon operated on a big scale, with upper-class customers like Lord Thomas Grave and thousands of pounds going through his accounts.

Harry Sabini was also arrested and interned in 1940, although it quickly became obvious that he had no trace of hostile intentions and that there were no grounds for his detention. In spite of this, he was swiftly charged with perjury, as in his appeal against his detention he'd denied that he'd been known as Harry Handley. Flimsy evidence was found to refute this, and in July 1941 he was sentenced to nine months' imprisonment.[739] When racing resumed at the end of the war, Harry Sabini started up again as a commission agent, putting on bets for other people. On one occasion, he was driven to Newmarket by Bert 'Battles' Rossi, for whom it was a special day.

> On the way, he takes out these yellow telegrams, opens them up and starts making notes. You learn as you go along. Now, he was a commission agent and had the trust of the trainers to get their bets down. And of

course he gets paid, and he also knows for himself what horse is trying and which isn't.

When we get there and I've got parked Harryboy goes into the Members [enclosure] and talks to one or two people about the horses. This impressed me no end.

One of those he spoke with was either the Earl of Roseberry or Lord Derby, who passed on the information to bet on a certain horse owned by the King because it was trying. Rossi backed it and it won: 'I thought it was marvellous; a different world from a slum in Clerkenwell'. After that, he often took Harryboy and Joe Sabini racing.[740] In 1978, and a few months before Darby's widow, Harry Sabini died. He was still living in Hamilton Park and he left £31,000.[741]

The list of gangster-type criminals compiled in 1940 for MI5 included British subjects who were associated with Italian gangsters. Amongst them was Jim Ford, one of the inner circle of the Sabini Gang, who was now living in Brighton. Imprisoned in 1929 after assaulting a bookmaker, he was fined two years later for assault, but since then had seemingly followed Darby Sabini and Georgie Langham away from gangsterism.[742] Edward Emanuel, alias Edward Smith, was also listed, in his case as the 'financier of the Sabini gang and other bullies'. As with Ford and Darby Sabini, the evidence for his inclusion was outdated. Emanuel had financed the Sabinis in the early 1920s, but for over a decade he had been a respectable and wealthy businessman. By 1930, he, his wife and their two daughters were living in a large house in Finchley Road, Golders Green – a district that was attracting middle-class Jewish families. He died in 1943, followed by his wife seven years later. She left £22,656.[743]

The leaders of the Birmingham Gang were nowhere near as successful as some of the Sabinis. Andrew Towey carried on selling his dots and dashes cards in the Midlands and the North until the 1940s but there is no trace of a will; and Cunny Cunnington continued to live in a jerry-built back-to-back in Ladywood.[744] As for Ike Kimberley, a quick-walking man fond of drink and the company of prostitutes, it was too late for him to be anything other than an incorrigible rogue, as he was branded in 1929 when imprisoned for loitering. Purportedly a tic-tac on dog tracks, he was living in Paddington in London. Five years later, he was even arrested trying to pick pockets at an unruly fascist meeting in Brighton. After his release, he was imprisoned twice in 1935, and within days of the outbreak of war, he was sentenced to three months' hard labour for loitering. Now ostensibly a painter, he was living in Notting Hill.[745] Kimberley's older brother, Mo, remained in Birmingham. In 1926, he was condemned as 'a parasite on society' when imprisoned for theft in Hereford. Within weeks of his release, he was convicted in Liverpool and went on to be arrested for frequenting at Uttoxeter races in 1932, when he said he was a bookmaker's clerk.[746] Nothing more is known of either Ike or Mo Kimberley.

The charabanc trip for the Epsom Road Battle had been organised by Edward 'Ted' Banks. He was a persistent criminal, but on a bigger scale to the Kimberleys. He was named as an organiser of crime and a former financer of criminals when he was finally brought to book in 1934 for a well-planned scheme to receive a large delivery of stolen bacon at his shop in Digbeth. Sentenced to four months' hard labour, as he descended the steps of the dock, women shouted 'Good-Bye, Ted. Good luck'.[747] After his release, he returned to his real name of Edward

Pankhurst and, in 1939, he, his wife and two sons were living on Belgrave Road, Balsall Heath. Recorded as a master grocer, his home fronted the street, which was higher status than a back house up a yard. He died in 1950.[748]

Billy Kimber was the only one of the Birmingham Gang for whom crime paid. It paid for his transformation from backstreet pickpocket to a respectable bookmaker living in a fine house on the English Riviera. That remarkable change did not benefit his first wife, Maude, and their two daughters, Maude and Annie, whom he abandoned when they were eight and six. His great-granddaughter, Juliet Banyard, believed that he must have stayed in touch with Annie as she was his favourite, 'but he was not much bothered with Maudie and she didn't care for him either. Maudie used to say, "You owed our dad money, you paid with your life".[749] They were chilling but prophetic words. By 1921, Kimber was making big sums from his criminality, but Maude and her daughters were struggling to get by in a back-to-back in Hockley.[750] Battling against poverty must have worn her out, and in 1926 she died aged just forty-three. Maude was buried in a pauper's grave.[751] A communal burial place with nothing above it to mark the lives of those within, it was the ultimate indignity for a poor person.

Kimber knew that she had died, for he stated he was a widower when, within days, he married Eliza Garnham, a sister of his friend and ally, John Garnham of the Chapel Market Gang.[752] Following the truce with the Sabinis, Andrew Towey returned to operating his 'services' within the Midlands and North but Kimber remained in London, though more inconspicuously than in the past. He took no part in Sage's Camden Town Gang and from at least 1923 he was living in Warren Street, Islington in the Garnham family home.[753] From that base, Kimber worked point-to-point meetings. With little supervision, they gave racing rogues plenty of scope, and in March 1925, he was at one in North Devon. A welching bookie was surrounded by a hostile crowd, but as he was about to be taken away by a policeman, another bookmaker called Kimber said, 'I will offer a hundred pounds to a shilling that he is not the man.' Immediately the welcher was surrounded by bookmakers' bullies, protecting him from the angry crowd.[754]

From the intriguing family stories passed on to him, Brian McDonald believed that Kimber also had interests in West End clubs. If he did, these ended in about 1927, when he and Bert McDonald shot through the windows of the Griffin, a pub in Clerkenwell favoured by the Sabini Gang. The two men escaped from the police by going to America, where Kimber may have killed a man in Arizona who did not pay him the money owed for a favour. After moving on to Los Angeles to meet up with Wag McDonald, who had been there since fleeing after the Epsom Road Battle, Kimber was said to have gone to Chicago. Brian McDonald was told that he was hidden by Murray Humphreys, who was prominent in Al Capone's notorious gang, before returning to England in 1929.[755] Kimber's Birmingham daughters also knew that he had to leave for America, and he did disappear from London in this timeframe. After 1927 he was no longer on the electoral register at Warren Street, but by 1930 he had reappeared on the managerial staff at Wimbledon Greyhound Course.[756] Dog racing was a highly popular new sport, but Kimber also continued to work point-to-points in the South West of England. They were now better run and, in 1938, he placed several advertisements in local newspapers. These publicised a Yeovil telephone number with the slogan, 'Bet with a reliable man – Bill Kimber'. But Kimber himself no longer needed to attend meetings and was operating through representatives.[757] Making plenty of money, he was spending it.

In 1932, he bought the freehold of a house called Beltinge in East End Road, East Finchley, moving there from a flat above a shop in Upper Street, Islington.[758] As with Sabini's move to Brighton, it symbolised a social and cultural shift away from old associates and their neighbourhoods. Kimber was propelling his family, especially his two daughters from his second marriage, into an affluent middle-class lifestyle. Born in 1920 and 1923, they had very different lives to their half-sisters in working-class Birmingham, benefiting from luxuries such as expensive cruises. A photograph sent to Eliza Kimber's relations in Islington showed her and her two daughters dressed smartly in summer clothes standing in front of a garden and an elegant building with a balustrade balcony and shuttered windows. Written across the bottom were the words, 'Boxing Day 1934 Madeira'. Four years later, the Kimbers returned to Southampton on the *Arundel Star* after a lengthy trip to South Africa that took in Durban, East London, Port Elizabeth, Cape Town and Madeira. The passenger list recorded Billy Kimber as a commission agent still living in East Finchley.[759]

During this time, he sent his daughter Annie in Birmingham 'a very expensive dressing table set, but they had to sell it as they were so poor . . . She also had a picture of him on the deck of a ship with a woman.' Annie also knew that Kimber had moved to Torquay on the English Riviera, which he did by 1939.[760] Ironically, he became president of the Devon and Cornwall Bookmakers' Association – ironically as it was the founding of the 'Bookmakers' and 'Backers' Racecourse Protection Association in London in late 1921 that had sounded the death knell for his rackets on southern England's racecourses.[761] But Kimber's new life was highlighted in 1941 when his eldest daughter, an officer in the Women's Auxiliary Air Force, married a flight-lieutenant from the RAF.[762] Four years later, Billy Kimber died after a prolonged illness. His obituary in the local newspaper affirmed that 'his great interest in life, both personal and professional, was racing and he was well known and respected on every racecourse in England'. His funeral was attended by many, but few would have known of his upbringing and past – few except for his brother Joe, part of Kimber's original pickpocketing gang.[763] Having spent large sums on the good life, Kimber still died a prosperous man, leaving his widow the large sum of £3,665.[764] Though a far cry from his youth fighting and thieving in the back streets of Birmingham, Kimber died one of the last of the peaky blinders.

AFTERWORD

Alfie Solomon's life was changed irretrievably when he was beaten up by Thomas Armstrong in 1921. Once of good character, he was transformed into one of the most dangerous men in the race gangs. A razor merchant as ready to use a shooter as a knife, he returned to violent ways following his release in 1927 for the manslaughter of Barney Blitz.[765] With Darby Sabini having left London and Alf White taking over the remnants of the Sabini Gang, Solomon formed his own 'gang of thieves' blackmailing bookies, which included Jackie Burman, originally one of Emanuel's tearaways. Although extortion was less profitable, and would soon be limited to the open parts of racecourses and some dog tracks, it also attracted Dodger Mullins when he came out of prison and restarted his Bethnal Green mob. The two gangs feuded but Mullins was soon back inside, sentenced in 1931 to six years for demanding money with menaces. A notorious terror who hated the Sabinis and their associates, he was released in December 1935 and reignited the vendetta with Solomon's gang. In early 1936, led by a gangster known as 'Conky', they slashed Mullins badly across his face and back. Vengeful, he teamed up with the Hoxton Gang led by Jimmy Spinks and the Elephant Boys under Wag McDonald.

In June, they all set off to Lewes to 'to wipe out the Jewish toughs', arriving with hatchets, knuckledusters, truncheons, hammers and chisels. When they saw Solomon, Spinks shouted, 'There they are, boys, get your tools ready.' Flourishing a hatchet above his head, he led the charge at Solomon, who was struck with several blows and wounded on his head but still managed to run away. His clerk was not so fortunate and was beaten savagely. Having been alerted to trouble by anonymous sources, the police were prepared and swiftly stopped the violence. Mullins and McDonald escaped, but heavy sentences were passed on the sixteen men who had been arrested and found guilty. It has been presumed by most writers that the attack was aimed at the Sabini Gang.[766] It was not, as there was no longer such a gang and amongst those arrested was Thomas Mack, who had been a prominent member of the Sabinis. The attack was clearly against Solomon and his men, as emphasised by the arrest of Albert Blitz, supposedly a relation of Barney Blitz who was killed by Solomon.[767] This was the last reference to Solomon, one of the most violent gangsters of the 1920s.

The misnamed 'Battle of Lewes' gave Graham Greene the idea for his first masterpiece, *Brighton Rock*.[768] Starting out as a thriller, as Norman Sherry remarked, the strangest aspect of the novel was 'the development of the religious theme, which changed it from a story about gang warfare into a struggle between good and evil'.[769] Yet it's the 'gangster' aspect of the novel that gained popular attention. Greene avidly read the newspaper reports of the Lewes affray and soon after, invited his brother to join him at Brighton races.[770] A frequent visitor to the town, he later wrote that 'I once spent an evening with a member of a gang who introduced me to a certain amount of slang in use and took me to one of the meeting places of his fellow gangsters'.[771] Though from an upper middle-class background, Greene's research brought a reality to the novel with its blackmailed bookies, their fear of a carving, the Bank Holiday racing scene, the lines of bookmakers, the changing of the odds, the half-crown enclosure, the race-gang attack, and the razor slashing of Pinkie, the main character. Though but a teenager, he heads his own mob. A murderer who is merciless towards his enemies, he falls foul of Colleone, a major gang leader. Small and with a neat round belly, he wears a grey double-breasted suit, whilst his hair is thin and grey and his eyes gleam like raisins. And his base is the grand Cosmopolitan Hotel.[772] Was Pinkie named after Jimmy Spinks, who was known as Spinkey by his pals?[773] And was Colleone based on Darby Sabini, for Greene did acknowledge that, 'My novel *Brighton Rock*, it is true, deals a little with something similar to the Sabini Gang'.[774]

Whether or not Sabini was the inspiration for Colleone, it was the Sabini Gang rather than its rivals that linked most strongly with London's organised gangs after the Second World War. Yet when Darby Sabini moved to Brighton and Hove in 1926 and began his move away from criminality in the capital, the Sabini Gang could have disintegrated like the Camden Town Gang and Birmingham Gang. It did not do so because he had formed a well-organised band of loyal gangsters, and those who were not 'legitimised' by the bookmakers looked for leadership to one of Sabini's tight inner circle. Following his release from prison, Joe Sabini was not interested, whilst although Harry Sabini continued to have some connections with the gang, he was mostly focused on his legal earnings as a commission agent. Of the other potential leaders, George Langham was also shifting away from gangsterism, Jim Ford followed Sabini to the south coast, and Alfie Solomon was in prison. This left only one of Sabini's original lieutenants – Alf White. It is likely that he had begun to take over operations in the capital as early as 1925, when Sabini was embroiled in the libel case with D. C. Thomson, and it is noteworthy that White was the Sabini Gang leader that year who was beaten up by Benneworth and Mullins and their mob.

There were no Sabini brothers in the Sabini Gang led by White, and whilst it wasn't as big and powerful as it had been, it remained a feared force. This successor gang included Thomas Mack, who had been with Darby Sabini from the start, as well as younger Anglo-Italians. No longer operating racecourse rackets, White and his 'confederates' deliberately used violence to 'impress' publicans and illegal street bookmakers 'with a view to intimidating them and subsequently to extort money'.[775] He was a dangerous man himself and, in 1927, aged forty and still also running his floristry business, White was charged with a brutal attack on two policemen, one of whom was lucky not to lose his sight. White was imprisoned for merely three months.[776] Seven years later, he and his sons were damned as 'the most notorious hooligans in North London' against whom no one would come forward and testify.[777]

Those accusations were proven in April 1935, when the Whites were at a charity dance and attacked a man they didn't know, 'without apparent rhyme or reason, striking him on the face and body with fists, kicks, tables and chairs'. The assault was so extremely violent that the victim lost the sight of his left eye. White and two of his sons were arrested, but the injured man's wife was the only witness to come forward on his behalf, whilst the Whites summoned twelve people to say that they had not been involved. The jury didn't believe them and the Whites were each sentenced to twelve months' imprisonment. During the proceedings, forty of their 'confederates attended either at or in the vicinity of the courts', and after the conviction, the prosecuting counsel received a threatening letter and sought police protection. In a police report of the case, White was described as 'one of the leading lights of the Sabini Gang', but although the name lingered on, it was now clearly White's gang.[778] Later known as the King's Cross Mob, its leadership was passed on to one of his sons, Harry. He controlled the protection rackets in the West End, and following Darby Sabini's internment in 1940, Harry White took over the running of the bookmakers' pitches on the free parts of meetings like Epsom and Brighton and also of the point-to-points. These racecourse interests were forcibly taken over by Jack Spot (Jacob Cromer) early in 1947, and as James Morton indicated, soon afterwards the Whites were finally routed by an alliance of Spot and Billy Hill, who would quickly become enemies.[779]

The power exhibited by the Whites until their fall was matched by other noteworthy figures in London's post-war gangland – men who had once been considered part of the ranks of the old gangs. One such prominent personality was Bert Marsh, who had been in the Sabini Gang. Born in 1901, his real name was Pasqualino Papa. A hairdresser from Clerkenwell and later an illegal off-course bookie, he had been a very good boxer. One of London's foremost bantamweights, he had been picked out as amongst those youngsters who would go to the top of the tree if only he had plenty of practice.[780] He was trained for a time by Darby Sabini, who recalled that Marsh 'did not turn out as good as we thought'.[781] Wonderfully game though he was, unfortunately he possessed 'the common fault amongst many of our boxers – a deep dislike of any form of strenuous training, which has hitherto kept him from earning titular honours'. Marsh did not mend his ways and, in 1925, he stopped boxing soon after he was imprisoned with others in the Sabini Gang for the beating of two bookies at Wye races.[782]

Having convictions for unlawful wounding and common assault, in 1936 he was found guilty of the manslaughter of a childhood friend, Massimino Monte-Colombo. It is no wonder that he was regarded by the police as 'a most violent and dangerous individual and leader of bullies who frequent racecourses and clubs'. Marsh was interned with Darby and Harry Sabini in 1940.[783] Morton, an expert on London's gangs after the Second World War, revealed that after his release, Marsh became a major figure in Soho and supporter of gambler and high-profile gangster, Albert Dimes. Once Jack Spot had been pushed out and Billy Hill had all but retired, Dimes was regarded as the 'King of the Point-to-Points' and 'the almost unseen Godfather' in the late 1950s.[784] It is clear that the Sabini name still had a magnetism, and as late as 1955, five years after Darby Sabini had died and almost thirty since he had moved away from his gang, Dimes was identified as the leader of the Sabini Gang.[785]

Although there was no longer such a thing as the Sabini Gang itself, the name continued to resonate in post-war Britain. But what of the peaky blinders and the fearsome Birmingham Gang that was formed by some of the most vicious amongst them? Contrastingly, its name was not even a faint echo. Lacking the overall leadership of Kimber after the truce with the Sabinis, the Birmingham Gang fell apart. With no nightclubs or any other opportunities for protection rackets in strongly-policed Birmingham, it disappeared so quickly and completely that it didn't pass into Brummie folklore let alone gangland mythology. Yet it had been the first major gang in England to operate on a national scale, and after it took over the rackets on the southern racecourses in 1920, it had seemed in an unassailable position of power. Such power, though, was illusory because of the very nature of the Birmingham Gang. It never became a fully organised combination of criminals, but instead remained a rampaging, ramshackle jumble of disparate groups of ruffians. Dangerous and frightening they may have been, but apart from Kimber they were petty-minded villains who carried on acting as peaky blinders, relishing fighting and violence above all else. What they extorted and stole, the majority of them 'blew' on drink and good times. Feckless, thoughtless and unruly as they were, they were incapable of creating a disciplined force to consolidate their hold in the South, as was shown by their racist persecution of Jewish bookmakers.

It was that hatred that provoked a fierce backlash, instigating the rise of the Sabini Gang and the most vicious gang rivalry Britain had ever seen. This disturbing development alarmed not only journalists but also police chiefs and even the Home Secretary. Rightly abhorred for their brutality and blackmailing, these British gangsters did however become a distinctive though unfortunate feature of the Roaring Twenties. Would that have happened without the peaky blinders? Perhaps it might have, but as it was the legacy of the peaky blinders was the Birmingham Gang and Britain's most notorious 1920s gangs.

ACKNOWLEDGEMENTS

I had heard of the race gangs growing up, but I first learned about them in detail in 1987 when I was researching a social history of illegal betting and bookmaking, which was prompted by my background. My granddad, Richard Chinn, had started up as an illegal back-street bookie in Sparkbrook, Birmingham in 1922, and my dad, Alfred 'Buck' Chinn, then oversaw the move into betting shops after cash betting away from the racecourse was legalised in 1961. I was born five years before, and I worked part-time in the business from the age of thirteen, throughout most of my secondary schooling and university education, taking over its running between 1978 and 1984, when we sold up. For several years afterwards, Dad remained a leading figure in the local Bookmakers' Protection Association and, through his contacts, I was fortunate to meet men who taught me about racecourse bookmaking and its history, something with which my family had not been involved. Their contribution to my book was much valued.

A few of those bookies from London gave me first-hand

information about Billy Kimber and the Birmingham Gang and Darby Sabini and the Sabini Gang, all of whom have been dramatised in the television series, *Peaky Blinders*. These bookmakers included Dave Langham, the son of Darby Sabini's best friend and right-hand man George Langham; Simmy Solomon, the younger brother of Alfie Solomon; Lou Prince, who was present when the Birmingham Gang went on the rampage at Alexandra Park races in 1921; Charles Maskey, who grew up in Hoxton, the stronghold of the Titanics; Alan Smith, a well-informed London bookie; and Sam Dell, who had a deep knowledge of racecourse bookmaking in the 1920s. I am grateful to them as I am to Joe Martin, Jim Cooper, Horace Bottrell, Mr Gilliver, Hilda Burnett and Steve Nicholls, who provided me with information from a Birmingham perspective. I also appreciate the memories of the Sheffield Gang War shared with me by Frank Harris especially.

My book on illegal betting was published in 1992, and although it had a section on the Racecourse War of 1921, there was much that I was unable to include. That material has been brought into this book, along with years of research since then. I am grateful, therefore, to John Blake Publishing for giving me the opportunity to write extensively on the gangs of the 1920s, and I appreciate the input of the whole team involved in bringing out *Peaky Blinders – The Legacy*. In particular, however, I wish to thank Ciara Lloyd, Editorial Director, for her belief in my work and enthusiastic support, and Ellie Carr, editor, for her thoughtful, informed and careful editing. My family has played the most important role in my approach to history and I thank my late mom and dad, Sylvie and Buck, my grandparents, Lil Perry, Arthur Perry and Richard Chinn, and my great-aunt Win Martin and great-uncle George Wood for inspiring me

ACKNOWLEDGEMENTS

through telling their stories of working-class life in Sparkbrook and Aston. For giving me the confidence to uphold the value of such stories, I pay tribute to Dorothy Thompson, an influential and pioneering historian who supervised my doctoral thesis. Finally, I thank my wife, Kay, whose stories of growing up in Finglas West, Dublin, keep me grounded and without whose backing I could never have become a historian.

SELECT FURTHER READING

The detailed Endnotes list many books and articles for further reading. This list highlights those that are most pertinent to reading on the peaky blinders, Sabini Gang and Sheffield Gang War.

J. P. Bean, *The Sheffield Gang Wars* (Sheffield, 1981).

Carl Chinn, *Peaky Blinders. The Real Story. The true history of Birmingham's most notorious gangs* (London, 2019).

Brian McDonald, *Elephant Boys. Tales of London and Los Angeles Underworlds* (Edinburgh and London, 2005).

Brian McDonald, *Gangs of London. 100 Years of Mob Warfare* (Wrea Green, 2010).

James Morton, *Bert Battles Rossi. Britain's Oldest Gangland Boss* (London, 2017).

James Morton, Frankie Fraser as told to James Morton, *Mad Frankie. Memoirs of a Life of Crime* (London, 1995 ed.).

James Morton, *Gangland. London's Underworld* (London, 1993 edn.).

Raphael Samuel, *East End Underworld. Chapters in the Life of Arthur Harding* (London, 1981).

Heather Shore, *London's Criminal Underworlds, c. 1720 – c. 1930. A Social and Cultural History* (London, 2015).

ABBREVIATIONS

BCWG Bath Chronicle and Weekly Gazette

BDG Birmingham Daily Gazette

BDP Birmingham Daily Post

BLA BirminghamLives Archive MS 1902, Archives and
Collections, Library of Birmingham

BM Birmingham Mail

CCBA Carl Chinn Bookmaking Archive, US39, Cadbury
Research Library, University of Birmingham

CID Criminal Investigation Department

DC Dundee Courier

DET Dundee Evening Telegraph

DH Daily Herald

DM Daily Mail

DMH Hull Daily Mail

DTC Daily Telegraph & Courier [London]

ED Evening Despatch [Birmingham]

EN	Empire News
GRO	General Register Office
IPN	Illustrated Police News
LM	Leeds Mercury
LMA	London Metropolitan Archives
MG	Manchester Guardian
NEP	Nottingham Evening Post
PG	Police Gazette
PMG	Pall Mall Gazette
SDT	Sheffield Daily Telegraph
SI	Sheffield Independent
SL	Sporting Life
SP	Sunday Post [Glasgow]
TBL	The British Library
TEN	The Evening News [London]
TG	The Guardian
TNA	The National Archives
TP	The People
TS	The Scotsman
TT	The Times
WG	Westminster Gazette
WSG	West Sussex Gazette
YPLI	Yorkshire Post and Leeds Intelligencer

SOURCES

The research for this book is based overwhelmingly on primary evidence. Unless otherwise stated in the Endnotes, information has been gleaned from the following sources:

Newspapers
'Men in Custody', *Birmingham Daily Gazette* (4 June 1921)
'Persons Wanted in Custody', *The Police Gazette* (8 June 1921)

The National Archives
CRIM: Records of the Central Criminal Court
HO: Home Office
MEPO: London Metropolitan Police
WO: War Office
PCOM: Home Office and Prison Commission

Census Records 1871, 1881, 1891, 1901 & 1911 & 1939
Register.

CRIM 1/209: Defendant: Cortesi, Augustus Cortesi, George
Cortesi, Paul Cortesi, Enrico Tomaso, Alexander. Charge:
Attempted murder.

HO 45/23691: WAR: Octavius Sabini, alias Darby Sabini, alias
Frederick Handley, notorious race-course gangster and
racketeer: internment.

HO 45/25720: WAR: Defence Regulation 18B detainees:
SABINI Harry.

HO140: Calendar of Prisoners.

HO 144/10430: BETTING AND GAMBLING: racecourse
ruffians: activities of the 'Sabini' gang.

MEPO 3/346: Affray at Ewell known as 'The Epsom Hold-
Up' on 2 June 1921 following race meeting. Twenty-eight
persons charged with causing grievous bodily harm to a
party of bookmakers.

MEPO 3/352: Race Gang Affray in Waterloo Road and
malicious damage: forfeiture of recognisances previously
entered into.

MEPO 3/366: Various members of a race gang charged at
different times with demanding money with menaces,
assault, and conspiring together.

MEPO 3/374: Alfred SOLOMON charged with wilful murder
of Barnet BLITZ and attempted murder of Michael
ABELSON on 201/MR/549 afterwards sentenced for
manslaughter, here seeks police protection from race gangs.

MEPO 3/444: Attempts to bribe two Maidstone Warders to
convey correspondence to Joseph SABINI.

MEPO 3/9190: Alfred and William White and others causing
grievous bodily harm to John McCarthy Defferary.

SOURCES

MEPO 3/1579: Five members of the 'Camden Town Gang' convicted of feloniously shooting at Detective Constable J. Rutherford with intent to kill at Gray's Inn Road on 28 July 1922.

MEPO 3/1581: Shooting Affray between the 'Italian or Sabini Gang' and the 'Birmingham Gang' at Mornington Crescent, Camden Town, on 19 August 1922.

MEPO 6: Criminal Record Office: Habitual Criminals Registers and Miscellaneous Papers.

PCOM 2: Prisons Records, Series 1.

PCOM 8/58 CAPITAL. FOWLER, Lawrence at Leeds on 13 July 1925.

PCOM 8/59 CAPITAL. FOWLER, Wilfred at Leeds on 13 July 1925.

WO 96: Militia Attestation Papers.

WO 329: Service Medal and Award Rolls, First World War.

WO 363: Soldiers' Documents, First World War 'Burnt Documents'.

WO 364, Soldiers' Documents from Pension Claims, First World War.

ENDNOTES

Introduction

1 A Victim, 'Letter to the Editor', *DTC* (20 August 1898).

2 'Our Note Book', *Sporting Times* (20 August 1898) & 'Racing Notes', *The Sketch* (21 September 1898).

3 C., Letter to the Editor, *DTC* (18 August 1898) & Noel Fairfax-Blakeborough (ed.) *'J.F.B.' The Memoirs of Jack-Fairfax-Blakeborough, OBE MC* (London, 1978) p.87.

4 'Roughs on the Turf', *DTC* (13 August 1898).

5 Cited in J. Fairfax-Blakeborough, 'The Ring in the Merry Past', *Banyan* (December 1948) & p.19 Ron Whytock, Southern Bookmakers' Protection Association, *History File* (n.d.) p.4.

6 'Scene at Hamilton', *DET* (10 September 1904).

7 J. Fairfax-Blakeborough, 'Secrets of the Old Tyneside Race Gang', *Sunday Sun* [Newcastle] (20 January 1935) & Fairfax-Blakeborough (ed.), p.87.

8 'Roughs on the Turf', *DTC* (13 August 1898).

9 Geoffrey Pearson, *Hooligan. A History of Respectable Fears* (London, 1983) p.74 & Heather Shore, *London's Criminal Underworlds c. 1720 – c. 1930. A Social and Cultural History* (London, 2015), pp.144–165.

Chapter One

10 'The Epsom Road Ambush', *TEN* (London) (4 June 1921).

11 'Twenty-Eight Men Charged at the Police Court', *TG* (4 June 1921).

12 'Story of the Epsom Ambush', *BDG* (4 June 1921).

13 'The Epsom Road Ambush', *TEN* (London) (4 June 1921).

14 'Identity of the Twenty-Eight', *BDG* (21 July 1921).

15 'The Epsom Road Ambush', *TEN* (4 June 1921).

16 'Denials of Epsom Prisoners', BDG (22 July 1921).

17 'Acts of Violence', *BDG* (29 December 1903).

18 'Sequel to the Nottingham Jewellery Robbery', *NEP* (22 April 1904).

19 'Charge of Housebreaking', *NEP* (16 June 1904).

20 'The End of the Peaky Blinders', *SI* (28 June 1923).

21 See Carl Chinn, *Peaky Blinders. The Real Story. The true history of Birmingham's most notorious gangs*, pp.173–189.

22 'The Dartmouth Street Vendetta', *BDG* (3 May 1909).

23 'A Birmingham Vendetta', *BDG* (26 August 1910).

24 'Edward Pankhurst', Midlands, England, Electoral Registers, 1832–1955 (Deritend 1922).

25 'Men of Means in Epsom Ambush', *BDG* (11 June 1921) & 'The Epsom Road "Battle"', *BDG* (27 June 1921).

26 Anonymous, *BLA*.

27 'Quarrel Over Football', *BDG* (6 April 1909).

28 'Birmingham Gambling Raid', *BDG* (10 May 1910).

29 After the Epsom Races', *WSG* (28 July 1921).

30 'Assaulting Jews', *BDP* (9 February 1892) & Chinn, pp.30–1.

31 Chinn, pp.223–4.

32 'A Judenhetze at Birmingham' *Bristol Mercury* (9 February 1892).

33 'Assaulting Jews', *BDP* (9 February 1892).

34 'Lady to a Policeman's Rescue', *Central Somerset Gazette* (4 September 1897).

35 MEPO 3/346, Birmingham Chief Constable's Office, Report (10 June 1921).

36 'Gaming at Gosforth Park', *Newcastle Daily Chronicle* (28 June 1919).

37 'Lichfield City Police', *Lichfield Mercury* (18 August 1905).

38 'After the Epsom Races', *WSG* (28 July 1921).

39 'An Expert Scamp', *Liverpool Echo* (28 May 1914).

40 'Racecourse Gang', *TS* (5 July 1926).

41 'Pocket-Picking in Newcastle', *Newcastle Evening Chronicle* (3 July 1919).

42 'Aston Police Court', *BM* (12 August & 27 March 1887).

43 'Assault' *BDP* (4 September 1894).

44 'An Alibi that Failed', *BDP* (10 October 1914).

45 'A Soldier's Return', *BM* (11 February 1918); and PWC.

46 Lesley & Robert Staight, Email (18 April 2015).

47 'Assaulting the Police', *BDP* (26 May 1893).

48 'Burglary at Yardley', *BDP* (11 December 1895).

49 'Drinks in the Tap Room', *BDG* (23 February 1907).

50 'Lincoln Racecourse Cases', *NEP* (22 March. 1911) & PWC.

51 'Street Tragedy', *BDG* (7 March & 14 March 1912).

52 'City Assizes', *BDG* (21 March 1912).

53 MEPO 3/346, Infantry Record Office, Letter (8 July 1921), Sergeant G. Rawle, Birmingham Police (6 July 1921).

54 'Result of a Holiday', *BM* (8 July 1901).

55 See Chinn, pp.173–189.

56 'Fierce Police Court Struggle', *BDG* (2 September 1903).

57 'Quarter Sessions', *BDG* (1 July 1908).

58 'After the Jewels', *Surrey Advertiser* (2 July 1917).

59 'After the Epsom Races', *WSG* (28 July 1921).

60 *Bedfordshire Mercury* (12 March 1909).

61 'Robbery with Violence', *BDG* (10 March 1909).

62 Andrew Davies, 'Histories of Hooliganism', in Dick Hobbs (ed.) *Mischief, Morality and Mobs: Essays in Honour of Geoffrey Pearson* (New York and London, 2017) p. 89.

63 'Other Trials', *BDG* (6 March 1914).

64 'Assaulting the Police', *BDP* (24 August 1916).

65 'Shopbreakers Sentenced', *BDP* (1 October 1918).

66 'Working the Queues', *BDG* (9 August 1919).

67 Mr and Mrs Gilliver, Interview, *BLA* (6 January 1989).

68 'Warwick Borough', *Leamington Spa Courier* (19 September 1919).

69 TNA WO 97, Royal Hospital Chelsea: Soldiers Service Documents, Box 6013, Record 85, Attestation Service Number 10601 (31 July 1907).

70 '"A Dangerous Thief"' Sentenced', *ED* (13 February 1914).

71 TNA WO 86: Judge Advocate General's Office: District Courts Martial Registers, Home and Abroad: Piece 071 (1916–1917) WO 86/71 (21 September 1916); 'Dangerous Thief' *ED* (13 February. 1914); 'Alleged Shopbreaking and Assault', *BM* (28 September 1917); & MEPO 3/346, Infantry Record Office, Letter (8 July 1921).

72 'Trading on Army Service', *BDG* (29 January 1920).

73 MEPO 3/346, Infantry Record Office, Letter (8 July 1921).

74 WO 364 – First World War Pension Claims, William O'Brien, Service Number 19769.

75 'Suspicious City Loiterers', *Manchester Evening News* (23 July 1918).

76 'Alleged Notorious Pickpockets at Blackpool' & 'Jostled Blackpool Crowd', *Lancashire Evening Post* (2 & 3 August 1918).

77 'Suspect Sentenced for Loitering', *BDP* (31 December 1918).

78 *The National Roll of the Great War, 1914–1918. Section VI, Birmingham* (London, 1920) p.419.

79 Western Front Association, WWI pension ledgers and index cards, 6 MV 1 498959 & WO329; Ref: 615.

80 MEPO 3/346, Chief Constable, Report (10 June 1921) & 'After the Epsom Races', *WSG* (28 July 1921).

81 Eric Rickman, *On and Off the Racecourse* (London, 1937) p.256.

Chapter Two

82 'Racing Rogues Held Off By Armed Man', *TEN* (London) (24 March 1921).

83 For a full discussion of Kimber's early life see Chinn, pp.191–208.

84 'Thomas Templar', *IPN* (20 February 1913).

85 Moss Deyong, 'Everybody Boo . . .' (London, 1951), p.53.

86 Thomas Dey, *Leaves from a Bookmaker's Book* (London, 1931) pp.208–10.

87 'Englishmen Charged in Dublin', *Dublin Daily Express* (11 May 1917).

88 Tommy Garnham, Interview (July 2013).

89 'A Charge of Stabbing', *IPN* (20 February 1913).

90 'Alleged Wounding', *East London Observer* (15 March 1913).

91 Brian McDonald, *Gangs of London. 100 Years of Mob Warfare* (Wrea Green, 2010) p.188.

92 Raphael Samuel, *East End Underworld. Chapters in the Life of Arthur Harding* (London, 1981) p.182.

93 Wray Vamplew, *A Social and Economic History of Horse Racing* (London, 1976), pp.62–7.

94 Chinn, pp.200–2.

95 Rickman, p.252.

96 'Easter Racing Features', *LM* (19 April 1919).

97 Rickman, pp.252–5.

98 Tom Divall, *Scoundrels and Scallywags (And Some Honest Men)* (London, 1929) p.208.

99 'Detectives v Crooks', *Sunderland Daily Echo and Shipping Gazette* (15 September 1919).

100 'Station Disturbance', *SDT* (8 October 1919).

101 'Racecourse Pests', *DM* (9 July 1920).

102 'Rogues of the Racecourse', *TT* (17 July 1920).

103 'Racecourse Roughs', *Ibid.* (23 August 1920).

104 McDonald, p.139.

105 'Racecourse Roughs', *IPN* (12 August 1920).

106 McDonald, pp.139–40.

107 Ali Harris, Interview, *CCBA*. (3 July 1987).

108 McDonald, p.152.

109 'Applauds His Sentence', *Globe* (15 June 1920).

110 'Blackmail Charge', *Glasgow Herald* (11 September 1922).

111 Sam Dell, Interview, *CCBA*. (1987).

112 HO 144/10430, CID, Report (1 December 1922).

113 'Sabini's Admissions in Bankruptcy Court', *DET* (29 June 1926).

114 Dell, Interview.

115 Dell, Interview.

116 Charlie Maskey, Interview, *CCBA* (18 April 1988).

117 Jim Cooper, Interview, *CCBA* (4 April 1988).

118 Simeon Solomon, Interview, *CCBA* (3 July 1987) & Dave Langham, Interview, *CCBA* (1987).

119 Dell, Interview & 'Bookmakers' Accessories', *SL* (17 January 1939); & Lou Prince, Interview,

CCBA (1987).

120 Garnham, Interview.

121 Prince, Interview.

122 Divall, p.199.

123 'Racecourse Bullies', *TT* (12 April 1921).

124 For a full discussion of Solomon's early life see Chinn, pp.208–11.

125 Deyong, p.55.

126 'Fatal Blow at the Races', *DH* (2 August 1921).

127 'Sandown Park Riot Sequel', *PMG* (3 August 1921).

128 'Racing Men's Feud', *BDG* (18 August 1921) & 'Racecourse Fight', *Derby Daily Telegraph* (10 September 1921).

129 'Pleaded Guilty', *BDG* (17 December 1889).

130 TNA WO 9602, Militia Service Records 1806–191, Box 94, Record Number 233 (2 February 1891).

131 'Racing Man's Death', *BDG* (3 August 1921).

132 Solomon, Interview.

133 Alan Harris, Interview.

134 Dell, Interview.

135 Prince, Interview.

136 Samuel, Interview.

137 Ralph L. Finn, *Grief Forgotten* (1st published 1968, 1985 edn. London) pp.23–5.

138 Dell, Interview.

139 'The Story of the Rival Gangs', *BDG* (4 June 1921).

140 Prince, Interview, & Divall, p.199.

141 Solomon, Interview.

142 HO 45/23691, Ottavio Sabini, Statement (3 December 1940).

143 See Chinn, pp.216–20.

144 For the Italians of Saffron Hill see David R. Green, 'Little Italy in Victorian London. Holborn's Italian Community', *Camden History Review*, vol.15 (1988) pp.2–6.

145 Shore, pp.186–7 and p.178.

146 McDonald, photograph p.2.

147 'Free Fights at a Trotting Match', *PMG* (24 March 1921).

148 'Racecourse Pests', *WG* (31 March 1921).

149 McDonald, p.156 & Samuel, pp.204–5.

150 'Blackmail Gangs on Racecourses', *PMG* (31 March 1921).

151 HO 144/10430, CID, Report (1 December 1922).

152 McDonald, pp.125, 139–40 & 158.

153 Edward T. Hart, *Britain's Godfather* (London, 1993), p.56.

154 Shore, p.11.

155 Hart, pp.56–60.

156 Edward Greeno, *War on the Underworld* (London, c. 1960), p.17.

157 'Hit First, Then Shot', *BDG* (20 April 1921).

158 'A Shadow and a Revolver', *WG* (19 April 1921).

159 'Shot after Orgy', *BDG* (6 April 1921).

160 'King's Cross Mystery', *Nottingham Journal* (29 March 1921).

161 'Hit First Then Shot', *BDG* (20 April 1921).

162 'A Gang of Terrors', *Nottingham Journal* (28 April 1921).

163 Garnham, Interview.

164 'Shot after Orgy', *BDG* (6 April 1921).

165 Greeno, p.18.

166 Deyong, p.54.

167 Prince, Interview.

168 'Racecourse Gangs', *DM* (5 July 1921) & Greeno, p.18.

169 'Racecourse Fracas', *DH* (5 April 1921).

170 'Racecourse Scenes', *WG* (4 July 1921) & 'Fracas at Races', *DH* (5 July 1921).

171 'Rival Race Gangs', *BDG* (5 July 1921).

172 Joe Martin, Interview, *BLA* (1987) p.23.

173 'Shooting on a Racecourse', *MG* (5 April 1921).

174 Martin, Interview.

175 'German Bomb Handed to Policeman', *DET* (21 April 1921) & 'Shooting Affray', *DH* (22 April 1921).

176 Greeno, p.18.

177 MEPO 3/346, Chief Constable, Report (10 June 1921).

Chapter Three

178 'Racecourses Infested with Ruffianly Gangs', *DET* (13 April 1921); Black Mail Gangs on Racecourses', *PMG* (31 March 1921); 'Racing Roughs Riot at Alexandra Park', *IPN* (7 April 1921); 'Race-Course Riot' & 'Ruffianism at the Races', *TT* (4 April & 2 August 1921); 'Racecourse Gangs in Conflict', *DET* (21 April 1921); 'Rival Race Gangs', *BDG* (5 July 1921); 'Racecourse Fracas', MG (5 July 1921).

179 'Racing Roughs Riot at Alexandra Park', *IPN* (7 April 1921).

180 'Racecourse Riot,' & 'Meeting at Alexandra Park', *TT* (4 April 1921).

181 'More Ruffianism', *Sporting Times* (9 April 1921).

182 'Midland Men Resent Blackmail Charges', *BDG* (6 June 1921).

183 Hilda Burnett, Letter, *BLA* (1995).

184 'Mr Bigland's Trial', *SP* (19 February 1922).

185 Richard Lane, 'The Battle of Kingston Hill' (May 1951). This was published in a magazine, but it has not been possible to find out which one.

186 Steve Nicholls, Interview, *BLA* (30 March 1989).

187 'A Battle after the Races', *Gloucester Citizen* (4 June 1921).

188 The 'Hold-Up' at Epsom, *LM* (17 June 1921).

189 'Epsom Race Riot', *BDG* (17 June 1921).

190 'Police Find at Inn', *BDG* (25 June 1921).

191 'The Epsom Road Battle', *YPLI* (17 June 1921).

192 Hart, pp.47–9.

193 'Leader of the S– Gang', *EN* (6 August 1922).

194 'The Epsom Ambush', *Western Mail* (20 July 1921).

195 'After the Epsom Races', *WSG* (28 July 1921).

196 MEPO 3/346, Charles Schwartz, Statement (2 June 1921).

197 'Epsom Road Battle', *TT* (4 June 1921).

198 Chief Inspector James Berrett, *When I was at Scotland Yard* (London, 1932), pp.116–9.

199 MEPO 3/346, Divisional Detective Inspector James Berrett, Report (28 July 1921).

200 'Epsom Road Prisoners Sentenced', *TT* (25 July 1921).

201 MEPO 3/346, Assistant Commissioner, Report (21 July 1921).

202 'Epsom Road Prisoners Sentenced', *TT* (25 July 1921).

203 MEPO 3/346, Berrett, Report (28 July 1921) & Assistant Commissioner, Report (21 July 1921).

204 '"Birmingham Boys"', *TEN* [London] (4 June 1921).

205 'A Brutal Assault', *BM* (27 June 1883).

206 'Quarter Sessions', *BDG* (31 October 1907).

207 See Chinn, pp.164–89.

208 'Blackmailed "Bookies"', *BDG* (4 June 1921).

209 HO 144/10430, CID, Report (1 December 1922).

210 The 'Hold-Up' at Epsom, *LM* (17 June. 1921).

211 Dell, Interview & 'Race day Feud', *NEP* (19 July 1921).

212 McDonald, p.162 & Fairfax-Blakeborough (ed.) p.99.

213 Brian McDonald, *Elephant Boys. Tales of London and Los Angeles Underworlds* (Edinburgh and London, 2005).

214 MEPO 3/346, Superintendent W. May, CID, Birmingham Chief Constable's Office, Report (28 June 1921).

215 *Ibid.*, Sergeant Hall, Staffordshire Constabulary, Report (8 July 1921).

216 'Matrimonial' & 'A Bookmaker's Clerk and His Matrimonial Affairs', *Smethwick Telephone* (21 January & 29 January 1921).

217 Horace Bottrell, Interview, *CCBA* (1987).

218 This assessment is based on unrecorded conversations with people who knew Cunnington.

219 'Calendar of Prisoners, 1870–1935. Birmingham Quarter Sessions, 1839–1971', QS/B/20/81 (27 January 1909).

220 *Ibid.*, QS/B/20/111 (1 March 1913).

221 'Birmingham Police Court', *BDP* (20 May 1918).

222 MEPO 3/346, Ernest Seigenberg, Statement (2 June 1921).

223 'Attack on Lady Cashier', *BDG* (14 November 1907); 'Suspects at Snow Hill Station', *BDG* (16 December 1908); 'Christmas Day Scene in Hurst Street', *BM* (27 December 1911); & 'Persons in Criminal Custody', *PG* (10 April 1917).

224 'Moat Thieves Sentenced', *Irish Independent* (12 December 1917).

225 Berrett, p.120.

226 'Violent Gangs at Salisbury', *Western Gazette* (8 July 1921).

227 McDonald, *Gangs of London*, p.163.

228 'Violent Gangs at Salisbury', *Western Gazette* (8 July 1921) & 'After the Races', *Western Times* (20 July 1921).

229 Rickman, p.262.

230 'Wild Scenes at Bath Meeting', *YPLI* (18 August 1921).

231 'Sensational Scenes in Bath' *BCWG* (20 August 1921).

232 'Murderous Race Gangs', *IPN* (25 August 1921).

233 'Sensational Scenes in Bath',
     BCWG (20 August 1921).

234 'Rival Bookies' Vendetta', *SP*
     (21 August 1921).

235 'Sensational Scenes in Bath'
     BCWG (20 August 1921).

236 Divall, pp.200–1.

237 'Ugly Racecourse Scenes',
     Courier [Dundee] (18 August
     1921).

238 'Racecourse Feuds', *Observer*
     (21 August 1921).

239 'Rival Bookies' Vendetta. Sequel
     to Wild Scenes at Racecourse',
     SP (21 August 1921).

240 'Suspicious Persons at the Races',
     Cheltenham Chronicle (25 May
     1907).

241 Bottrell, Interview.

242 'Mounted Police Clear
     Racecourse', *DC* (20 August
     1921).

243 'Racecourse Feuds', *TT*
     (23 August 1921).

244 '"Your Time Draws Near"', *NEP*
     (30 August 1921).

245 'Racecourse Ruffianism', *YPLI*
     (24 August 1921).

246 'Always First to Start Betting',
     DH (7 September 1931).

247 'Heavy Penalties', *London Daily
     News* (22 May 1902).

248 'North London', *London Evening
     Standard* (24 December 1904).

249 'The East End Gambling Raid',
     East London Observer
     (10 February 1912).

250 'London Gambling Den', *NEP*
     (17 September 1917).

251 '£300 Fine for Gaming', *Daily
     Mirror* (18 September 1917).

252 Prince, Interview.

253 'Denied he was the King of the
     Sabini Gang', *SP* (4 July 1926).

254 Netley Lucas, *London and Its
     Criminals* (London, 1926), p.76.

255 'Ruffianism on the Racecourse',
     DH (30 August 1921).

256 Bookmakers' and Backers'
     Racecourse Protection
     Association, General
     Committee, *Minutes*
     (12 September 1921).

257 'Race Gang at the Old Bailey',
     WG (16 January 1923) &
     'Frightened Witnesses in Race
     Feud Trial', *YPLI* (25 October
     1922).

258 HO 144/10430, CO, Letter
     (1 December 1922).

259 Ron Whytock, *Southern
     Bookmakers Association: History
     File* (n.d.).

260 'Racecourse Rowdies', *TT*
     (30 August 1921) & 'The
     Bookmakers' and Backers'
     Racecourse Protection
     Association, What it has done
     and what it can do with YOUR
     help' (1921) [henceforth BBRPA
     1921] p.14–15.

261 'Hurst Park Free Fight', *TT*
     (26 July 1921).

262 Divall, pp.201–5.

263 BBRPA 1921, pp.6–7.

264 *Ibid.*, p.3 & 'Battle of the Race Gangs', *EN* (20 August 1922).

265 'Racing Gangs Feud', *BG* (21 August 1922).

266 Greeno, p.12.

267 'Sporting Items', *NEP* (20 September 1921).

268 'The Bubbly Armistice in the Great Turf War', *Sporting Times* (1 October 1921).

269 'Bath Race Day Scene', *BCWG* (8 October 1921).

270 Brian McDonald, Email (10 October 2013).

271 'Bath Race Day Scene', *BCWG* (8 October 1921).

272 'Neglecting Children', *BM* (5 March 1891).

273 'A Stabbing Affray', *BDP* (3 April 1895).

274 'The Boys' Early Start', *BDG* (20 March 1907).

275 'Under the Seats', *BDG* (28 October 1907).

276 '£25 Compensation for a Referee', *PMG* (21 February 1919).

277 Racecourse Feud', *MG* (5 October 1921).

278 BBRPA 1921, pp.6–8, 2 & 10.

Chapter Four

279 Finn, p.26.

280 Bryan Magee, *Clouds of Glory. A Hoxton Childhood* (London, 2004 edn.) pp.150–3.

281 'Turf Gangs' New Move', *DM* (28 August 1922).

282 HO 144/10430, CID, Report (1 December 1922).

283 'Extraordinary Burglary at Ponders End', *Middlesex Gazette* (7 November 1896).

284 Old Bailey Proceedings Online (www.oldbaileyonline.org, version 8.0, 22 March 2020) November 1896, trial of GEORGE SAGE (20) WILLIAM LOADER (20) BEN COOPER (19) (t18961116-18).

285 LMA, Church of England Parish Registers, St James, St Pancras, Camden (22 April 1900) & 'Miscellaneous Charges', *Islington Gazette* (11 July 1899).

286 'Walter Butler's Assault at Arms', 'Wonderland Tonight', 'Tom Loates Beat "Brummy" & Contests at Finsbury Park Hall' *SL* (9 February 1898, 6 September 1898, 4 November 1905 & 24 October 1905).

287 'Counterfeit Coins', *DTC* (20 January 1910).

288 LMA, St Mark, Battersea Rise, 'Irene Sophia Sage' (22 October 1911).

289 McDonald, *Gangs of London*, pp.111–2.

290 'Thomas Templer' & 'A Charge of Stabbing', *IPN* (20 February 1913).

291 WO 364, 'Soldiers' Documents

from Pension Claims, First World War', Piece 2489.

292 'Englishmen Charged in Dublin', *Dublin Daily Express* (11 May 1917).

293 Divall, pp.205–7.

294 McDonald, *Gangs of London*, p.218.

295 TBL England & Wales, Electoral Registers 1920–1932, Ref. SPR.Mic.P.316/BL.F.1 & SPR. Mic.P.316/BL.F.1 (1923 & 1927).

296 LMA, 'Parish Registers Hoxton St Mary', Reference Number: p91/mry2/005 (2 April 1893).

297 LMA, 'Poor Law Hospital Registers', Roll Number CBG/346/001 (2 November & 26 September 1899). Proof of John Gilbert's relationship to Fred Gilbert is in MEPO 3/336, Goodwillie, Report (15 October 1922).

298 'Boxing Notes', *SL* (10 March 1910); 'Matinee Boxing', *DH* (7 Feb. 1913); 'National Sporting Club', *The Referee* (14 April 1912); 'Six Rounds Contests', '&' Six Rounds Contests', *SL* (18 December 1911, 5 August 1912 & 16 April 1912).

299 'West London Stadium', *TP* (28 March 1915) & 'Fifteen Rounds Contests', *The Sportsman* (20 April 1917).

300 'Battle of the Race Gangs', *EN* (20 August 1921).

301 'New Charge against Racing Men', *DC* (7 September 1922) & 'Alleged Paddington "Hold Up"', *Kensington Post* (8 September 1922).

302 Our Commissioner, 'Battle of the Race Gangs', *EN* (20 August 1921).

303 'Rooting Out the Razor Rogues', *TP* (30 August 1925).

304 Maskey, Interview.

305 'Three Sabinis and Their Rivals', *EN* (10 September 1922).

306 Our Commissioner, 'Battle of the Race Gangs', *EN* (20 August 1921).

307 'Bookmakers Unafraid', *BCWG* (26 August 1922).

308 Samuel, p.146

309 Sidney Theodore Felstead, *The Underworld of London* (London, 1923), p.40.

310 'Founder of the Flying Squad', *TP* (24 May 1925) & '"Titanic" Gang', *PMG* (10 September 1921).

311 'Leader of the S– Gang', *EN* (6 August 1922).

312 'The Titanic Gang', *DH* (15 February 1921); 'The Titanic Gang', *Ealing Gazette and West Middlesex Observer* (19 March 1921); 'Pickpocket Gang on Underground', *WG* (23 August 1924); & 'Titanic Gang', *PMG* (10 September 1921).

313 Felstead, pp.41–5.

314 'Leader of the S– Gang', *EN* (6 August 1922).

315 'Battle of the Race Gangs', *EN* (20 August 1921).

316 Bryan Magee, pp.76 & 81.

317 Magee, p.81.

318 'Nile Street Battle', *Shoreditch Observer* (18 January 1908).

319 George H. Duckworth's Notebook: Police District 5 [Old Street, Finsbury and Shoreditch], District 6 [Hoxton and Haggerston], District 9 [Bethnal Green, North and South] (1898), LSE Library's Charles Booth archive, BOOTH/B/352, p.155.

320 Maskey, Interview.

321 'Greenford Revolver Shots', *Middlesex County Times* (2 April 1921).

322 'I Carry That', *WG* (21 April 1913) & 'Theft in Tube Lift', *Globe* (10 March 1909).

323 Maskey, Interview.

324 'Faro Till Serve in the Morning', *Yorkshire Evening Post* (13 February 1925) & 'Mr William Chandler', *DC* (26 March 1946).

325 'Chief of "Sabini Gang"', *EN* (3 September 1922).

326 'Blackmail Gangs at the Races' & 'Hunt for Turf Pests', *DM* (25 August & 26 August 1921).

327 'Gangs Who Make Thousands of Pounds', *SP* (27 August 1922).

328 'Blackmail Gangs at the Races' & 'Hunt for Turf Pests', *DM* (25 & 26 August 1921).

329 'Gangs Who Make Thousands of Pounds', *SP* (27 August 1922).

330 U.S. Department of Labor, 'Earnings and Hours of Labor of Workers in Great Britain and Northern Ireland, 1924', *Monthly Labor Review*, vol. 25, no. 3 (1927).

331 Greeno, p.18.

332 'Battle of Three Race Gangs', *EN* (20 August 1921).

333 'Hooligan Gangs in London', *Shoreditch Observer* (18 January 1908).

334 'Battle of Three Race Gangs', *EN* (20 August 1921).

335 Maskey, Interview.

336 'Battle of Three Race Gangs', *EN* (20 August 1921).

337 'Alleged Strand Pickpockets', *DTC* (23 May 1908) & 'Violent Gangsters Sentenced', *IPN* (30 October 1930). See also McDonald, *Gangs of London*, pp.104–5.

338 'Alleged Racing Ruffianism. Strange Story at Brighton Police', *WSG* (31 August 1922).

339 'Racing Men Charged at Brighton', *YPLI* (12 September 1922).

340 'Brighton Racing Feud Charges', *Gloucester Citizen* (12 September 1922).

341 'Three Sabinis and Their Rivals'

& 'Man in Fear of His Life', *EN* (10 September 1922 & 27 August 1922).

342 'Judge on "Influence" in Brighton Case', *WG* (12 December 1922).

343 HO 144/10430, CID, Report (1 December 1922).

344 MEPO 3/1579, Sir James Olive, Commissioner of Police of the Metropolis, Report (27 November 1922).

345 *Ibid.*, George Langham, Statement (9 August 1922).

346 *Ibid.*, Alfred White, Statement (6 August 1922).

347 *Ibid.*, Olive, Report (27 November 1922) & Hill, Report (9 August 1922).

348 *Ibid.*, Hill, Report (9 August & 22 September 1922).

349 *Ibid.*, Goodwillie, Report (1 August 1922).

350 *Ibid.*, Hill, Report (9 August 1922).

351 *Ibid.*, Goodwillie, Report (24 August 1922) & Droy, Statement (21 August 1922).

352 'Revolver Fracas Echo', *BDG* (23 August 1922).

353 MEPO 3/336, Goodwillie, Report (24 August 1922).

354 *Ibid.*, Jack Delew, Statement (20 August 1922).

355 *Ibid.*, Simeon Solomon, Statement (21 August 1922).

356 *Ibid.*, Samuel Samuels, Statement (20 August 1921).

357 'Racecourse Feuds', *Daily Telegraph* (31 August 1921).

358 'Racecpurse Feud Case', *PMG* (30 August 1922).

359 'Titanic Versus "Sabini"', *DC* (21 August 1922).

360 'Race Gang War', *WG* (31 August 1922).

361 'Public Prosecutor on Racing Gangs', *DH* (31 August 1922).

362 'Race Gang on Trial', *SDT* (24 October 1922) & 'Walking Stick Curio Half Revolver and Half Stiletto', *PMG* (30 August 1922).

363 'The Jewish Invasion', *WSG* (21 July 1921).

364 'London Shooting Affair', *TS* (4 October 1922).

365 'Racing Men's Feud', *YPLI* (7 September 1922).

366 Greeno, p.19.

367 'Shooting Affray at Camden Town', *WG* (23 August 1922) & 'Racing Feud Trials', *MG* (24 October 1922).

368 'Racing Gang Affray', *WG* (5 October 1922).

369 'Racing Feud Sensation', *PMG* (21 August 1922).

370 'Man in Fear of His Life', *EN* (27 August 1922).

371 'The Racing Feud', *Western Mail* (23 September 1922).

372 'Racecourse Feud', *PMG* (26 August 1922).

373 'Sequel to Race-Train Scene', *WG* (23 September 1922).

374 'Sabini's Record', *Nottingham Journal* (21 November 1922).

375 MEPO 3/1581, Hambrook, Report (4 November 1922).

376 'A Revolver-Stiletto Stick', *DH* (31 August 1922).

377 MEPO 3/1581, Hambrook, Report (4 November 1922).

378 'More "Fear" at Old Bailey', *PMG* (24 October 1922).

379 MEPO 3/1581, Hambrook, Report (4 November 1922).

380 'Shooting Affray after Hurst Park Races', *YPLI* (31 August 1922) & 'Racing Feud Case', *Western Morning News* (25 October 1922).

381 'Witnesses' fears', *SDT* (27 October 1922).

382 MEPO 3/1581, Hambrook, Report (4 November 1922) & 'Racing Gangs Feud', *TT* (4 November 1922).

383 'Racing Feud Sentences', *DH* (4 November 1922).

384 TBL, 'England & Wales, Electoral Registers 1920–32', Parliamentary Borough of Finsbury, Ref. SPR.Mic.P.316/BL.F.1 (1925)

385 'Three men remanded for Soho Affray', *IPN* (8 October 1925) & 'Lowfield Heath Charge', *Surrey Mirror and County Post* (20 May 1927).

386 'Tattersall's Scene', *WG* (16 December 1925).

387 GRO, Volume 1b, p.515 &Vol.5c, p.948.

Chapter Five

388 'Leader of the S– Gang', *EN* (6 August 1922).

389 MEPO 3/1581 'Shooting Affray', Anonymous, Letter (23 August 1922).

390 HO 144/1043, Tommy Atkins, Letters (21 September & 5 October 1922).

391 'The Liability of Bedding to Seizure', *Tower Hamlets Independent and East End Local Advertiser* (3 February 1900).

392 TBL, England & Wales, Electoral Registers 1920–1932, SPR. Mic.P.330/BL.H.11; 'Special Six Rounds', *IPN* (19 October 1901); & 'Boxing at the Baths' & *West London Observer* (10 March 1922).

393 See Chinn, *Peaky Blinders. The Real Story*, pp.211–5.

394 Heather Shore, 'Criminality and Englishness in the Aftermath: The Racecourse Wars of the 1920s', *Twentieth Century British History*, Vol. 22, No. 4, (201), p.497.

395 Frederick Porter Wensley, *Forty Years of Scotland Yard. The Record of a Lifetime's Service in the CID* (1ˢᵗ published 1930, New York edn. 1968) pp.301–2.

396 'Alien Criminals', *PMG*
(21 September 1901).

397 Lucio Sponza, *Italian
Immigrants in Nineteenth
Century Britain: Realities
and Images* (Leicester, 1988),
pp.241–2.

398 George R. Sims, 'Byways of
Babylon, vii Naples in London',
Pearson's Weekly (14 March
1907).

399 Sponza, pp.32–6.

400 Morton, *Bert Battles Rossi.
Britain's Oldest Gangland Boss*,
p.3.

401 'Leader of the S– Gang', *EN* (6
August 1922).

402 Thomas Burke, 'The London I
Know', *The Sphere* (6 December
1924).

403 'Battle of Three Race Gangs', *EN*
(20 August 1921).

404 'Leader of the S– Gang', *EN*
(6 August 1922) & Morton, *Bert
Battles Rossi*, p.5.

405 HO 45/23691, Octavious Sabini,
Letter (n.d.).

406 '"Give Me That Tenner"', *DH*
(28 August 1922).

407 'Chief of "Sabini Gang"', EN
(7 September 1922).

408 HO 45/23691, Frederick Sabini,
Letter (n.d.) & Ann Sabini,
Letter (27 February 1941).

409 LMA, Ottavio Sabini; Reference
Number: p76/phi/016 (21
December 1913); & LMA, Doris

Annie Amelia Sabini, Church
of England Parish Registers,
1754–1906; Reference Number:
p90/jud/005 (25 January 1916).

410 'Chief of "Sabini Gang"', *EN* (3
September 1922).

411 HO 45/25720, Detective
Inspector Greeno, Report
(27 July 1940).

412 'Chief of "Sabini Gang"', *EN*
(7 September 1922).

413 'Six Rounds Contest', *SL*
(4 October & 24 December
1912).

414 'Denied he was the King of the
Sabini Gang', *SP* (4 July 1926).

415 HO 45/23691, Chief Constable
of Hove, Report (20 August
1940).

416 'Chief of "Sabini Gang"', *EN* (3
September 1922).

417 CRIM 1/209, Charles Sabini,
Cross Examined (5 December
1922) & Evidence (28 November
& 5 December 1922).

418 Prince, Interview.

419 Divall, p.209.

420 Langham, Interview.

421 'Three Sabinis and Their Rivals',
EN (10 September 1922).

422 Samuel, Interview.

423 HO 45/25720, Harry Sabini,
Statement.

424 Langham, Interview.

425 Dell, Interview.

426 'Terry Martin Wins by Narrow
Margin', *DH* (6 May 1919),

'Boxing at the Baths', *Cheltenham Chronicle* (18 January 1919), & 'Starmer and Tully at N.S.C.', *DH* (8 March 1920).

427 HO140 (3 March 1903 & 8 April 1913); TNA CRIM9, Piece 59, 'Central Criminal Court: After Trial Calendars of Prisoners' (22 April 1912); & 'Gang of Separate Criminal', *Jarrow Express* (11 April 1913).

428 Langham, Interview & 'War Office Daily List No. 5632' (31 July 1918).

429 'Ripe in Ringcraft', *BDG* (9 November 1920) and 'Was Betting the Cause?', *Star Green'un* (13 November 1920).

430 Deyong, p.43.

431 MEPO 3/910, CID, Report, (5 July 1935).

432 McDonald, *Gangs of London*, p.100.

433 'A Border Farmer', *Shields Daily News* (24 June 1913).

434 *Bognor Regis Observer* (4 August 1920).

435 McDonald, *Gangs of London*, pp.102 & 139–40.

436 'Betting in City Road', *Hackney and Kingsland Gazette* (30 August 1907).

437 'Leader of the S– Gang', *EN* (6 August 1922).

438 Ted McLean, 'How We Outwitted a Rival Gang', *Topical Times* (12 April 1924).

439 Morton, *Bert Battles Rossi*, p.4.

440 Prince, Interview.

441 'Football', *Athletic News* (30 August 1926).

442 Southern BPA, Folio 47, 15 May 1933, 'Printing of Lists'.

443 'Sabini Racing Gang Feud', *Nottingham Journal* (16 January 1923).

444 BBRPA General Committee, Minutes, 15 May, 12 June and 4 September 1922.

445 'Amazing Scene on Sea Front', *Newcastle Daily Chronicle* (24 August 1922).

446 BBRPA 1921, p.1.

447 'Hunt of Phantom Desperadoes', *DH* (25 August 1922) & 'Terrorism on the Racecourse', *DH* (26 August 1922).

448 'Race Feud Revelations', *PMG* (18 January 1923).

449 'Twelve Months' War' & 'Dominic Marini', *London Daily News* (9 & 26 September 1907).

450 Old Bailey Proceedings Online (www.oldbaileyonline.org, version 8.0, 5 April 2020) 'GEORGE CORTESI, VINCENT SABINI. Breaking Peace: wounding.' (11 January 1910).

451 'Italians Charged', *Islington Gazette* (6 September 1909).

452 'Race Feud Revelations', *PMG* (18 January 1923), 'Foreigners at Strife', *Islington Gazette* (27 March 1912) & TNA WO 372/5,

'British Army Medal Index Cards, 1914–1920', Service number 46270.

453 CRIM 1/209, Augustus Cortesi, 'Certificate of Employment during the War'.

454 'Hunt for Turf Pests', *DM* (26 August 1922).

455 Ted Mclean, 'Confessions of a Turf Crook', *Topical Times* (5 & 12 April 1924).

456 'Race Feud Revelations', *PMG* (18 January 1923).

457 Lucas, p.74.

458 'Sabini Shooting Affair', *PMG* (15 January 1923).

459 'Bottle Salutes', *PMG* (17 January 1923).

460 CRIM 1/209, *Firearm Certificate* (10 January 1921).

461 *Ibid.*, John Corsi, Evidence (28 November 1922).

462 *Ibid.*, Louisa Doralli, Evidence (28 November 1922).

463 'Italian Club Affray', *LM* (29 November 1922).

464 'Race Gangs Feud', *DM* (21 November 1922).

465 CRIM 1/209, Detective Inspector Grosse, Evidence (21 November 1922).

466 '"A Sidelight of the Turf"', *PMG* (21 December 1922).

467 CRIM 1/209, Charles Sabini, Evidence (28 November & 5 December 1922).

468 'Race Feud Shooting Affray', *WG* (22 December 1922).

469 'What Is a Riot?', *PMG* (16 January 1923).

470 'Used Pistol for a Zeppelin', *LM* (17 January 1923).

471 'Sabini Shooting Affray', 'What Is a Riot?' & 'Race Feud Revelations', *PMG* (15, 16 & 18 January 1923).

472 'Six and Half a Dozen', *WG* (19 January 1923).

473 England & Wales Government Probate Death Index 1858–2019 (8 April 1968).

474 GRO, England & Wales Deaths 1837–2007, Vol., 5C, p.1340.

475 'Scene at Wembley', *Hendon & Finchley Times* (19 June 1925).

476 GRO England & Wales Deaths 1837–2007, Vol. 5C, p.588.

477 HO 144/10430, Charles Haughton Rafter, Letter (17 February 1923 & 20 December 1922).

478 'Sequel to Sabini Case', *WG* (27 February 1923).

479 MEPO 3/444, Matt. Freight, Letter (16 February 1923).

480 *Ibid.*, E. Blackwell, Letter (19 February 1923).

481 *Ibid.*, Chief Inspector Brown, Report (9 May 1923).

482 'Sabini Feud Echo', *PMG* (30 July 1923).

483 'After a Betting Dispute', *PMG* (28 May 1923) & 'Magistrate on Cowardice', *LM* (6 June 1923).

484 'He is what may be described as a racing desperado', *IPN* (12 July 1923).

485 'Tancy Lee in Feud Drama' & 'Bookmaker in the Box', *PMG* (28 May & 9 June 1923) & 'Race Feuds Ended', *DH* (7 July 1923).

486 'Sabinis at Epsom', *PMG* (8 June 1923).

487 'Sabini Boys Freed', *DH* (19 June 1923) & 'Fracas at Epsom', *News of the World* (24 June 1923).

488 HO 144/10430, Anonymous, Letter (11 June 1922).

489 Samuel, p.204.

490 'Leader of the S– Gang', *EN* (6 August 1922).

491 HO 144/10430, *Memorandum* (8 December 1922).

492 'Blackmail by Police?', *WG* (9 December 1922).

493 H. Daley, *This Small Cloud. A Personal Memoir* (London, 1985), p.95; & 'Police Bribery Charges', *DM* (3 February 1923).

494 'Who's Who at a Night Club', *Dundee People's Journal* (25 October 1919).

495 'Blackmailers' Haunts', *Globe* (3 December 1920).

496 'Round the Nightclubs of London', *Sunday Post* (19 March 1922).

497 'The Thugs' Haunts', *HDM* (19 January 1923).

498 'Death of Mrs Meyrick', *NEP* (20 January 1933).

499 Mrs Kate Meyrick, 'When Terror Reigns in Night-Clubland', *Sunday Sentinel* (24 February 1929).

500 'Raid on Night Club Sequel', *IPN* (31 January 1924).

501 'Eighteen Months for Goddard', *LM* (30 January 1929).

502 'London Letters', *HDM* (19 January 1923).

503 There were a series of articles on lesser nightclubs in *DM* in January 1923.

504 'The secrets behind the sets', https://www.bbc. co.uk/programmes/ articles/29nTX6cZHtPs2flYz8 G8fjP/the-secrets-behind-the-sets (accessed 12 April 2020).

505 Samuel, p.185.

506 MEPO 3/374, Chief Inspector Brown, Report (27 October 1924).

507 *Ibid.*, Maurice Burn, Statement (2 October 1924).

508 *Ibid.*, Brown, Report (27 October 1924).

509 *Ibid.*, 'Wanted for Crime' (23 September 1924).

510 *Ibid.*, Anonymous, Letter (26 September 1924).

511 *Ibid.*, Brown, Report (27 October 1924).

512 'Street Stabbing Affray', *DET* (24 September 1924).

513 'Manslaughter in Club Case',

The Morning Advertiser (19 November 1922) & 'A Silent Quarrel', *Sheffield Daily Telegraph* (10 October 1924).

514 'Joy of the Sabini Gang', *TP* (23 November 1924).

515 'Racecourse Fiends' & 'Turf Gangs Break Truce', *HDM* (30 August 1924).

516 'Attacked by Race Gang at Wye', *Whitstable Times and Herne Bay Herald* (11 October 1924).

517 'Assault at Races', *WG* (14 October 1924).

518 'Mancini Was Nearly Four Months Awaiting Death', *Manchester Evening News* (31 October 1941).

519 'Joy of the Sabini Gang', *TP* (23 November 1924*)*.

520 For Glasgow see Davies, *City of Gangs*. There were also razor gangs in Sydney, Australia, see Larry Writer, *Razor: A True Story of Slashers, Gangsters, Prostitutes and Sly Grog* (Sydney, 2001).

Chapter Six

521 'New Phase in Feud of Race Gangs', *TP* (28 December 1924).

522 Frank Harris, Interview, *CCBA* (26 April 1988).

523 'The Raid Upon the Cold Well Gambling School', *Nelson Leader* (20 October 1922).

524 Carl Chinn, *Better Betting with a Decent Feller. A Social History*

of Bookmaking (London, 2004), pp.87–8.

525 Arthur Hopcraft, *The Great Apple Raid & Other Encounters of a Tin Chapel Tiro* (London, 1970), pp.71–2.

526 Michael Doyle, Interview (1987).

527 Máirín Johnston, *Around the Banks of Pimlico* (Dublin, 1985), p.75.

528 'Dublin's Animal Gang', *Belfast News-Letter* (16 October 1934).

529 'The Bradley Gaming Case Re-Opened', *Yorkshire Evening Post* (6 September 1928).

530 'To Supress Gangs', *SDT* (12 January 1927) & A. W. Cockerill, *Sir Percy Sillitoe: the biography of the former head of MI5* (London, 1975) p.91. This discussion on the Sheffield Gang wars benefitted from discussions with Alex Marshall, an undergraduate student at the University of Birmingham who graduated in 2015 and whose final-year dissertation on this subject I supervised.

531 'City Gambling Rings', *SI* (18 March 1921).

532 'Smart Police Coup', *Ibid.* (26 June 1917).

533 'On Sky Edge', *SDT* (26 June 1917).

534 '"Under or Over"', *Yorkshire Telegraph and Star* (1 April 1913).

535 'Mooney Gang', *Ibid.* (28 November 1913).

536 TNA 'A Calendar of Prisoners Tried at the Epiphany Quarter Sessions of the Peace for the Year 1903', Piece 229 (7 June 1902) & Piece 309 (2 April 1913).

537 'Married at Sixteen Separated at Seventeen', *SDT* (29 October 1907).

538 'Sheffield Gangs Who Invade Licensed Houses', *SDT* (16 February 1911); & 'Hard Labour for Sheffield Mooney-ites', *SDT* (11 September 1913).

539 'Sharp Sentence' *SDT* (24 February 1913).

540 'Mooney Convicted', *SDT* 11 July 1914) & 'Scene in a Bar', *SDT* (15 January 1913).

541 'Bitten Ear', *SDT* (6 May 1914) & 'One of the Gang', *SI* (11 July 1914).

542 'Mooney Again', *Sheffield Evening Telegraph* (29 October 1914).

543 'George Mooney', *PG* (12 July 1918) & 'Theft on a Leeds Tramcar', *Yorkshire Evening Post* (8 July 1918).

544 'Rowdyism in the Park District', *SDT* (29 July 1921).

545 'Racecourse Melee' & 'Shots at Club', *SI* (12 September 1921 & 13 April 1922).

546 'Notorious Sheffielder', *SI* (11 September 1919) & 'Notorious Gang of Thieves', *Lancashire Evening Post* (21 July 1919).

547 'A Lame Excuse', *SI* (1 October 1909).

548 West Glamorgan Archive Service, 'Records of Glamorgan Calendar Prisoners 1877–1922' (21 April 1915) & 'Arrests at Gosforth Park', *Newcastle Evening Chronicle* (24 June 1910).

549 'Terrorist Gang', *SDT* (25 May 1911).

550 'Hooliganism', *SDT* (29 June 1912).

551 'Foulkes's New Role', *SDT* (10 July 1915).

552 'Samuel Garvin', *PG* (28 December 1917).

553 'Mooney Puts His Case', *SI* (28 June 1923).

554 'A Charge against Samuel Garvin', *SDT* (13 April 1920).

555 PCOM 8/58 & 59, 'Chief Superintendent J. W. Hollis, "Activities of Rivals Gangs in Sheffield"' (5 July 1923) & 'Besieged House', *SDT* (26 June 1923).

556 'Park Sensation', *SDT* (28 May 1923).

557 PCOM 8/59, 'Chief Superintendent Hollis, "Activities of Rivals Gangs in Sheffield"' (5 July 1923).

558 'Midnight Shots at Mooney's

House', & 'Street Battles in Sheffield', *SI* (23 & 26 June 1923).

559 'Sheffield Feud Scenes', *SI* (26 June 1923).

560 Brian McDonald, *Alice Diamond and the Forty Elephants* (Wrea Green, 2015).

561 'The Passer-By' & 'Mooney Puts His Case', *SI* (28 June 1923).

562 'Sheffield Crime', *SDT* (7 May 1923).

563 PCOM 8/58 & 59, Hollis, 'Activities' (5 July 1923).

564 'When Friends', *SDT* (3 July 1923) & 'Sequel to a Gang Feud', *SI* (19 October 1923).

565 'House Raided', 'Sheffield Feud', *SDT* (27 December 1923 & 9 January 1924).

566 'Assistant Recorder on Gangs', *SDT* (April 1925).

567 'Election Night Case Dismissed', *SDT* (4 December 1924).

568 PCOM 8/58 & 8/59, 'Chief Superintendent J. W. Hollis, 'Activities' (1 June 1923) & 'Sheffield Affray', *SDT* (10 December 1924).

569 'Recorder of Sheffield and Stories of the Gangs', *SDT* (22 January 1925).

570 'A Fierce Struggle', *SDT* (23 December 1924).

571 '"The G.O.C."', *SDT* (22 January 1925).

572 'Recorder of Sheffield and Stories of the Gangs', *SDT* (22 January 1925); 'A Fierce Struggle', *SDT* (23 December 1924); 'Gang Feud Ends', *SDT* (8 January 1925); 'Sheffield Gangs', *SDT* (4 December 1924); & 'Gangs' Feud', *SDT* (23 January 1925).

573 PCOM 8/58 & 59, 'Chief Superintendent J. W. Hollis, "Activities of Rivals Gangs in Sheffield"' (1 June 1925).

574 J. P. Bean, *The Sheffield Gang Wars* (Sheffield, 1981), pp.51–2 & 'Gang Feud Ends', *SDT* (8 January 1925).

575 'Sheffield Gangs', *YPLI* (21 January 1925).

576 '"The G.O.C."', *SDT* (22 January 1925).

577 'Recorder of Sheffield and Stories of the Gangs', *SDT* (22 January 1925); 'Sheffield Outbreak', *SDT* (23 January 1925); & 'Sheffield Gang Talk', *SDT* (5 February 1925).

578 'Gang Reference', *SDT* (20 February 1925) & 'Assistant Recorder on Gangs', *SDT* (April 1925).

579 'Intolerable', *SDT* (13 July 1925).

580 PCOM 8/58 & 59, Hollis, 'Activities' (1 June 1925).

581 *Ibid.* & 'Copy of Mr Justice Finlay's Notes'.

582 *Ibid.*, Elizabeth Plommer, Thomas Plommer, William

Hazelwood, William Holden, Albert Pollard, John Rigg, Percy John Playfield & James Ewart Scholefield, 'Coroner's Inquest Evidence' (18 May 1928).

583 'Impressive Scenes at Home of Murdered Glasgow Man', *SP* (3 May 1925).

584 'Threats to Witnesses', *DM* (28 May 1925) & 'Lurid Death Threats', *News of the World* (23 August 1925).

585 'Brothers Sentenced to Death', *DM* (1 August 1925).

586 PCOM 8/59, Wilfred Fowler, 'Petition' (24 August 1925).

587 'Fowler Brothers' Last Bid', *SP* (30 August 1925) & 'Double Execution', *DM* (4 September 1925).

588 'Plommer's Death', *SDT* (30 July 1925).

589 Keith Farnsworth, *Sheffield's East Enders. Life As It Was In the Lower Don Valley* (Sheffield 1987) pp.93 & 95.

590 Harris, Interview.

591 'The Sheffield Murder', *YPLI* (1 August 1925).

592 'Lawless Assaults', *SDT* (27 August 1932) & 'Sheffield Gang War Fear', *SI* (17 May 1934).

593 Harris, Interview.

594 'King Garvin', *SDT* (1 August 1925) & 'Sheffield Murder Case', *TT* (1 August 1925).

595 'Gang Chief' Sentenced', *SDT* (3 August 1925).

596 'Judge and Sheffield Gangs', *YPLI* (3 August 1925).

597 'Mooney and Garvin on Lincoln Racecourse', *SDT* (27 March 1925).

598 'Head of Sheffield Gang Sentenced', *YPLI* (22 October 1925).

599 'Sheffield C.I.D. Officer to Retire. In Charge of First "Flying Squad"', *SI* (16 January 1936).

600 'Solicitor Attacks Flying Squad', *SI* (1 January 1926).

601 Sir Percy Sillitoe K. B. E., 'Cloak without Dagger' (London, 1955), p.64.

602 'Gangs Recalled', *SI* (24 December 1937).

603 Sillitoe, p.64.

604 'Member of Police Flying Squad Retires', *SDT* (27 April 1927).

605 Harris, Interview.

606 A. W. Cockrill, *Sir Percy Sillitoe. The biography of the former head of MI5* (London, 1975), p.92–3.

607 Sillitoe, p.62.

608 'Gaol for Members of Mooney Gang', *SI* (11 March 1927).

609 'Boy Attacked', *SDT* (15 December 1928).

610 'Sheffield Street Affray', *SDT* (22 December 1928) & 'Promised to Be Good But', *SI* (22 December 1928).

611 'Gangs Recalled', *SI* (24 December 1937).

612 'Black Eyes Court', *SI* (23 July 1929) & 'Sheffield Man Sentenced', *SDT* (18 February 1930).

613 GRO, Volume 2d, p.280.

614 Sillitoe, p.68.

615 'Six Months' Sentence', *SDT* (11 October 1930).

616 'City Men Sent to Prison', *SI* (10 October 1931) & 'Garvin's "Vast Knowledge of Train Criminals"' (19 April 1937).

617 GRO, Volume 2d, p.21.

Chapter Seven

618 'The New Terrorism', *Western Daily Press* (28 August 1925).

619 'Race Gangs Get "Busy" Again', *SP* (14 June 1925).

620 'Racing Gang Fracas', *Western Daily Press*, 'Race Gang Fight', *WG*, & 'Slashed with Razor', *Portsmouth Evening News* (16 February 1925).

621 Greeno, pp.29–30.

622 Samuel, pp.133 & 215 & 'Decision Applauded in Court', *DET* (23 February 1925).

623 'Five Men Implicated in Razor Attack', *DET* (17 February 1925) & 'Bookmaker in Bandages', *DH* (24 February 1925).

624 McDonald, *Gangs of London*, p.196.

625 Samuel, p.132–3

626 Greeno, p.24.

627 LMA, Ref. p72/jsg/015.

628 England & Wales Deaths 1837–2007, London, Bethnal Green, Vol. 1C, p.118 (1903).

629 '"Nightmare of the East End"', *Daily Herald* (3 July 1926).

630 'Two Tempers', *IPN* (10 June 1920).

631 'Happy Prisoner', *Globe* (15 June 1920).

632 'Pat O'Keefe Prosecutes', *PMG* (20 July 1923).

633 'Epsom', *Surrey Mirror* (13 June 1924).

634 McDonald, *Gangs of London*, p.191.

635 'A Disorderly Scene in Leeds', *YPLI* (17 January 1925).

636 'Gunmen in a Motor Car', *DM* (22 May 1925).

637 '"More Behind This Case"', *DH* (2 June 1925).

638 'Alleged Race Gang Raid', *BDG* (2 June 1925).

639 Greeno, p.21.

640 McDonald, *Gangs of London*, p.200.

641 'Car Driver's Thrilling Night Adventure', *IPN* (28 May 1925).

642 'Maiden Lane Affair', *Lancashire Evening Post* (25 May 1925).

643 'Victim Who Said He Was Italian', *WG* (2 June 1925).

644 'Car Driver's Thrilling Night Adventure', *IPN* (28 May 1925).

645 'Derby Scenes', *TS* (28 May 1925).

646 'Dangerous Gang', *BDG* (4 June 1925).

647 Hart, p.140.

648 'Attacked in Public House', *BDG* (15 June 1925).

649 West Midlands Police Museum, Birmingham City Police, *Convicts on Licence*, Thomas McDonald, no. 184.

650 'Today's Cases', *Coventry Evening Telegraph* (25 July 1895).

651 'Penal Servitude for a Birmingham Soldier', *BDP* (3 July 1917).

652 'Birmingham Police Court', *Coventry Standard* (15 April 1922).

653 'Bound Over', *Tamworth Herald* (20 September & 27 December 1924).

654 'Englishmen Charged in Dublin', *Dublin Daily Express* (11 May 1917).

655 'Racecourse Gang at Chester', *MG* (9 May 1925).

656 'Slashed with a Razor' & 'Feud of Race Gang' *BDG* (17 & 23 June 1925).

657 '"Birmingham Boys"', *HDM* (7 August 1925).

658 'Blackpool Man Fined for Loitering', *Lancashire Evening Post* (1 April 1930) & 'Calendar of Prisoners, 1880–1891 and 1906–1913', Birmingham Autumn Assizes (Nov.), QS/B/20/108.

659 'Race Gang at Nightclub', *BDG* (7 August 1925), 'Three Bookmakers Committed', *Worthing Herald* (15 August 1925); & 'Race-Gang Fight', *YEP* (6 August 1925).

660 'Sequel to Race Gang Feud', *WSG* (24 December 1925).

661 GRO, Volume 6d, p.227.

662 'Fifty Men Fight with Razors', *Daily Express* (21 August 1921).

663 HO 144/10430, Superintendent Palmer, Report (24 August 1925) & Report to the Home Secretary (25 August 1925).

664 'War on Race Gangs', *SDT* (24 August 1925).

665 '40 Men in Race Gang Fight', *DM* (26 August 1925).

666 MEPO 3/352, 'Race Gang Affray at Waterloo Road', Detective Henry Corbett, Report (25 August 1925) & 'Race Gangs Feuds', *Morning Post* (2 September 1925).

667 'Three Men Remanded for the Soho Affray', *IPN* (8 October 1925).

668 'Special Police to Break Race Gangs', *TEN* (24 August 1925).

669 'Race-Gangs', *Daily Express* (25 August 1925).

670 'Home Secretary and Gang Feuds', *TT* (27 August 1925).

671 'Race Gangs', *Morning Post* (25 August 1925).

672 Ex-Chief Inspector 'Nutty' Sharpe, 'Fade out of the Race Gangs', *The Star* (4 January 1938).

673 Dell, Interview.

674 Dick Kirby, *The Guv'nors. Ten of Scotland Yard's Greatest Detectives* (Barnsley, 2010), pp.30–1.

675 'How Birmingham Ends Race Gang Wars', *Belfast Telegraph* (11 May 1931).

676 Rickman, pp.263–4.

677 W. Bebbington, *Rogues Go Racing* (London, 1947), pp.15–20.

678 'Gang War in London', *DM* (13 July 1931).

679 David Ashforth, 'Darby Sabini Emperor of The Racetrack', *Racing Post* (3 July 2006).

680 Greeno, p.22.

681 Ted McLean, Confessions of a Turf Crook' & 'How We Outwitted a Rival Gang', *Topical Times* (5 & 12 April 1924).

682 'Prominent Cases in Coming Terms', *WG* (3 October 1925).

683 Non-Appearance of a Plaintiff *YPLI* (16 December 1925).

684 'Sabini Bankruptcy', *DH* (11 June 1926).

685 'Sabini's Admissions in Bankruptcy Court', *DET* (29 June 1926).

686 HO 45/2369, Ann Sabini, Letter (5 March 1921) & Frederick Sabini, Statement (n.d.).

687 *Ibid.* Ottavio Sabini, Statement (3 December 1940).

688 'A Mixed Career', *TS* (30 June 1926).

689 'Sabini's Admissions in Bankruptcy Court', *DET* (29 June 1926).

690 Cooper, Interview.

691 'Bookmakers Protection Association', *BDG* (18 March 1925).

692 Langham, Interview.

693 Northern BPA, Letter (28 August 1940) & NAB File, 'Dots and Dashes'.

694 'Racing and Race Gangs', *SDT* (22 March 1926).

695 'Farm-Boy as a Police Chief', *The People* (18 July 1926).

696 'Race Day Scene at Yarmouth', *Yarmouth Independent* (5 June 1926).

697 'Stoning the Police', *Yorkshire Evening Post* (7 November 1913).

698 'Witnesses Fear', *SDT* (17 February 1925).

699 Bebbington, pp.96–7 & 'Race Day Scene at Yarmouth', *Yarmouth Independent* (5 June 1926).

700 '"Nightmare of the East End"', *DH* (3 July 1926), & Samuel, p.132.

701 Reg and Ron Kray with Fred Dinenage, *Our Story* (London, 1988), p.11.

702 'Blackmailers Smartly Sentenced', *Diss Express* (9 July 1926).

703 'Characters Told By Detective', *Norwood News* (26 March 1927).

704 Bebbington, pp.98–9, 'Beware of Pickpockets', *DET* (4 September 1929).

705 'Race Day Charge', *Essex Newsman* (30 November 1929).

706 What has the B.P.A. Done?' (Southern File, 'History', 1939), p.1.

707 *Ibid.* & Meeting between the Stewards of the Jockey Club and the Representatives of the Three Branches of the BPA, Report (16 October 1929) and NAB File, 'Pitches'.

708 'In Joseph Chamberlain's City Today', *The Sphere* (20 February 1932).

Chapter Eight

709 'I'm the Gangster Who Runs London's Underworld' & 'One Night of Terror', *TP* (5 & 19 September 1954).

710 HO 45/23691, Inspector Collyer, Brighton Police, Report (28 March 1941).

711 'As Others See Us', *West Sussex Gazette* (21 November 1957).

712 Tom Tullett, 'Sudden death again in Little Italy', *Daily Mirror* (17 October 1962).

713 Norman Lucas, *Britain's Gangland* (London, 1969), p.23.

714 'Ugly violent criminals of the past', *Telegraph* (22 April

2005) & Catharine Arnold, *Underworld London: Crime and Punishment in the Capital City* (London, 2012), pp.284–6.

715 'Gunfight at Columbus Circle', *Reading Evening Post* (13 December 1980).

716 Brian McDonald, *Gangs of London*, p.278.

717 Samuel, p.184 & 'Boxing for Charity', *DH* (9 June 1920).

718 'Public House Brawl in Soho' & 'Three Men Sentenced for Assault', *IPN* (13 February & 3 April 1930).

719 'The Seamy Side', *DM* (24 January 1931).

720 Hart, pp.1–5.

721 Kirby, pp.105–10.

722 TBL, England & Wales, Electoral Registers 1920–1932, Ref. SPR. Mic.P.243/BL.B.101.

723 Hart, p.194.

724 'Innocent Man's Night in the Cells', *DET* (6 July 1928).

725 'Everyone Goes in Fear of Him,' *EN* (29 October 1929).

726 'Pulled Inspector's Nose', *Belfast News-Letter* (4 April 1931).

727 James Morton, Frankie Fraser as told to James Morton, *Mad Frankie. Memoirs of a Life of Crime* (London, 1995 edn.), pp.13–14.

728 Langham, Interview.

729 HO 45/23691, Hillier, Report (20 August 1940).

730 HO 45/23691, Collyer, Brighton Police, Report; Assistant Commissioner Norman Kendall, Report (2 January 1941); Sabini, Statement; & Minutes (12 January 1941).

731 'Heavy Sentence on Receivers', *Kent & Sussex Courier* (25 June 1943).

732 '£50 Produced from Sock', *Mid Sussex Times* (16 May 1945); Civil Registration Death Index, 1916–2007, Volume: 5h, p.351, Hove, Sussex, Ollavio Sabini (December 1950); & Hart, p.232.

733 Annie Emma Sabini, Probate Registry: Brighton (30 October 1978).

734 GRO, Volume 5b, p.290 & Principal Probate Registry, London (25 April 1974).

735 LMA Electoral Registers (1931).

736 Harry Sabini, Probate Registry: London (27 June 1978) & HO 45/23691, Detective Inspector Greeno, Report (21 June 1940).

737 'Alleged Riot at Club' & 'Scene at a Soho Club', *TT* (21 & 27 May 1935.

738 James Morton, *Gangland. Volume 2. The Underworld in Britain and Ireland* (London, 1995 edn.), pp.7– 9.

739 'Harry Sabini Denies Perjury', *DH* (8 July 1941).

740 Morton, *Bert Battles Rossi*, pp.49–50.

741 England & Wales, National Probate Calendar, London, (27 June 1978).

742 'Disgraceful Scenes in a Club', *West Sussex Gazette* (29 January 1931); & 'Pulled Inspector's Nose', *Belfast News-Letter* (4 April 1931).

743 GRO, England & Wales, Civil Registration Death Index, Vol. 3, p.948, Edmonton, Essex, Edward Emanuel (March 1943); & Elizabeth Mary Emanuel, England and Wales National Probate Calendar (3 February 1951).

744 Jackie Currigan, Interview, *CBBA* (1987).

745 'Goddard Trial Echo', *DH* (22 February 1929); 'Fascists in Skirmish', *Liverpool Echo* (13 July 1934); 'Bow Street' & 'Pickpockets Struggle with Detective He Robbed' *IPN* (25 April & 26 December 1935); & 'Flying Squad Officer's Smart Capture', *Marylebone Mercury* (30 September 1939).

746 'Show Ground Till', *Western Mail* (6 January 1926); 'Shadowed Bank Customers', *Belfast Telegraph* (1 March 1926); & 'Sequel to Racecourse Incident', *Staffordshire Advertiser* (9 April 1932).

747 'What Police Saw at Back of Fruiterer's Shop', *BDG* (31 March 1936).

748 GRO, Volume 9c, p.209.

749 Juliet Banyard, Email (7 September 2013).

750 TBL England & Wales, Electoral Registers 1920–1932, Ref. SPR. Mic.P.226/BL.B.68 (1921).

751 GRO England and Wales Civil Registration Death Index, 1916–2007, Volume 6d, p.11 (1926) & Banyard, Email.

752 GRO England and Wales Civil Registration Indexes (1926) Volume 1b, p.1341 (19 July 1926).

753 TBL England & Wales, Electoral Registers 1920–1932, Ref. SPR.Mic.P.316/BL.F.1 & SPR. Mic.P.316/BL.F.1 (1923 & 1927).

754 'Angry Crowd', *Nottingham Journal* (24 March 1925).

755 McDonald, *Gangs of London*, p.187–8 & 344.

756 Dey, p.210.

757 For example, *Western Morning News* (12 April 1938).

758 'Freehold', *The London Gazette* (27 May 1932).

759 TNA Board of Trade: Commercial and Statistical Department and successors: Inwards Passenger Lists.; Class BT26, Piece 1160.

760 Banyard, Email.

761 'Late Mr Bradshaw Smith', *Devon and Exeter Gazette* (25 October 1940).

762 'Personal and General', *Bedfordshire Times and Independent* (5 December 1941).

763 'Mr W. Kimber', Newspaper Cutting.

764 William Kimber, England & Wales, National Probate Calendar, Llandudno (20 October 1945).

Afterword

765 'Eden Club Case Stabbing', *MG* (19 November 1924).

766 Magee, p.152.

767 Bebbington, pp.100–4; McDonald, *Gangs of London*, p.255; 'Story of Race-Gang's Hatchets and Truncheons', *DH* (10 June 1936); 'No Mercy for Gang Violence', *DM* (30 July 1936); & 'Alleged Wounding on Racecourse', *DET* (28 July 1936).

768 John Carey, 'Book Review', *Independent* (2 January 1993).

769 Norman Sherry, *The Life of Graham Greene, vol. 1, 1904–1939* (London, 1989), pp.634–6.

770 Carey, 'Book Review'.

771 Graham Greene, Letter to Carl Chinn (9 May 1988).

772 Graham Greene, *Brighton Rock* (1st published 1938, Middlesex edn. 1970), p.61.

773 'Alleged Wounding on Racecourse', *DET* (28 July 1936).

774 Jake Arnott, 'Mad, bad and dangerous to know', *TG* (20 July 2002) & Greene, Letter.

775　MEPO 3/9190, Detective Inspector Burt, Report (2 May 1935).

776　'Brutal Attack on Police Officers', *IPN* (12 May 1927).

777　MEPO 3/9190, Anonymous, Letter (May 1935).

778　*Ibid.*, Chief Inspector Sharpe, Report (5 July 1935).

779　Morton, *Gangland. London's Underworld*, pp.44–5.

780　'Bert Marsh of Clerkenwell', *SDT* (10 July 1923) & 'Premierland Boxing', *PMG* (11 January 1922).

781　HO 45/23691, Ottavio Sabini, Statement (3 December 1940).

782　'Assault at Races', *WG* (14 October 1924).

783　HO 45/23691, Detective Inspector Greens, Report.

784　Morton, *Gangland*, pp.27 & 70–3.

785　'Glinski on Trial for Perjury Charge', *Liverpool Echo* (7 November 1955).

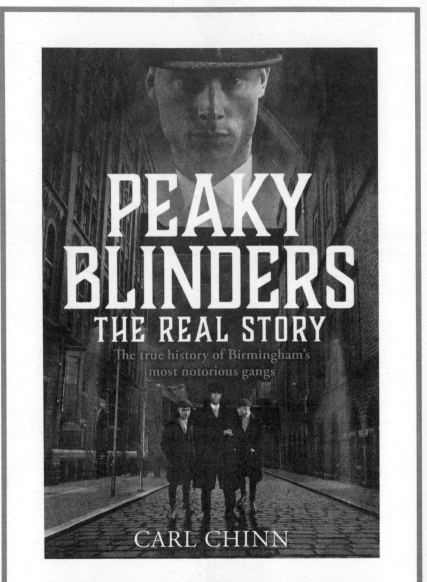

PEAKY BLINDERS
THE REAL STORY

The true history of Birmingham's
most notorious gangs

CARL CHINN

READ THE FIRST BOOK IN THIS SERIES NOW, AVAILABLE FOR £8.99.